Door County Living in Pictures, Vol. 2:

The Photography of Heather Harle Frykman & Lucas Frykman

First edition, first printing
Copyright © 2015 Peninsula Publishing & Distribution, Inc.
All photography copyright © Heather Harle Frykman & Lucas Frykman

All rights reserved. No part of this book may be reproduced, stored in a retrieval system, or transmitted in any form or by any means, electronic, mechanical, photocopying, or otherwise without prior permission of the publisher.

Editor: Stephen Grutzmacher
Editor in Chief: Madeline Harrison
Publisher: David Eliot

ISBN - 978-1-4951-5312-6

Published by
Door County Living, Inc.
A wholly owned subsidiary of
Peninsula Publishing & Distribution, Inc.
8142 Highway 57
Baileys Harbor, WI 54234

Printed in the U.S. of A.
in the State of Wisconsin by
Quad/Graphics
Commercial Specialty
Burlington, WI 53105

CHASING THE LIGHT

The Frykmans focus on photography for Sister Bay gallery

BY PATTY WILLIAMSON, PH.D.

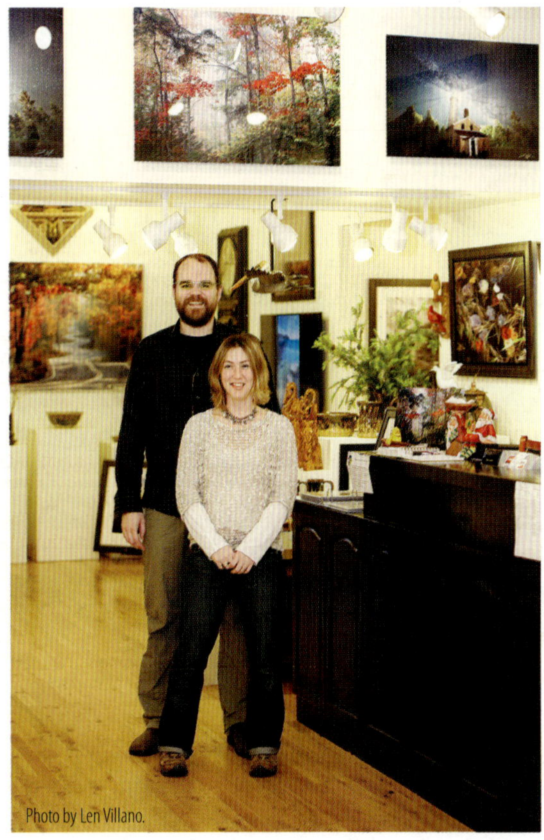
Photo by Len Villano.

It's said that long-married spouses sometimes grow to resemble one another and that pets and their owners may share features. Noted fine art nature photographers Heather and Lucas Frykman say their style has converged to the point that occasionally even they can't tell who took a particular picture. "Often, I'll take a picture of Heather as I pass a camera to her, so we'll know that the following shots are hers," Lucas says.

They met in Green Bay in 2001, when both had part-time jobs as hotel banquet workers. Heather was taking photography classes at the University of Wisconsin – Green Bay and also working at a portrait studio, but taking pictures was still just a hobby for her. It had always been a hobby for Lucas, who had been playing around with his dad's Nikon for years. (Dad is David Frykman, originally a potter, later a wood carver extraordinaire and, more recently, a painter.)

Heather freelanced as a photographer during a two-year stay in California, but hoped for a full-time career. Back in Door County for a vacation with family in 2004, they began looking at property for a gallery. "When I was growing up," Lucas says, "my folks let me know I could be anything I wanted to, that it was possible to make a living in art. They had a pottery studio in Sister Bay, and I knew that in Door County, if you have a good product and work hard, you don't have to be a starving artist."

"That concept was totally foreign to me," says Heather. "I grew up in Platteville, an engineering and farming community. I had no idea there was a place like Door County where this kind of life was possible."

"We owe all the credit to my parents," Lucas adds. "It was great to have them to guide us, to give us the opportunity to be our own bosses and be artists in Door County."

They opened their first gallery at Berch Tree in Ellison Bay in 2005, the year they were married. "That is a real artists' community," Lucas says. "We used to get together a few times a year, and we miss those shared experiences, but we outgrew the wall space."

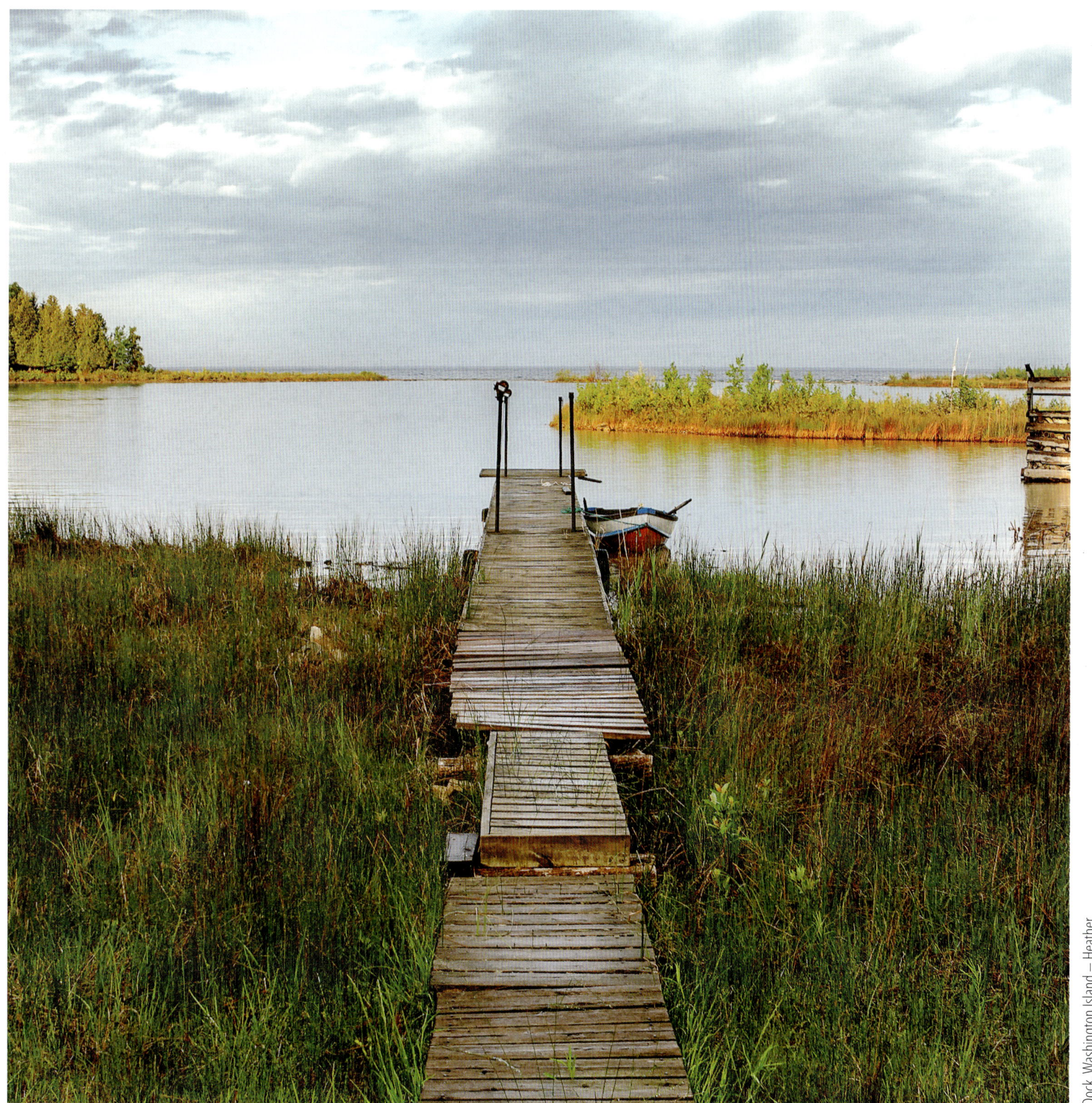

Dock, Washington Island – Heather.

The wall space in that first gallery was what prompted Lucas to get serious about photography.

"Heather was already an accomplished photographer," he says. "If I wanted to get any pictures on the walls, I had to become as good as I could. I did a lot of research, looked at lots of good work and practiced a lot. I learned her style quickly, and it became not just a hobby, but a passion."

"He started driving around with me," Heather says, "and it wasn't long before we had to get two good cameras – a pair of 5D Mark II Canons with a variety of lenses."

Heather is quick to point out that Lucas was always stronger in technical skills. "He still leans over my shoulder sometimes to check my camera settings."

"Yes," Lucas says, "but she has a real knack for composition. She can walk up to a scene and know immediately what she needs to do. She gets it in the first or second shot, while I may shoot dozens of pictures to get the best one."

They admit to being "a little competitive" with one another. If one goes out alone now, the other thinks, "Oh, I may be missing some good shots!"

They opened the Frykman Studio Gallery on Bay Shore Drive, just south of downtown Sister Bay, in 2008. Heather learned to mat and frame their work, while Lucas, a skilled woodworker, makes the frames and moldings in his home workshop. Most days in the summer are spent in the gallery talking with customers – with perhaps one day a week in the field. They shoot nearly every day in spring and fall, and even in the winter when snow sticks to the trees. Eventually, they'd like to be able to spend most of their time on photography, with help in other aspects of the business.

Their favorite locations are Peninsula State Park, Cana Island, Cave Point, Rock Island and Washington Island. They've also made photo trips to the Smoky Mountains and the north woods, where they canoe and camp. They spent January 2013 in Panama, shooting about half the time and absorbing the culture; next, they hope to visit Ecuador.

These days, the pair is best known for their Door County landscapes and incredible night sky photos. Using a wide-angle lens and a 20- to 45-second exposure, they shoot on clear, moonless nights – the moon "washes out" the sky – so they can concentrate on the stars. If conditions are good, they may spend the whole night shooting. "Basically, night photography is the same as day work," Lucas says. "The settings are different, but we're still looking for the dramatic view. June and July are prime time, because the Milky Way is highest on the horizon."

Light is the most important component in their work. "You can always tell another photographer," Heather says, "by their comments about light – how it plays across the grass, for instance."

A customer inquired about a photo Heather took a few years ago on the road to Northport.

"It had just stopped raining," Lucas said, "and for one minute, there was the most incredible light. It never occurred again that summer."

He also noted, with regret, that a high tree limb that "made the shot" has since been cut.

Many of their night sky shots are now printed on aluminum by Image Wizards in North Carolina. "They catch the eye like nothing else," Lucas said. "We hear gasps when customers see them. It's like a first glimpse of high-definition TV on a large screen. Some people even insist that we must be backlighting them somehow."

Along with leading some workshops at the Peninsula School of Art, Heather and Lucas also offer photo shoots specializing in sunrises, sunsets or night skies. "It's a very personal experience for just one or two people at a time," Heather says. "We cover as much ground as we can in two to three hours, chasing the light." Lucas adds that clients also really like to see how professionals work and that some of their own best photos have come from shoots with clients.

INFORMATION

FRYKMAN STUDIO GALLERY
ADDRESS: 2566 S. Bay Shore Drive, Sister Bay
WEBSITE: door-county-photography.com
PHONE: (920) 854-7351
HOURS: Open daily in season, weekends in winter and by appointment.

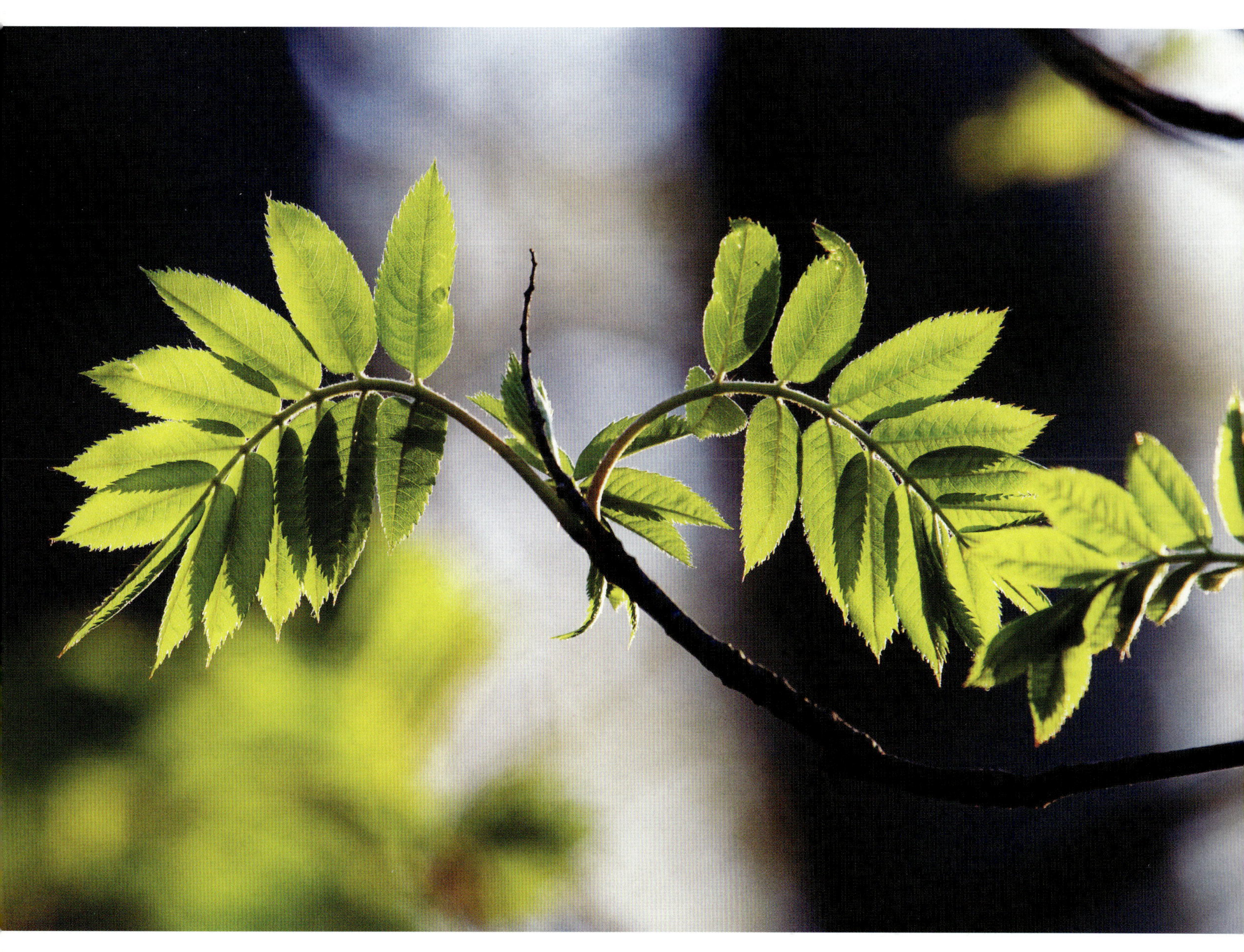

Spring foliage – Heather.

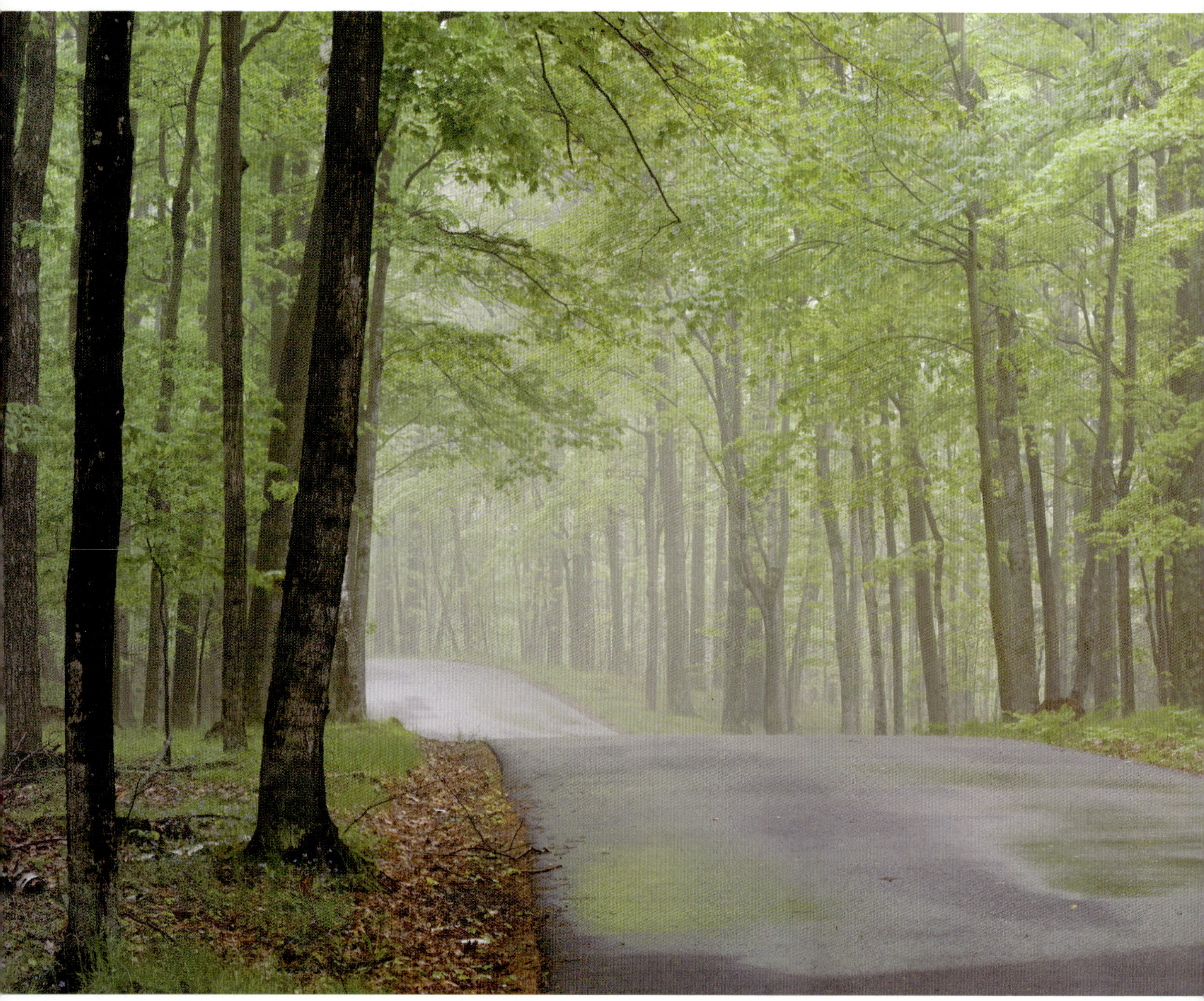

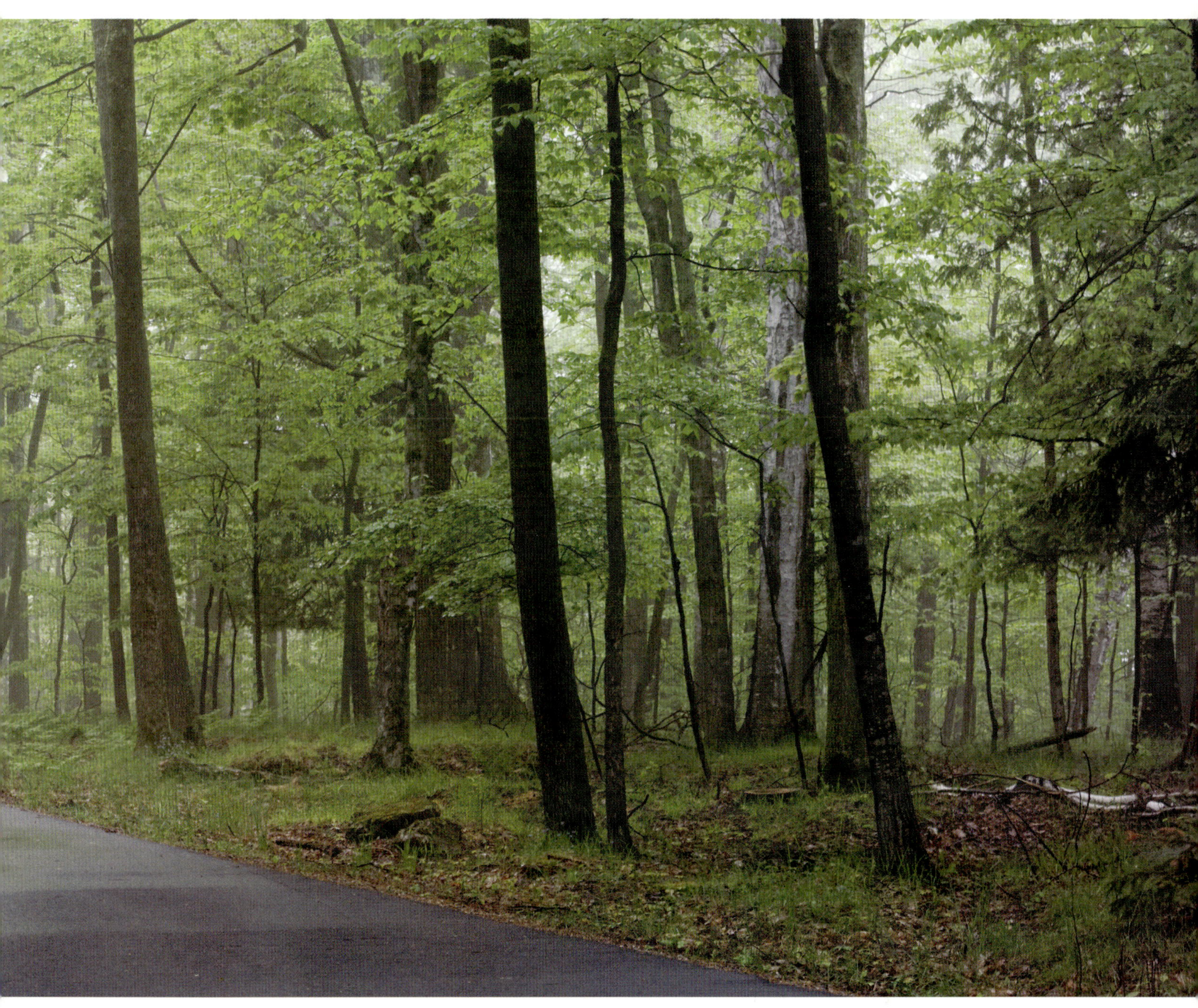

Skyline Road, Peninsula State Park – Lucas.

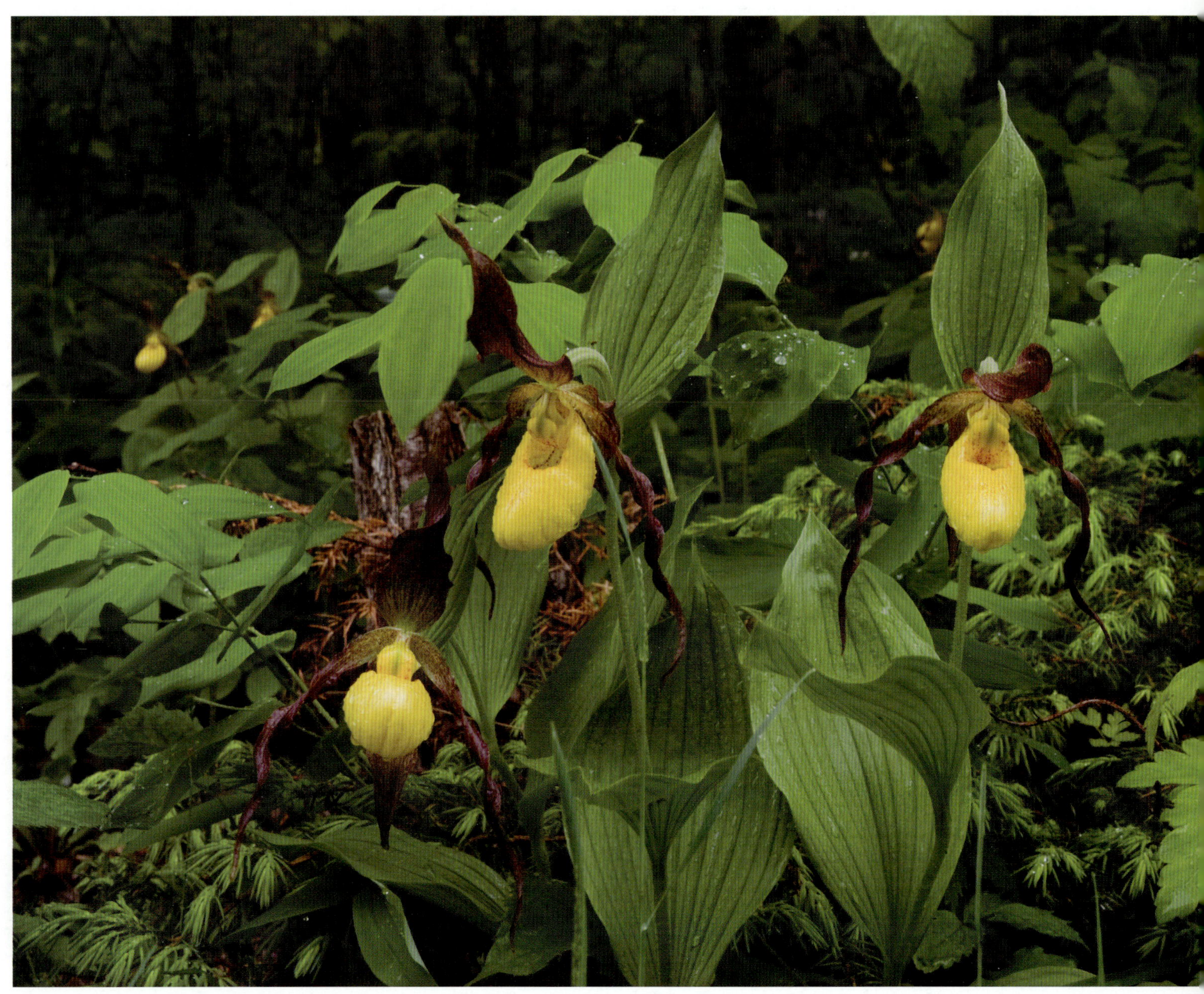

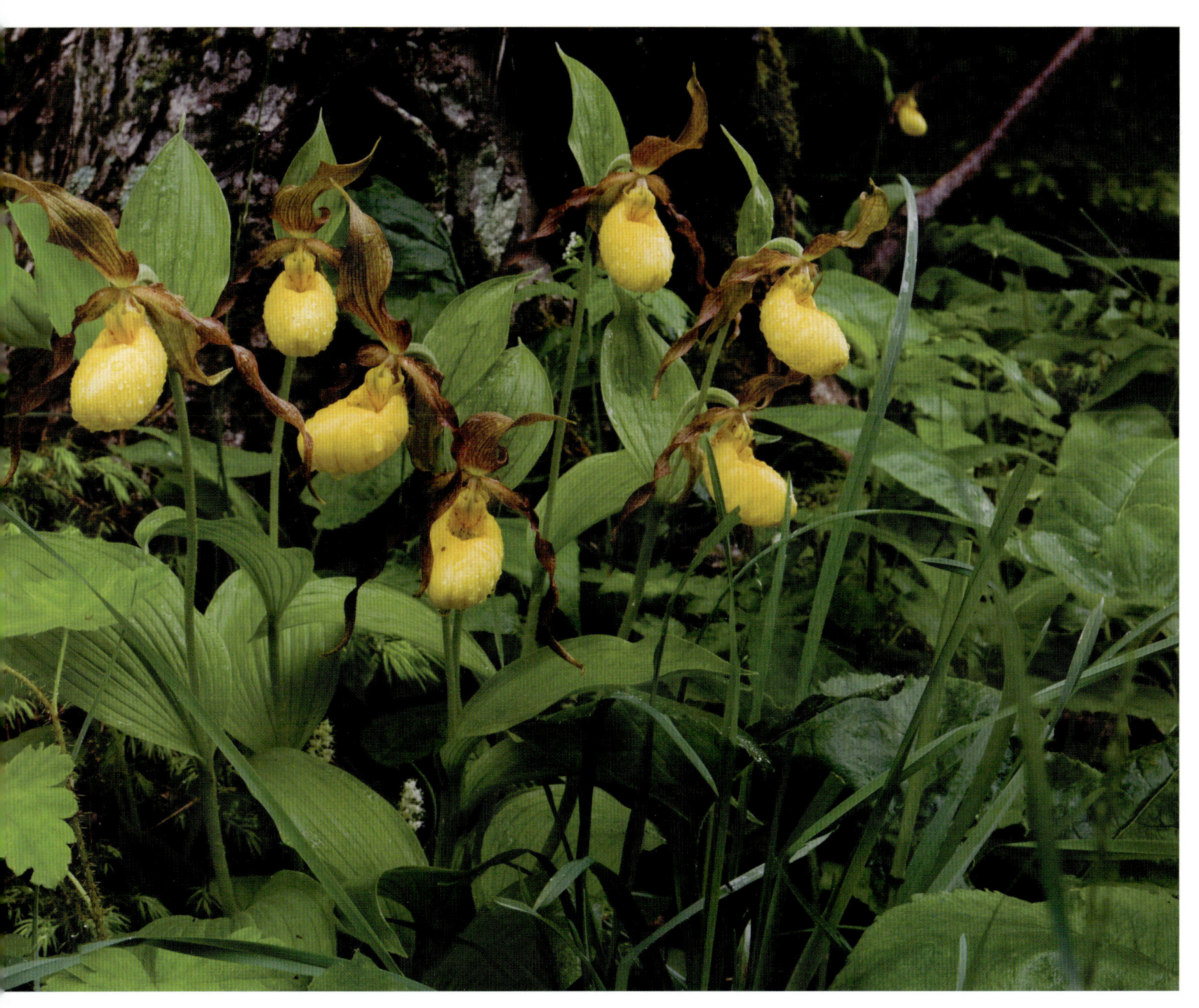

Yellow Lady's-slippers, Isle View Road, Gills Rock – Lucas.

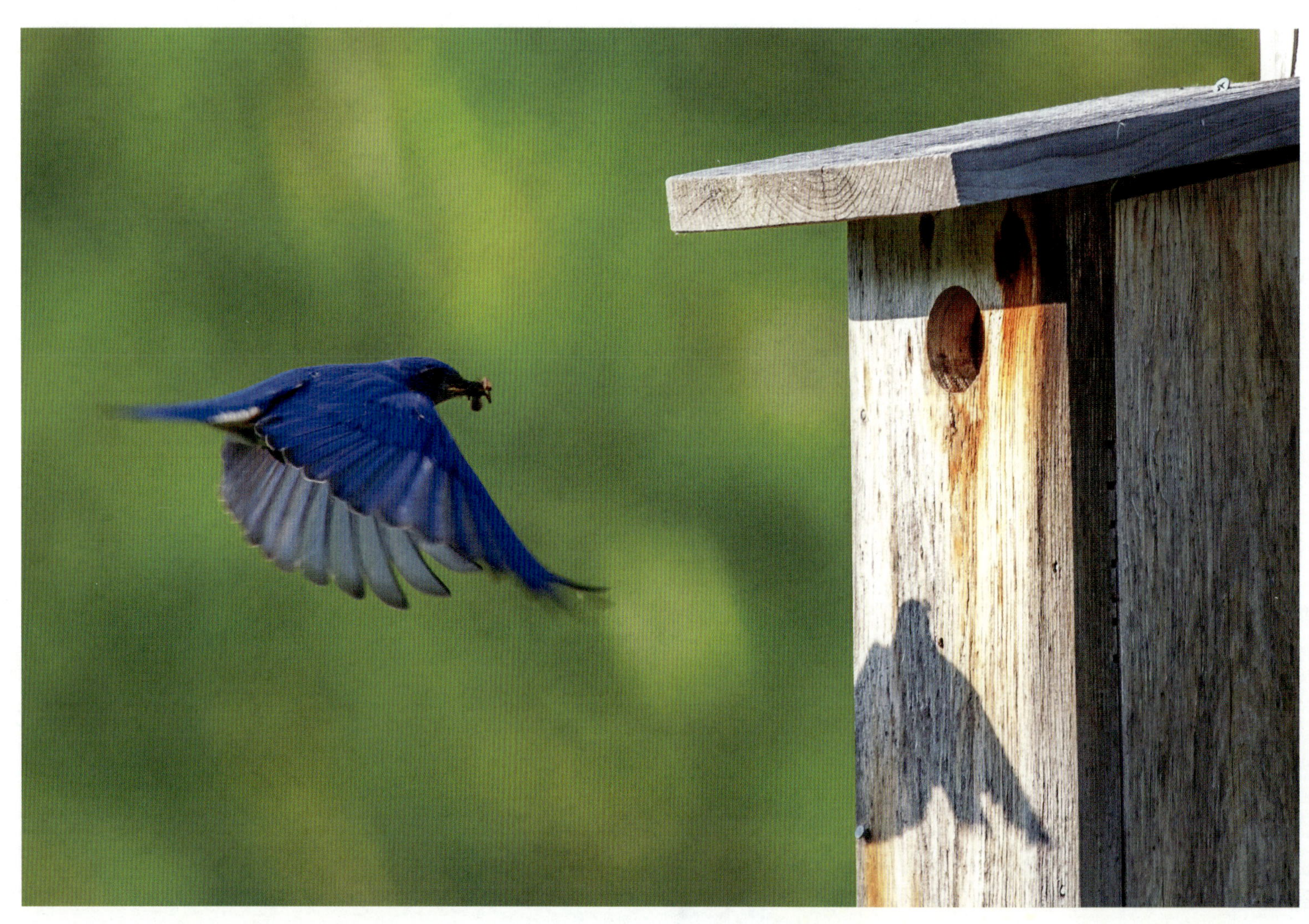

This page and the next: Eastern Bluebird, Ellison Bay – Heather.

Following pages: Trilliums, Ellison Bay – Heather; dandelions and cherry blossoms, Sister Bay – Heather.

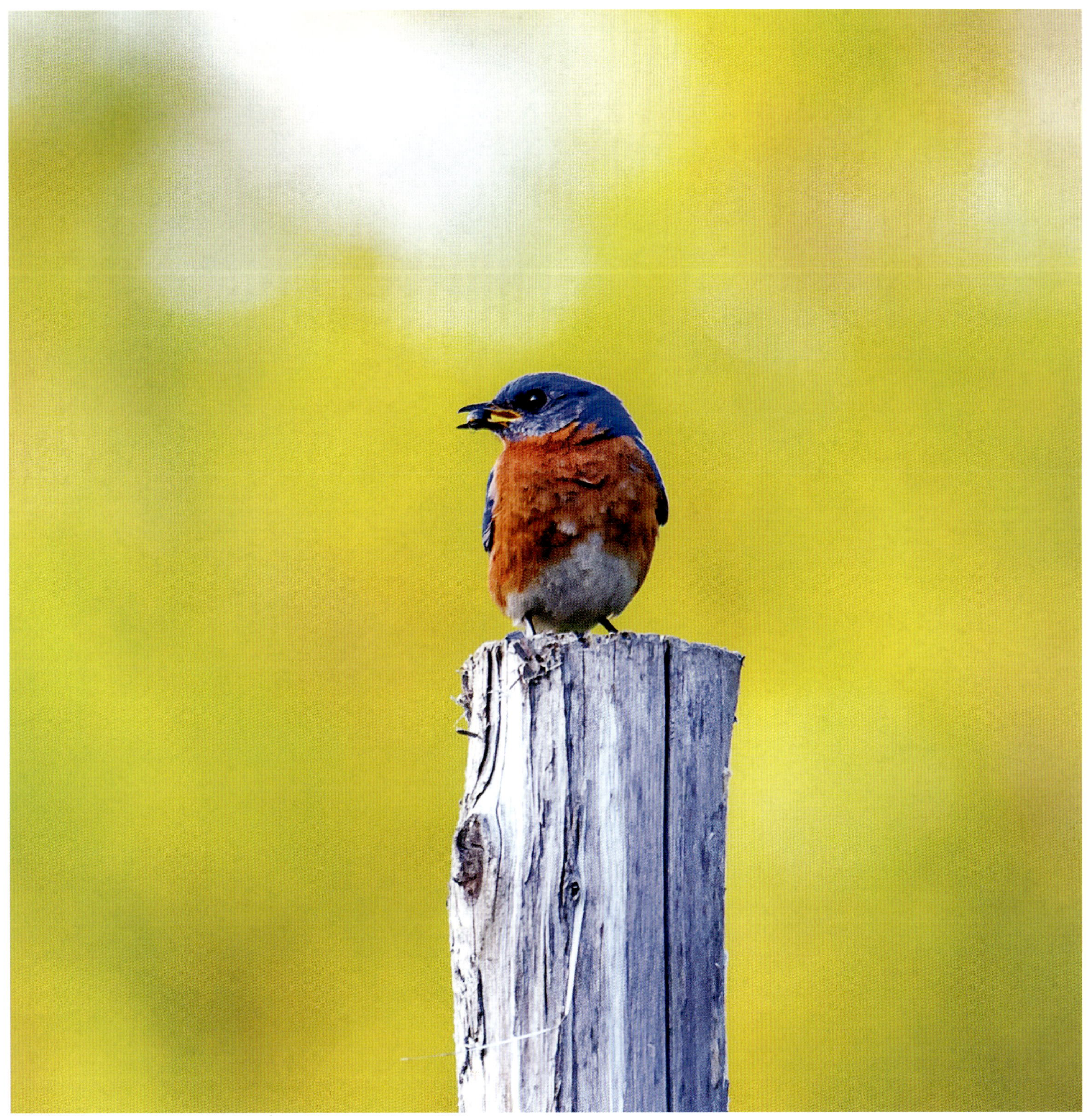

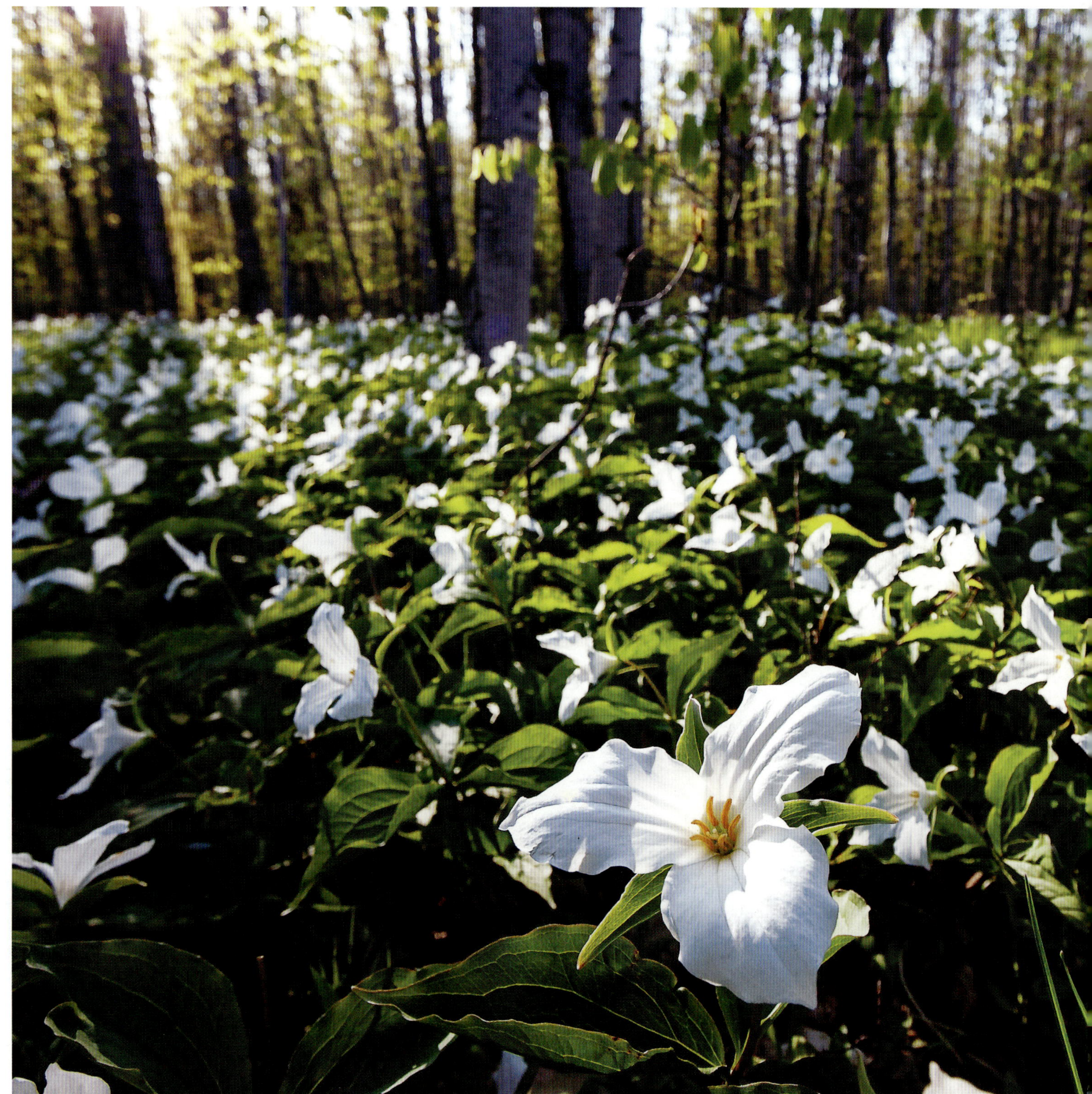

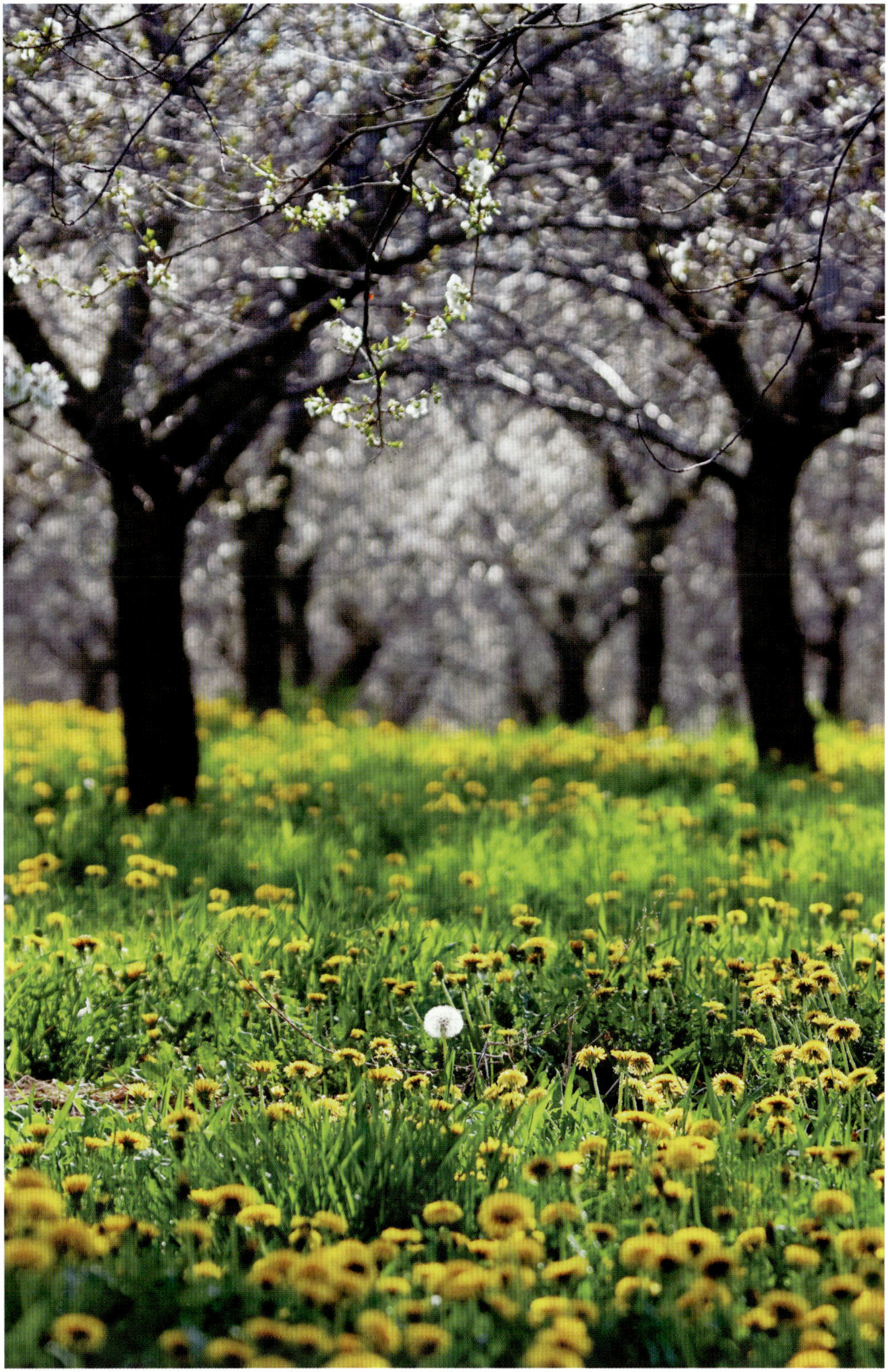

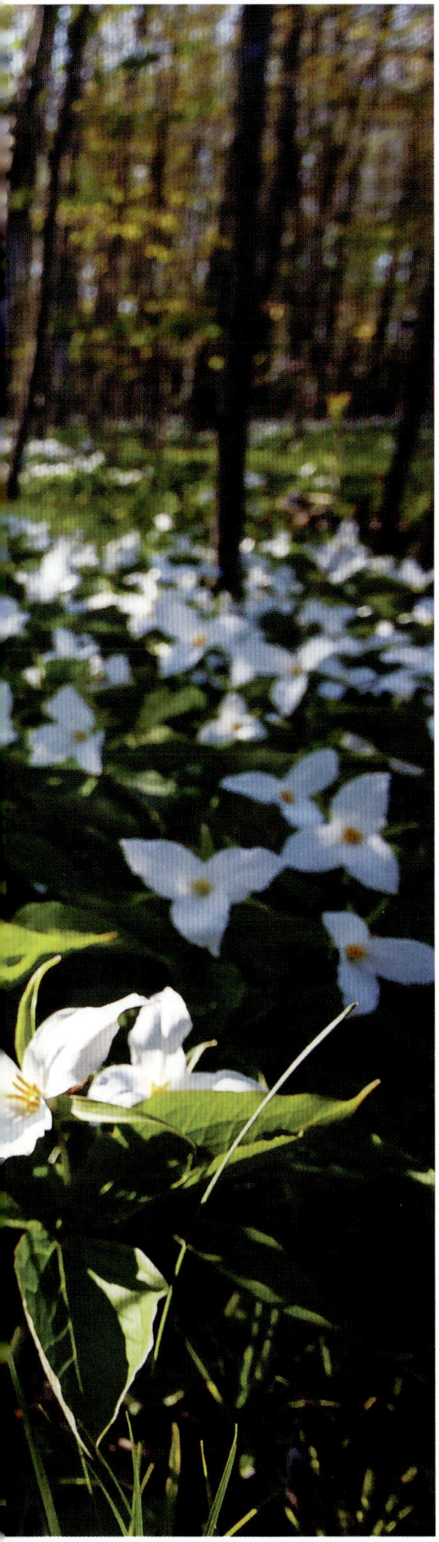

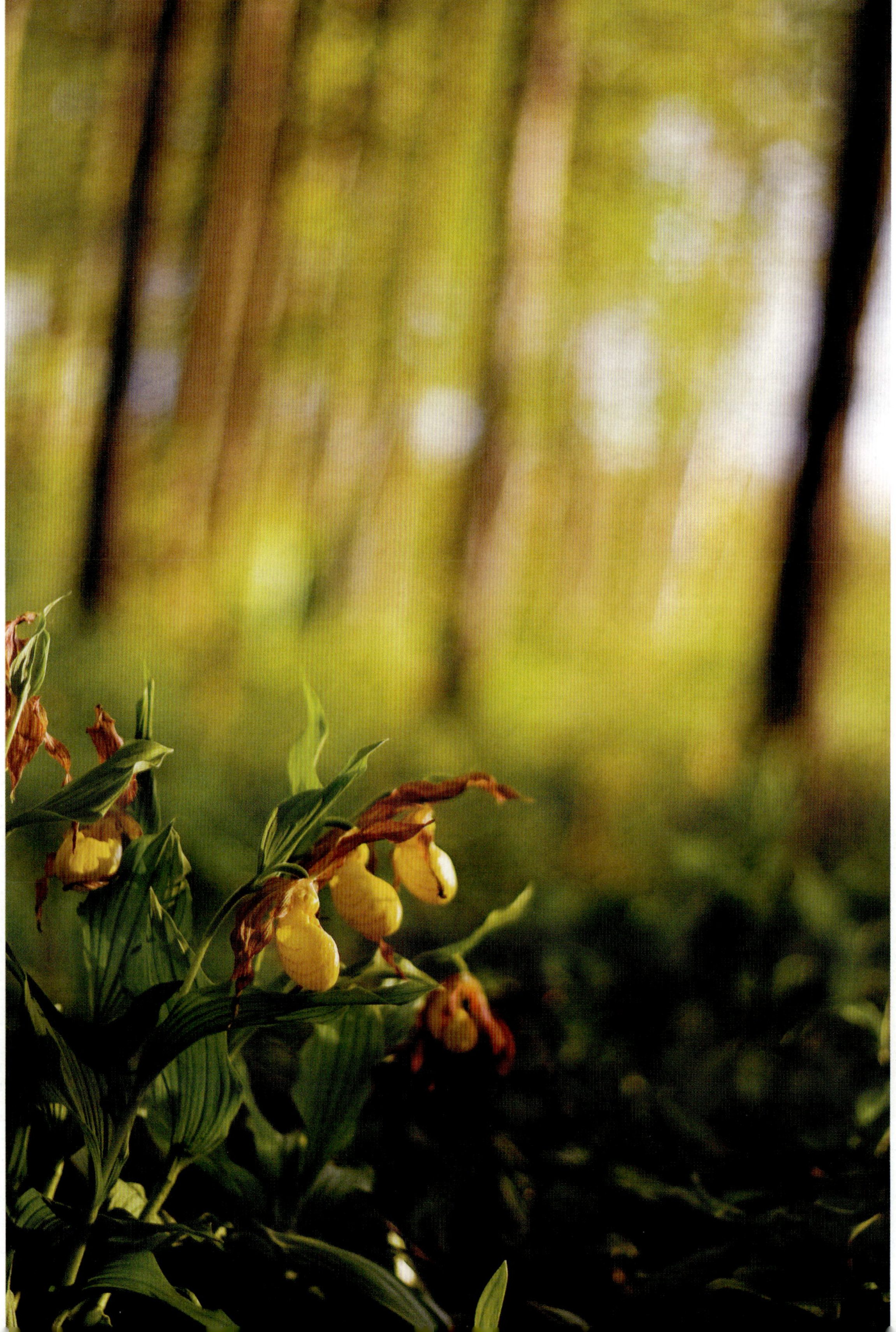

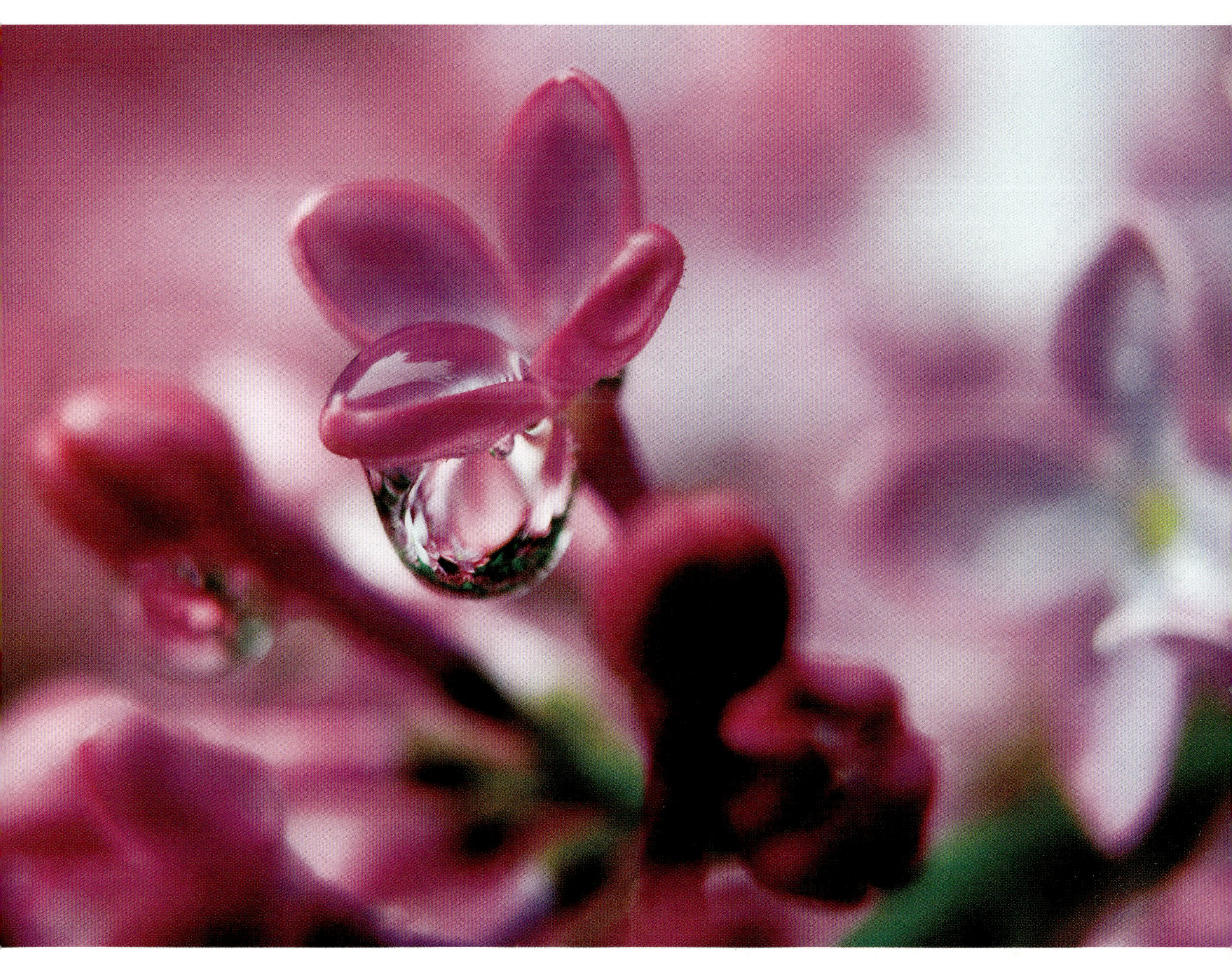

Previous page: Yellow Lady's-slippers, Egg Harbor – Heather.

This page: Water droplet on lilac, Fish Creek – Heather.

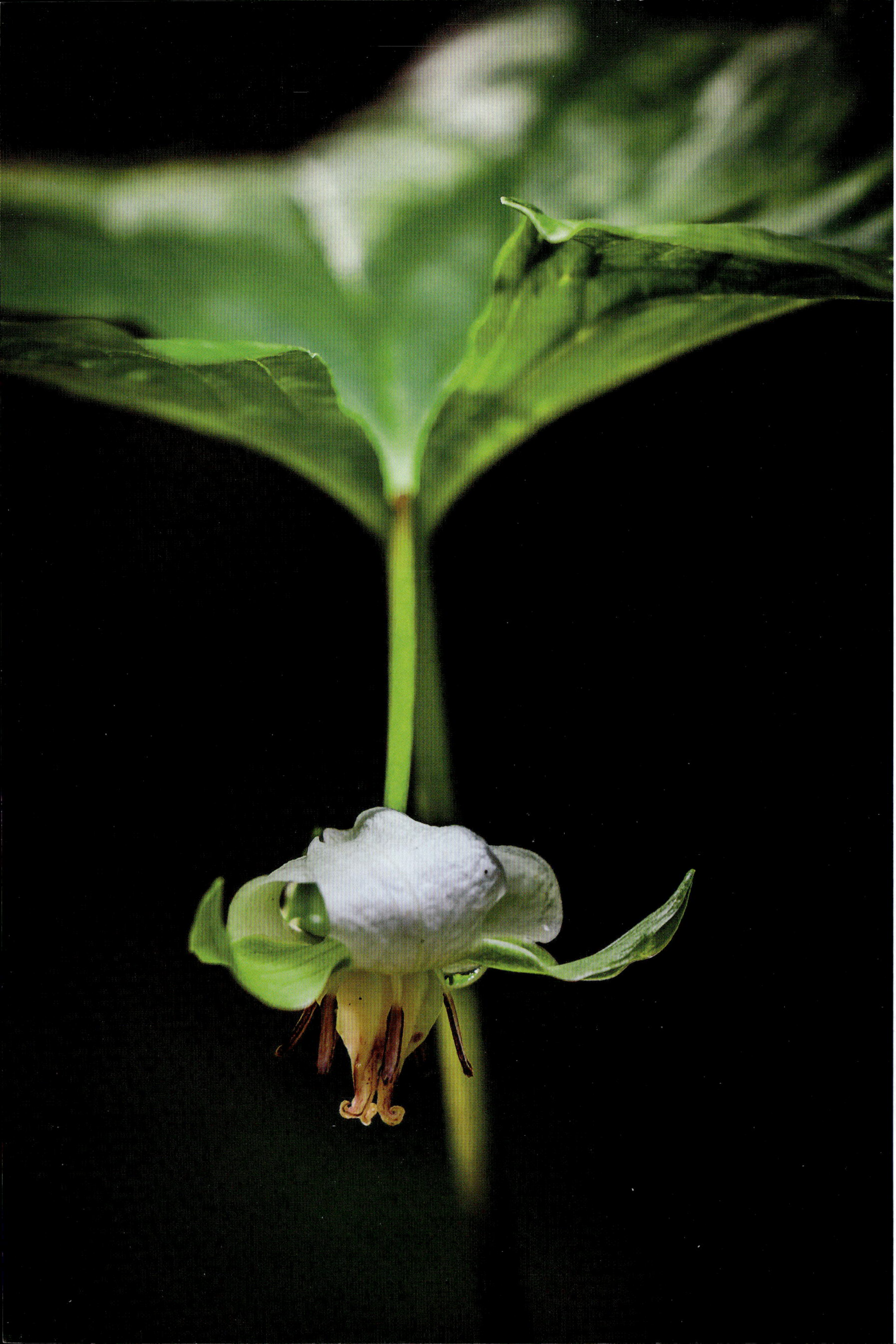

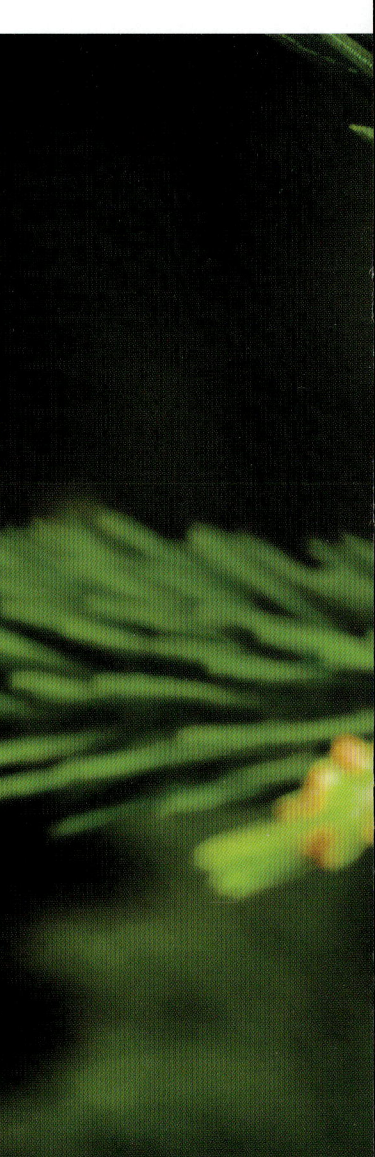

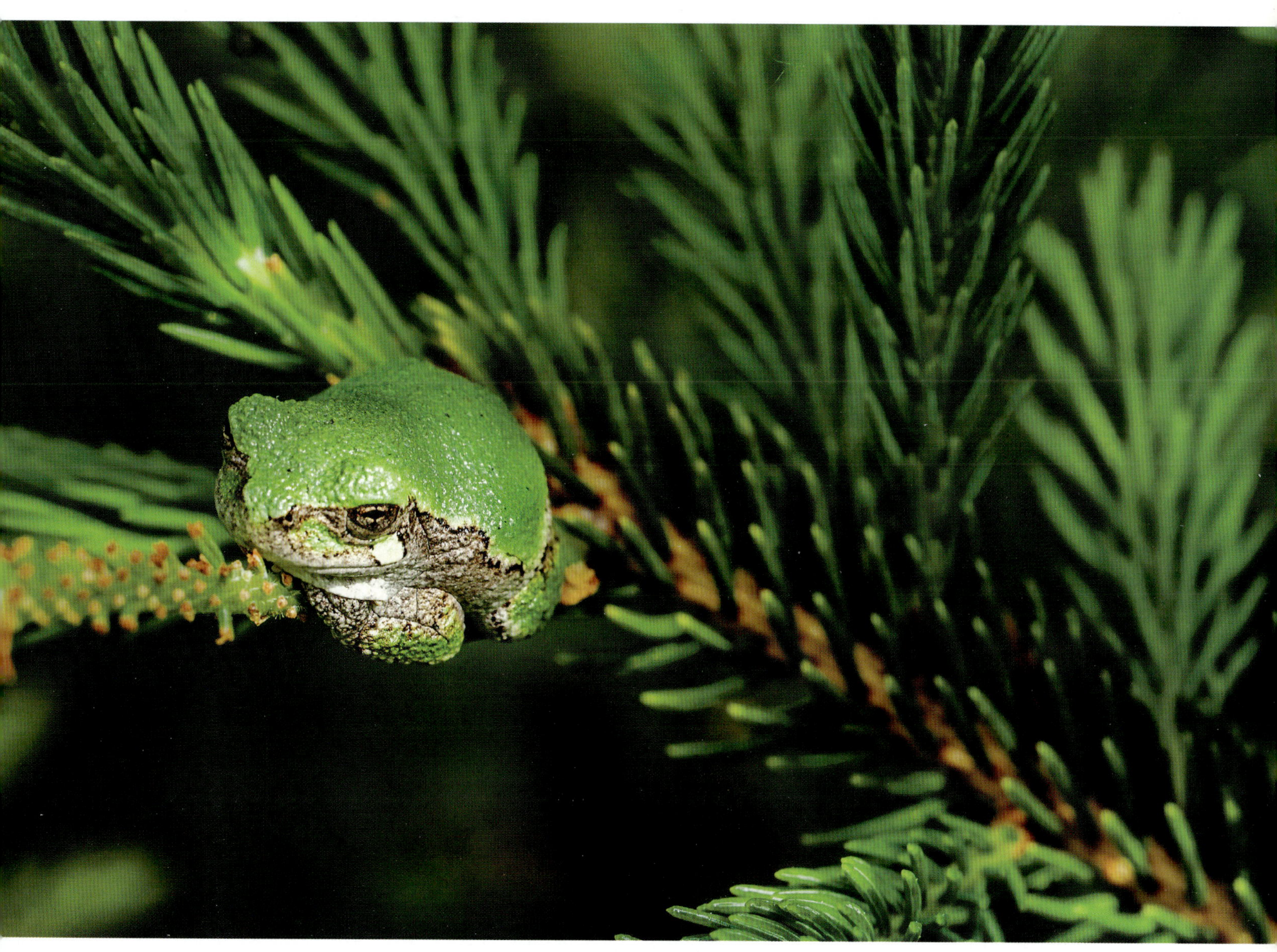

Previous page: Nodding Trillium, The Ridges Sanctuary, Baileys Harbor – Lucas.

This page: Gray Tree Frog on spruce, Logan Creek State Natural Area, Jacksonport – Lucas.

Following pages: Showy Lady's-slippers, The Ridges Sanctuary, Baileys Harbor – Heather; Pink Moccasin Lady's-slipper, The Ridges Sanctuary, Baileys Harbor – Lucas.

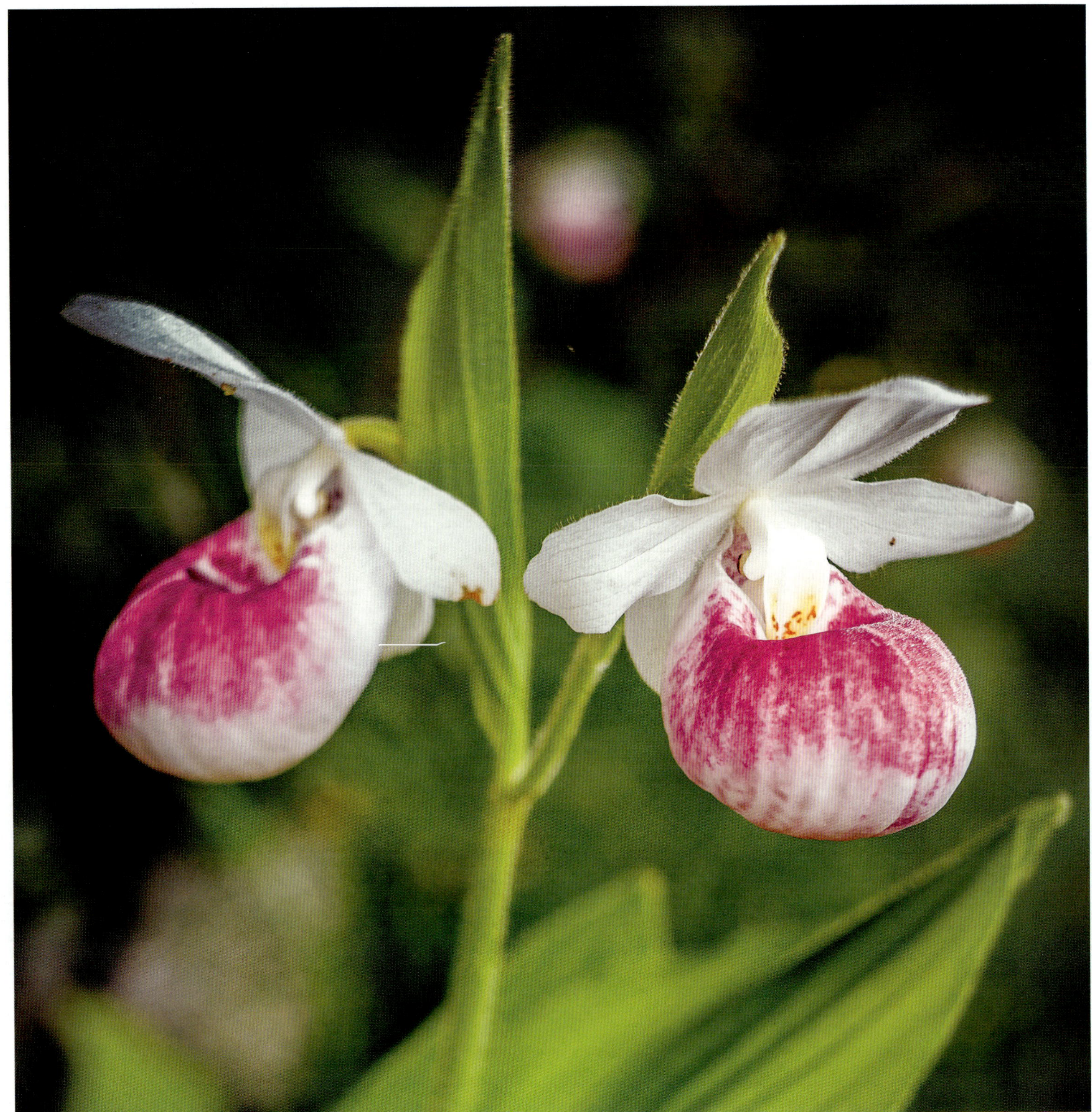

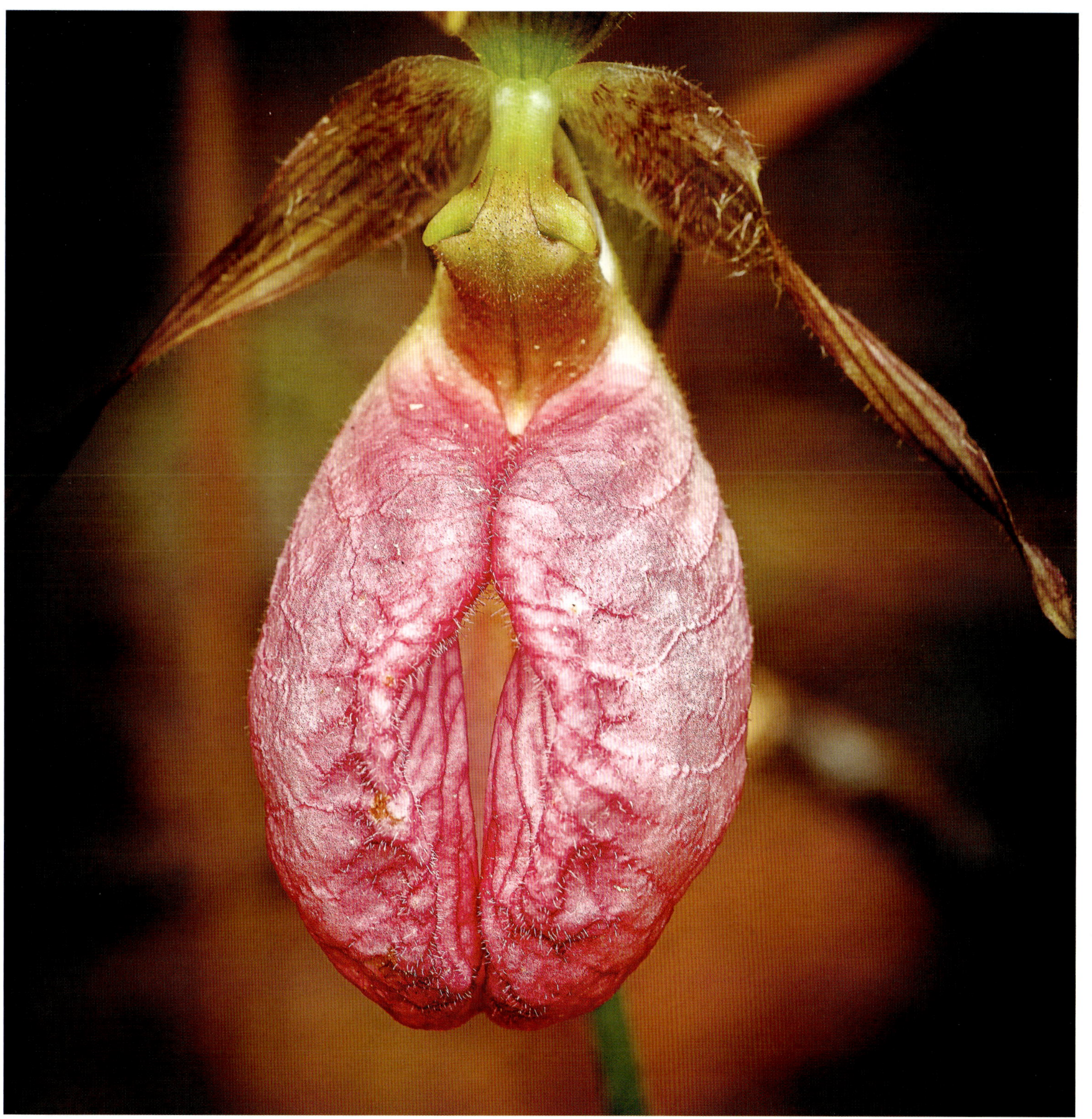

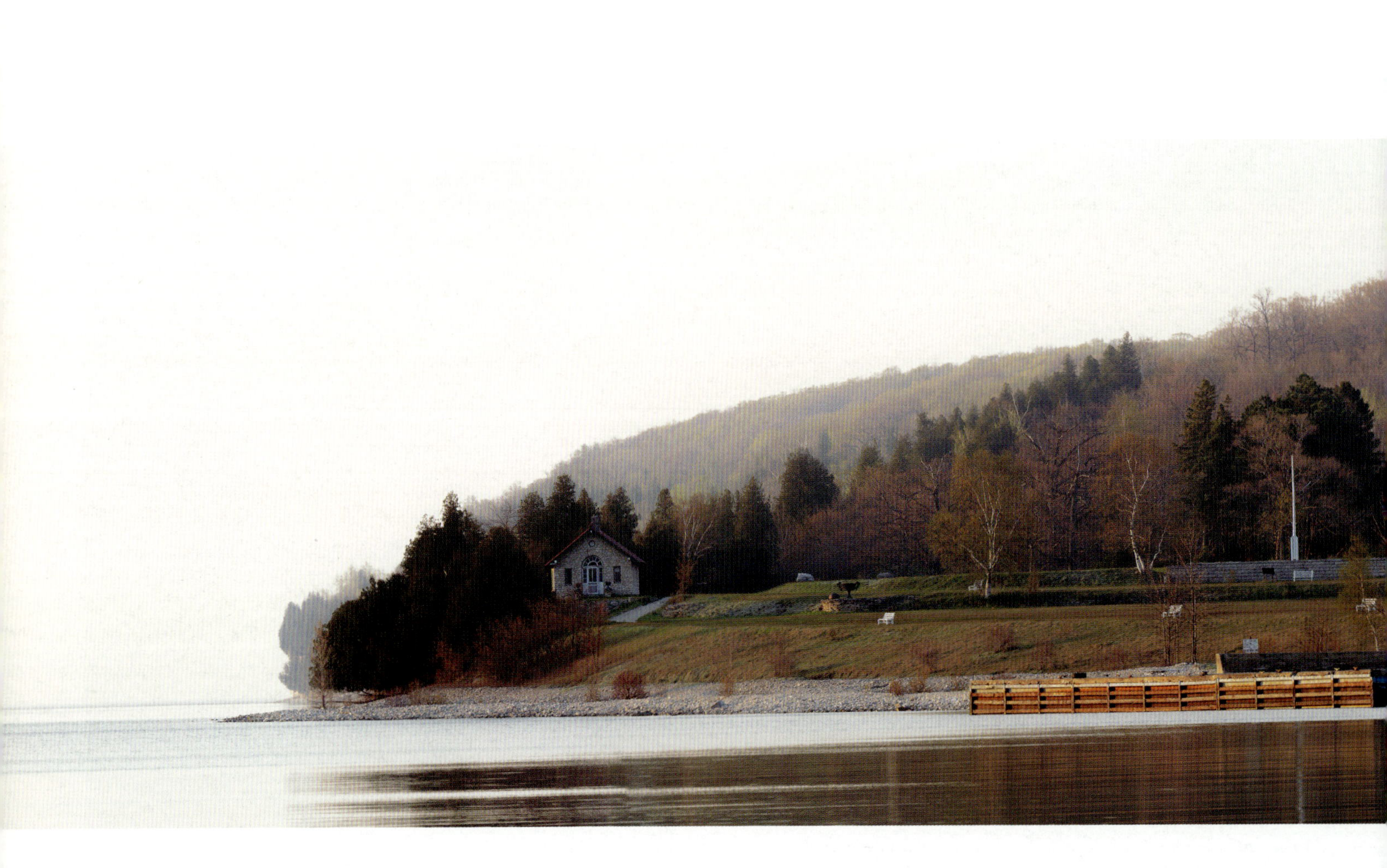

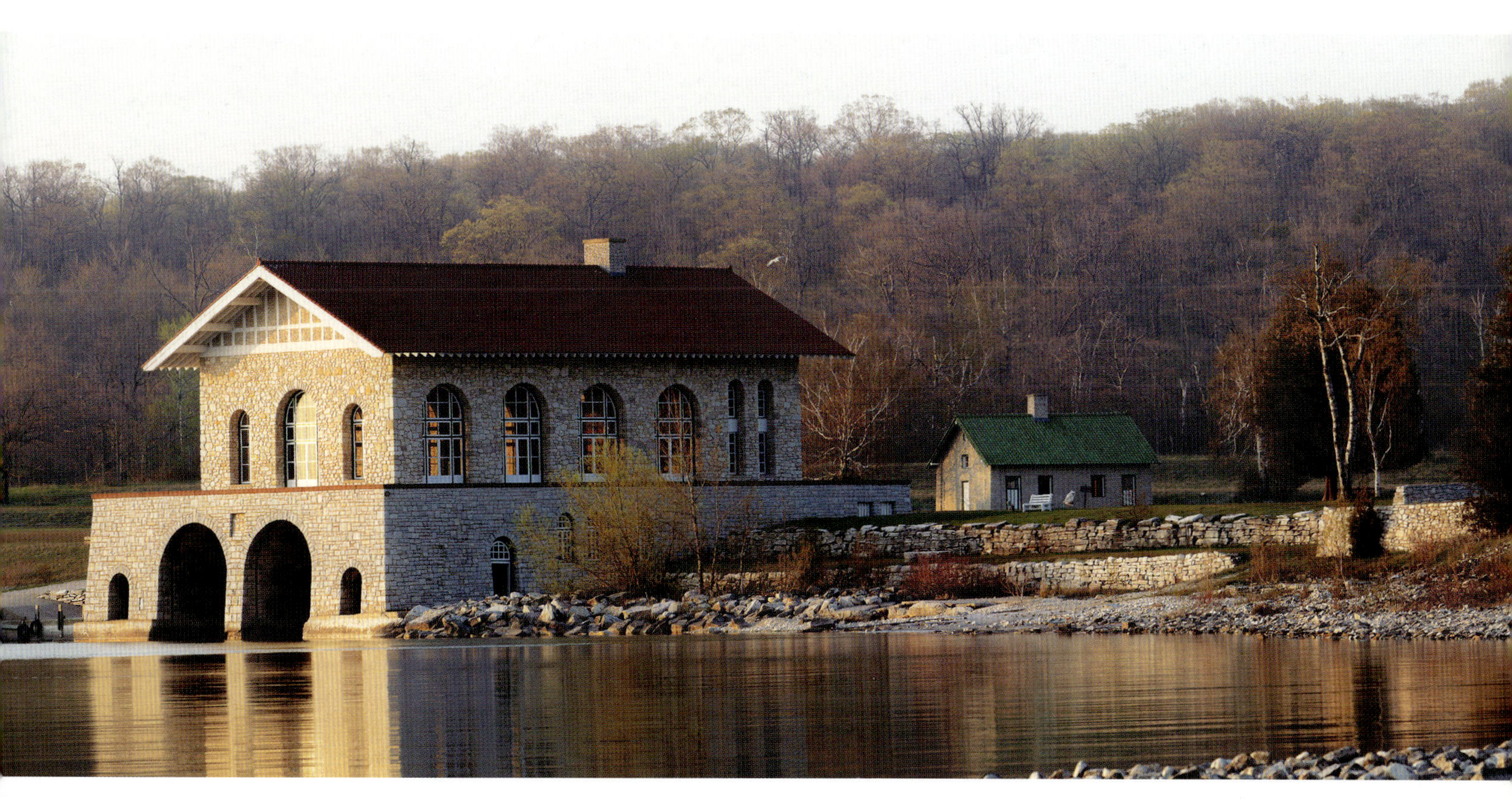

This page: Rock Island boathouse, Rock Island State Park – Lucas.

Following pages: *The Red Boat*, Washington Island – Heather.

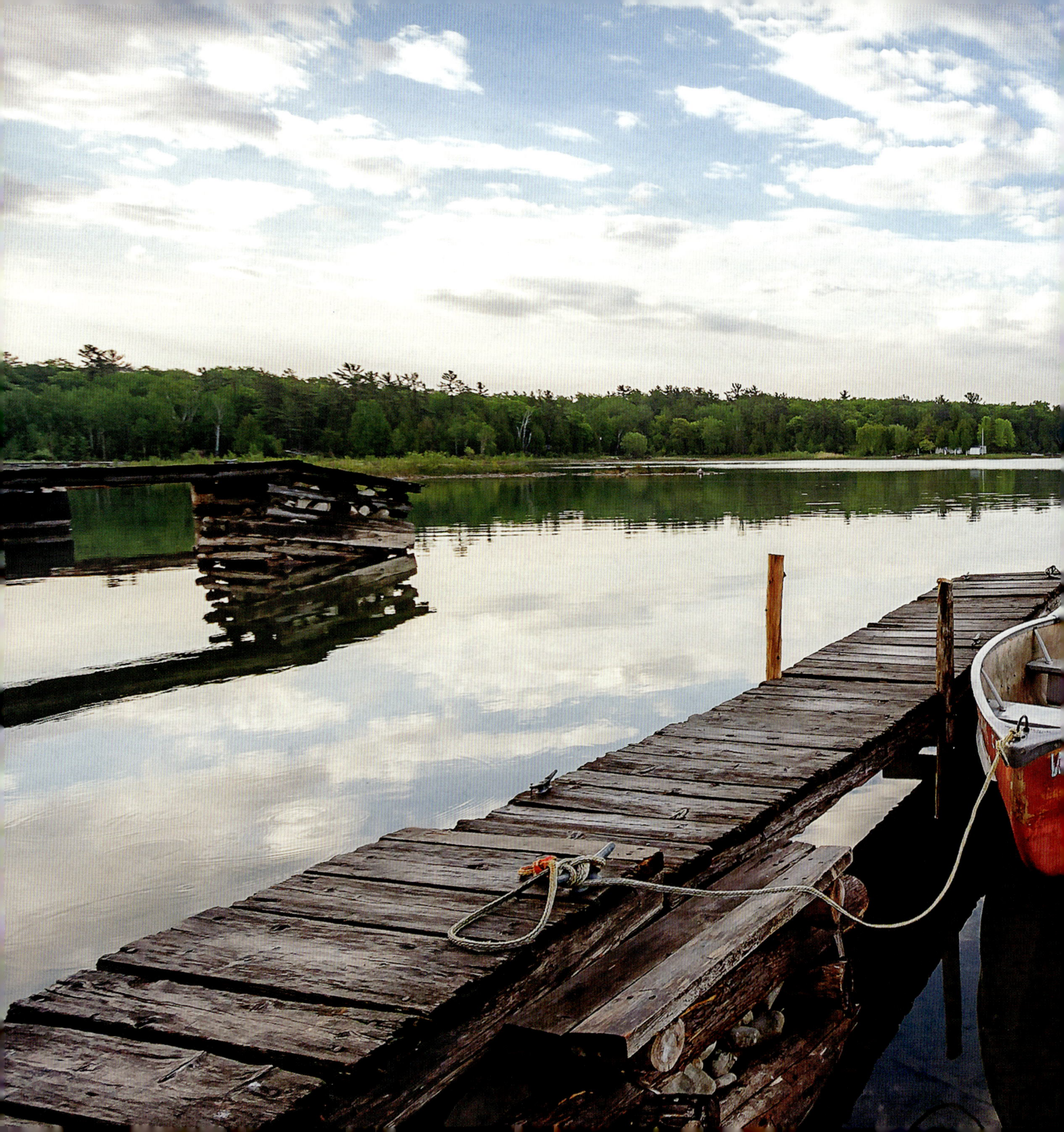

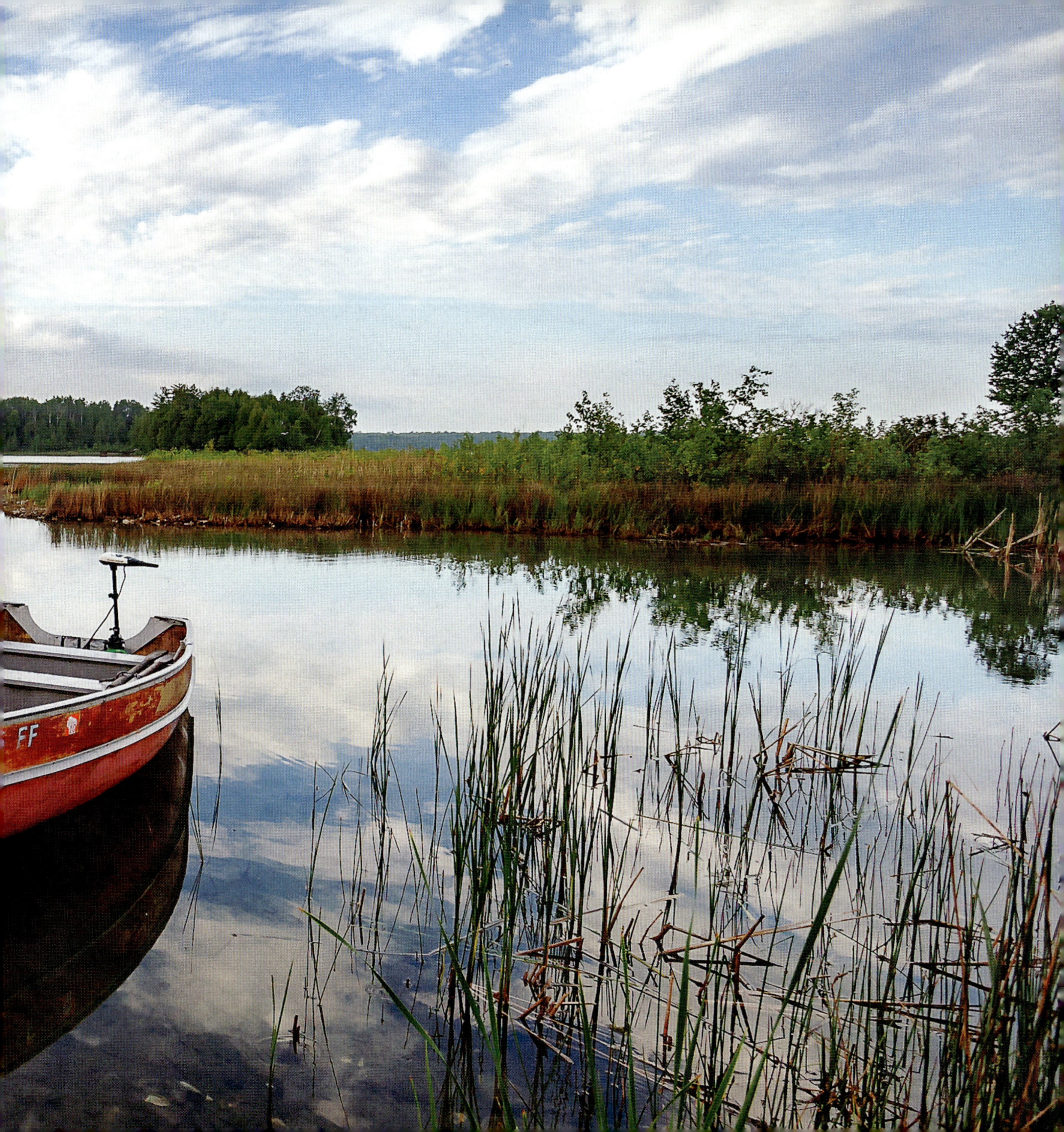
FF

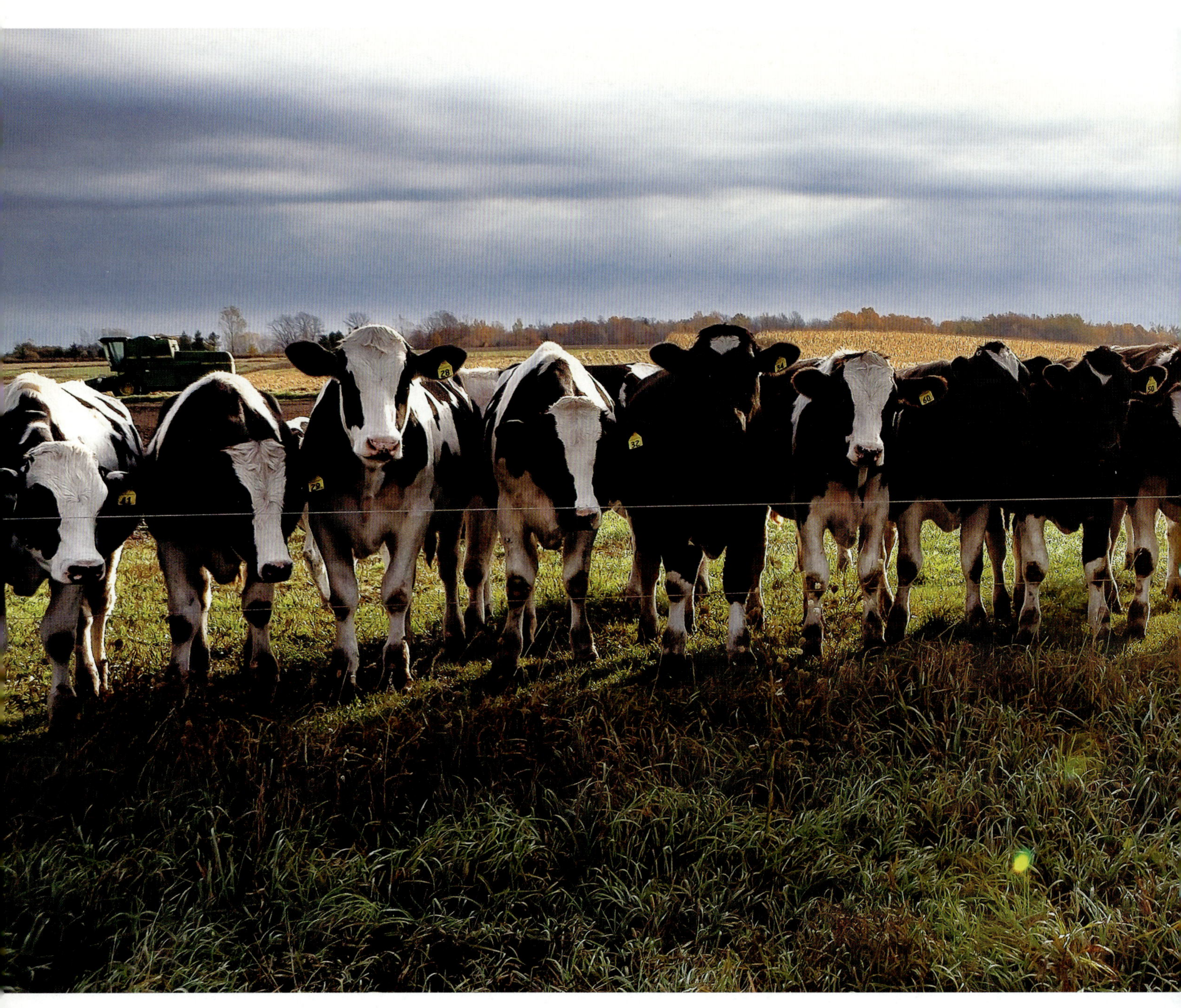

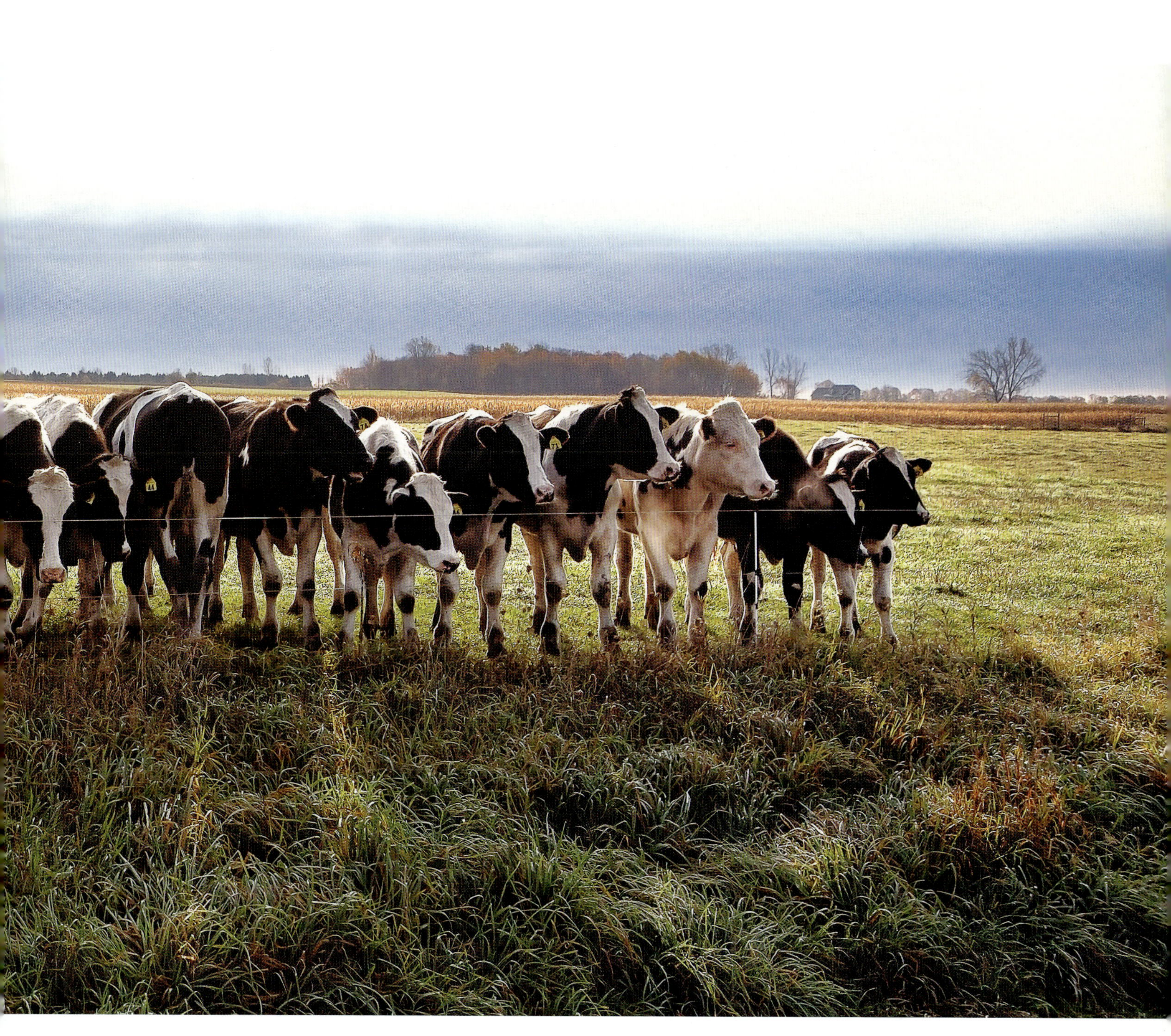

Holsteins, Institute – Heather.

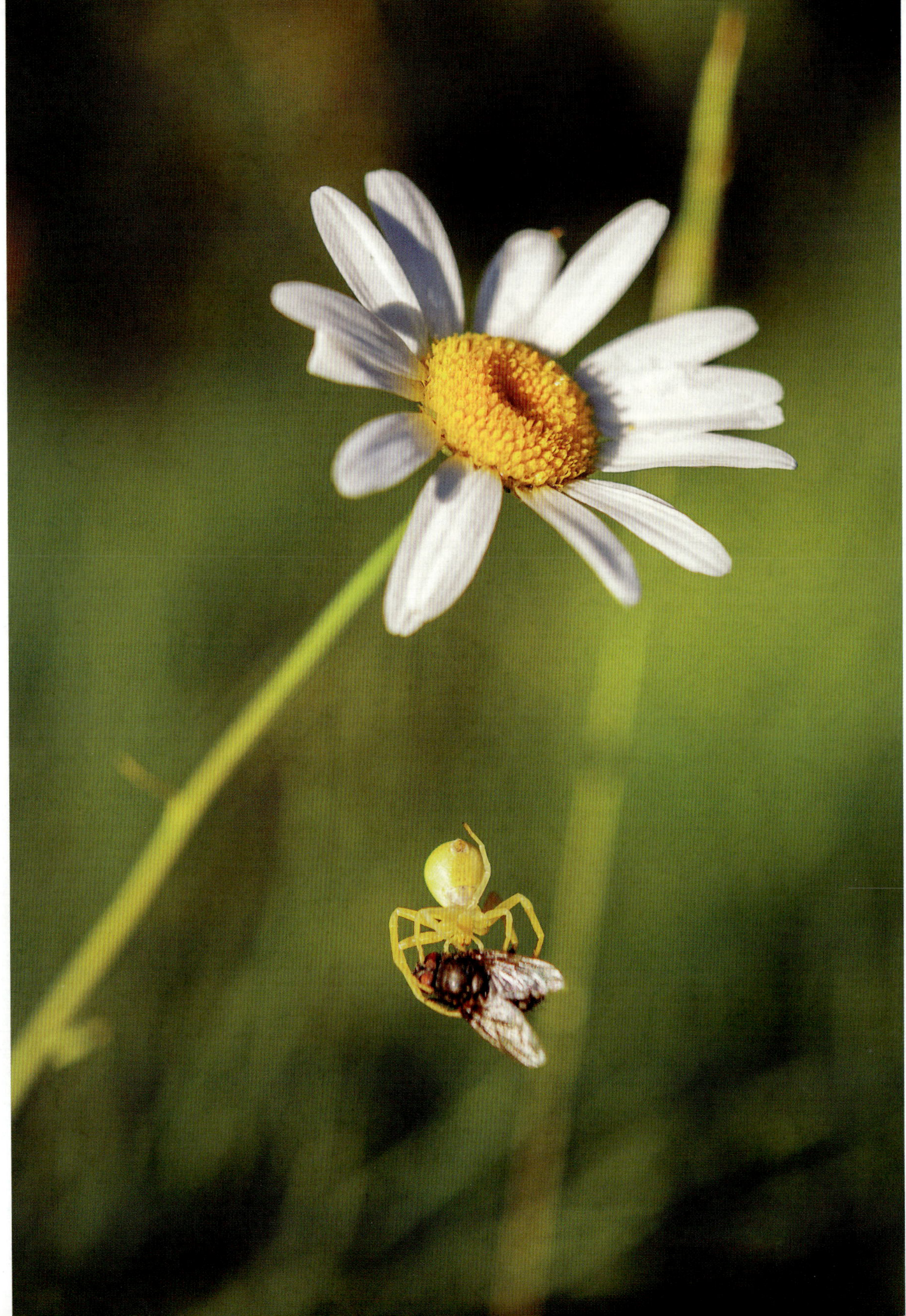

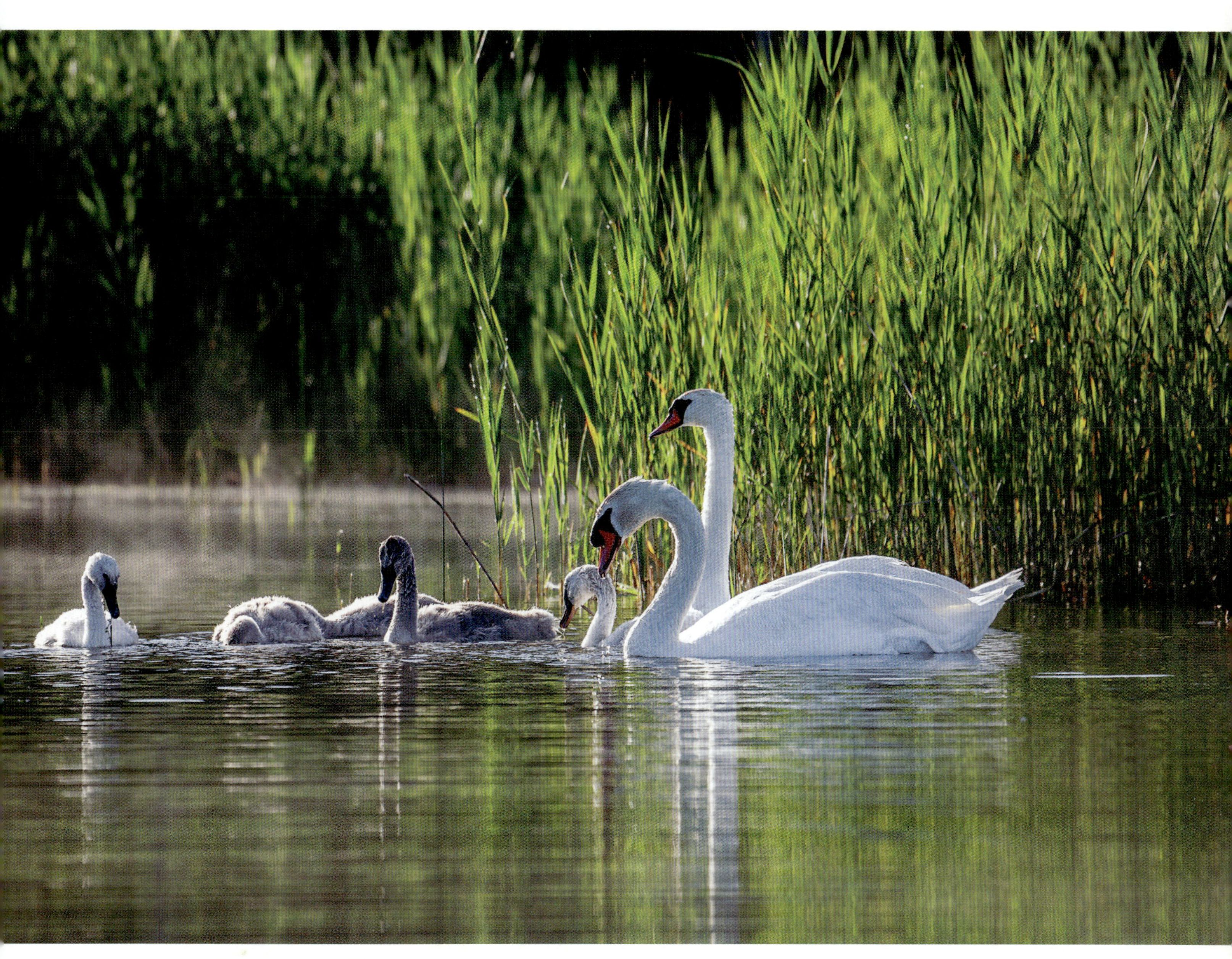

Previous page: *Catch of the Day*, Baileys Harbor – Heather.

This page: Swans, Washington Island – Heather and Lucas.

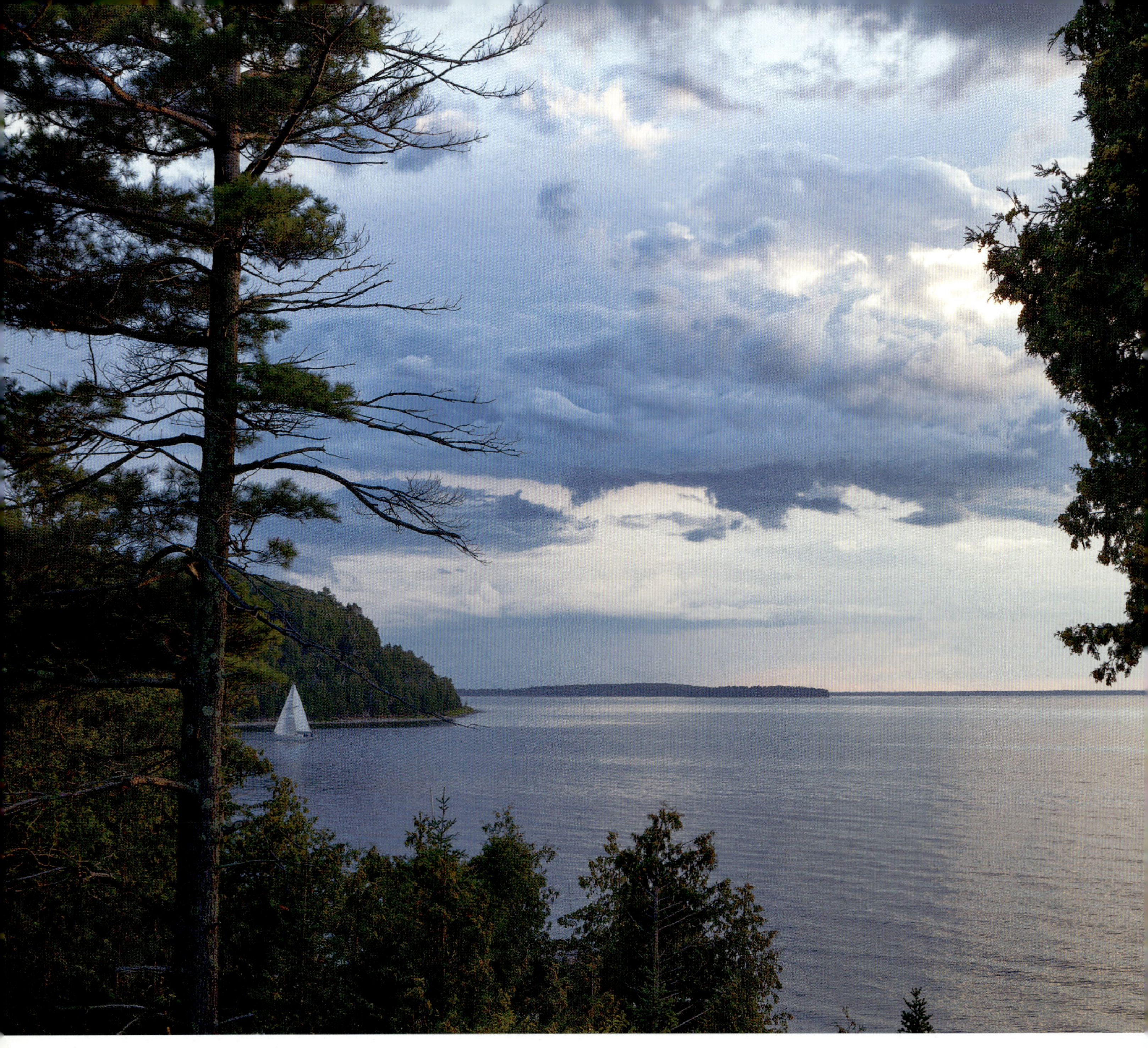

This page: Sailboat, Little Sister Bay – Lucas.

Next page: Wall cloud, Rock Island State Park – Heather.

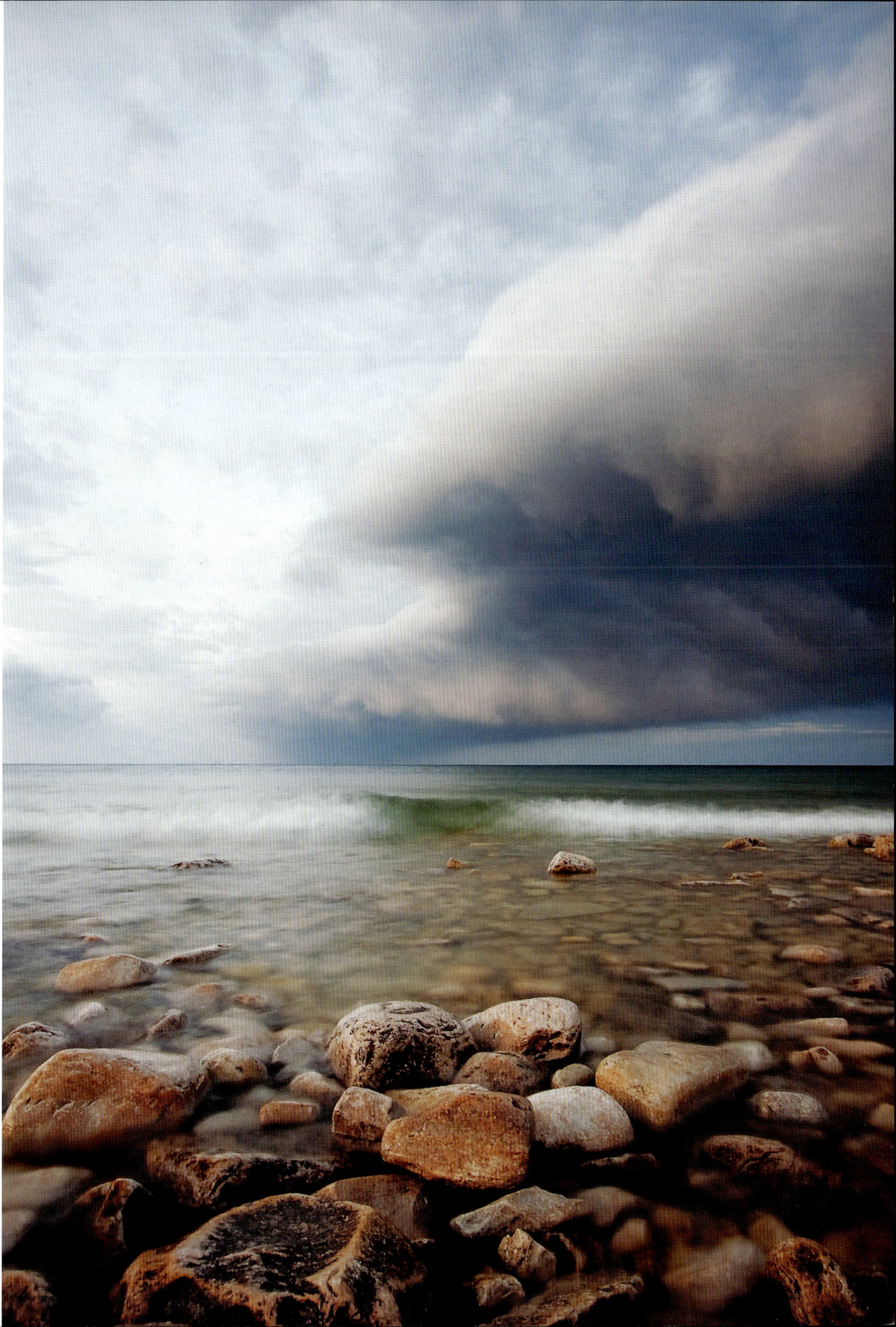

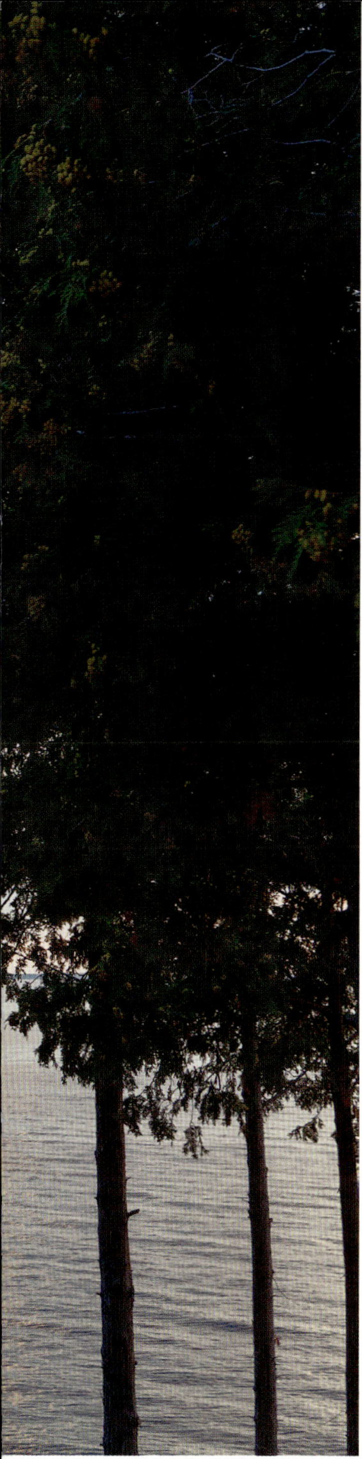

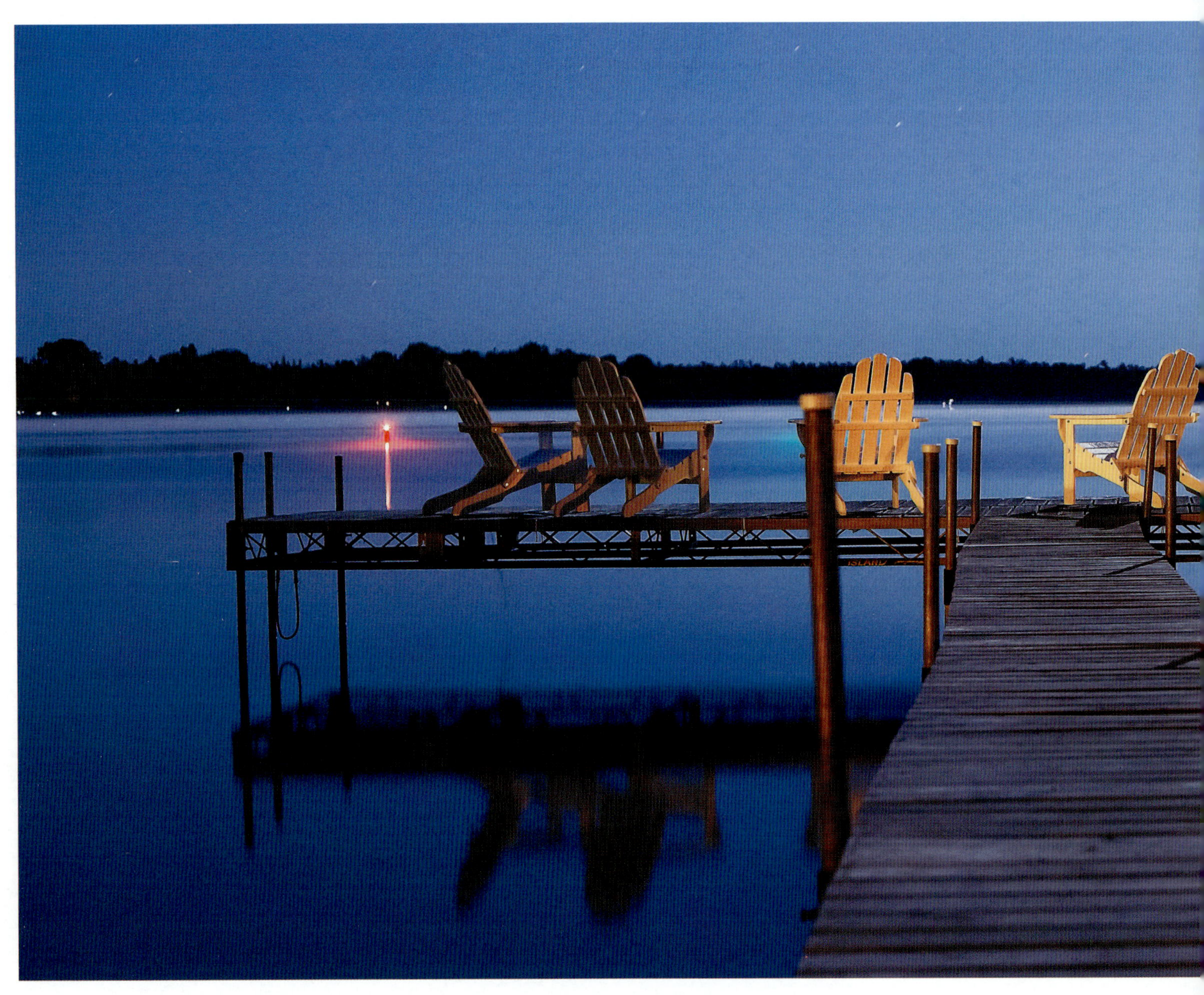

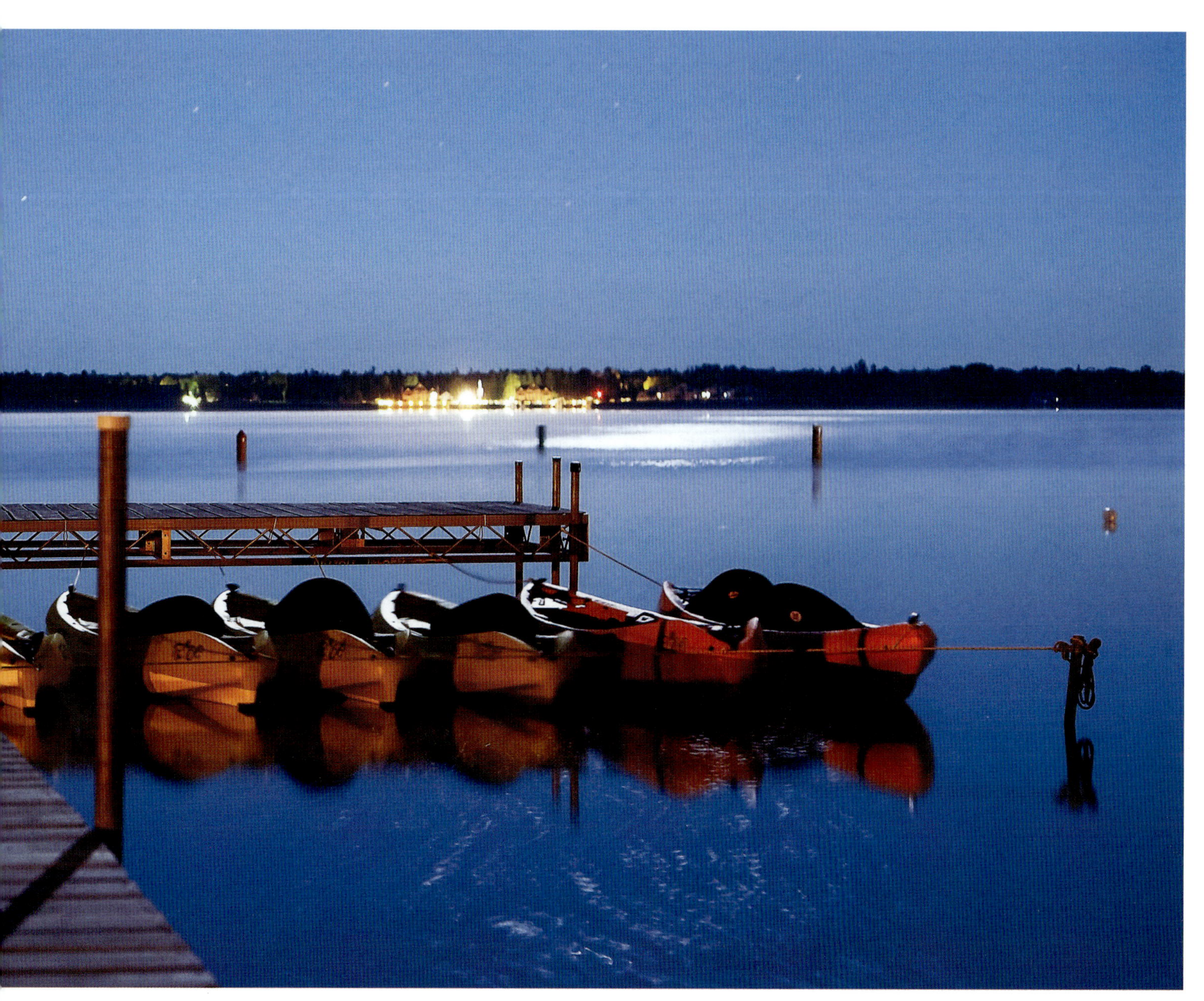

Moonlit chairs and kayaks, Baileys Harbor – Lucas.

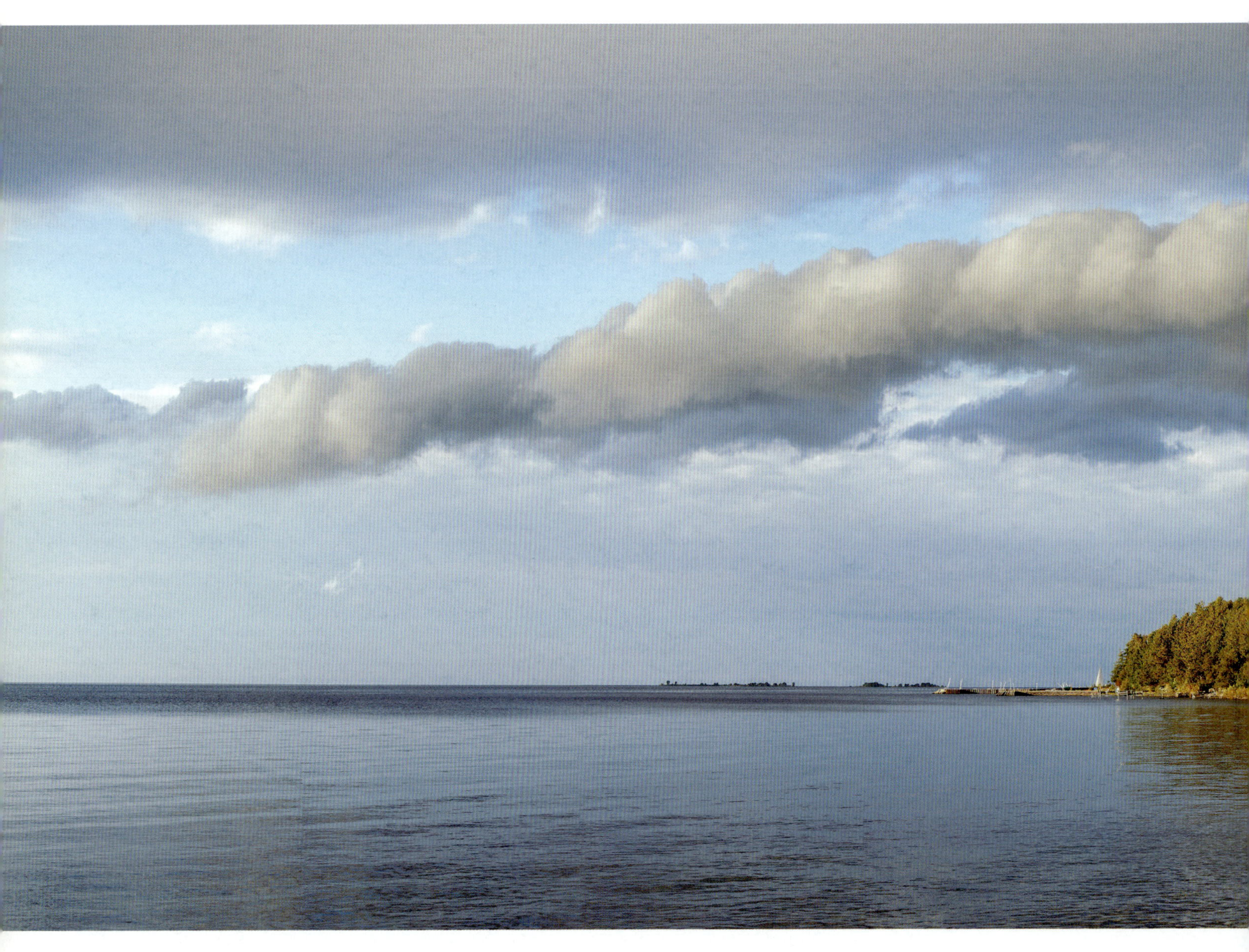

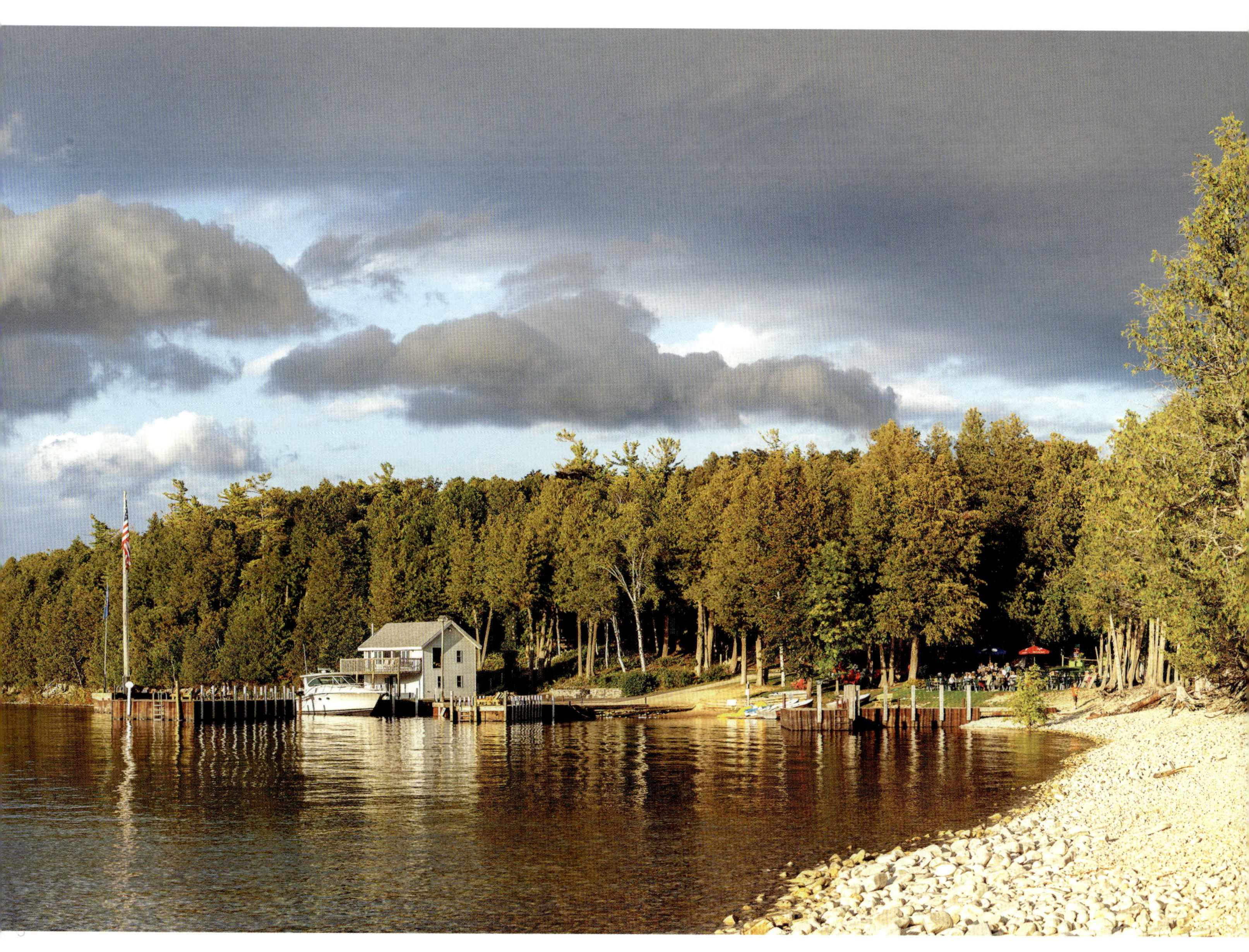

Storm clouds, Pebble Beach – Lucas.

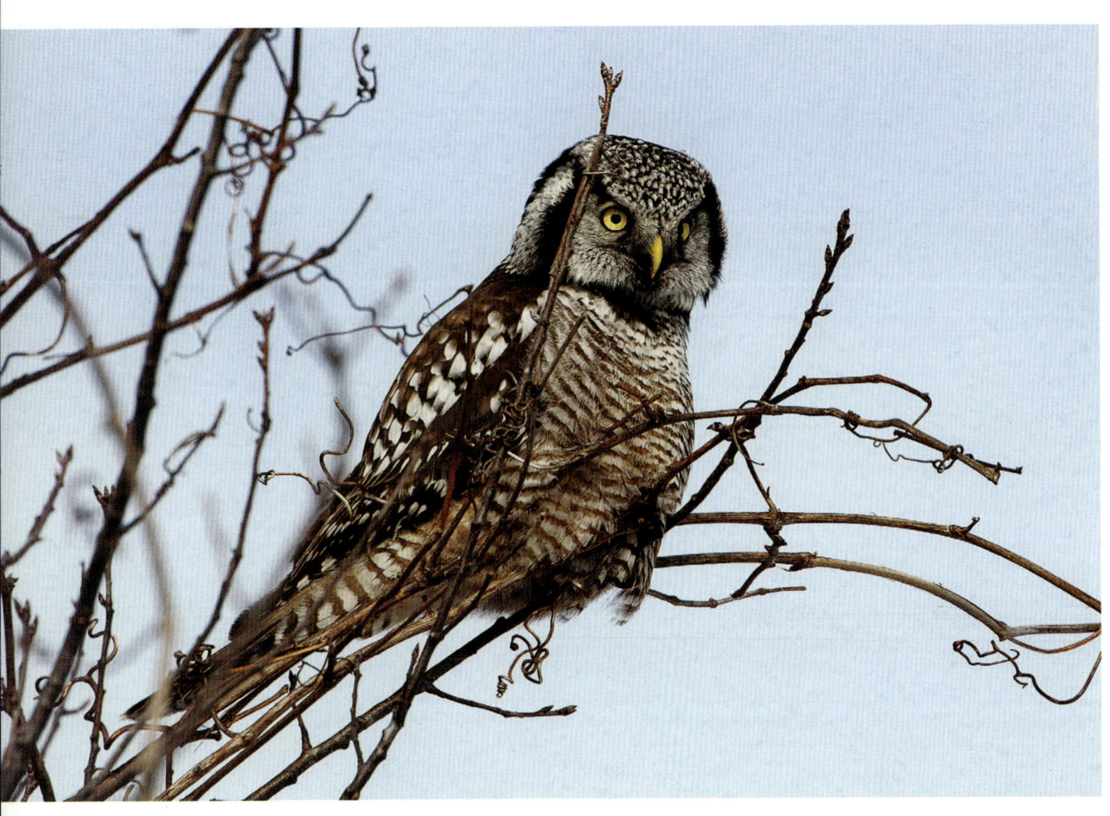

This page: Northern Hawk Owl, Sister Bay – Lucas.

Next page: Gray Fox, Sister Bay – Lucas.

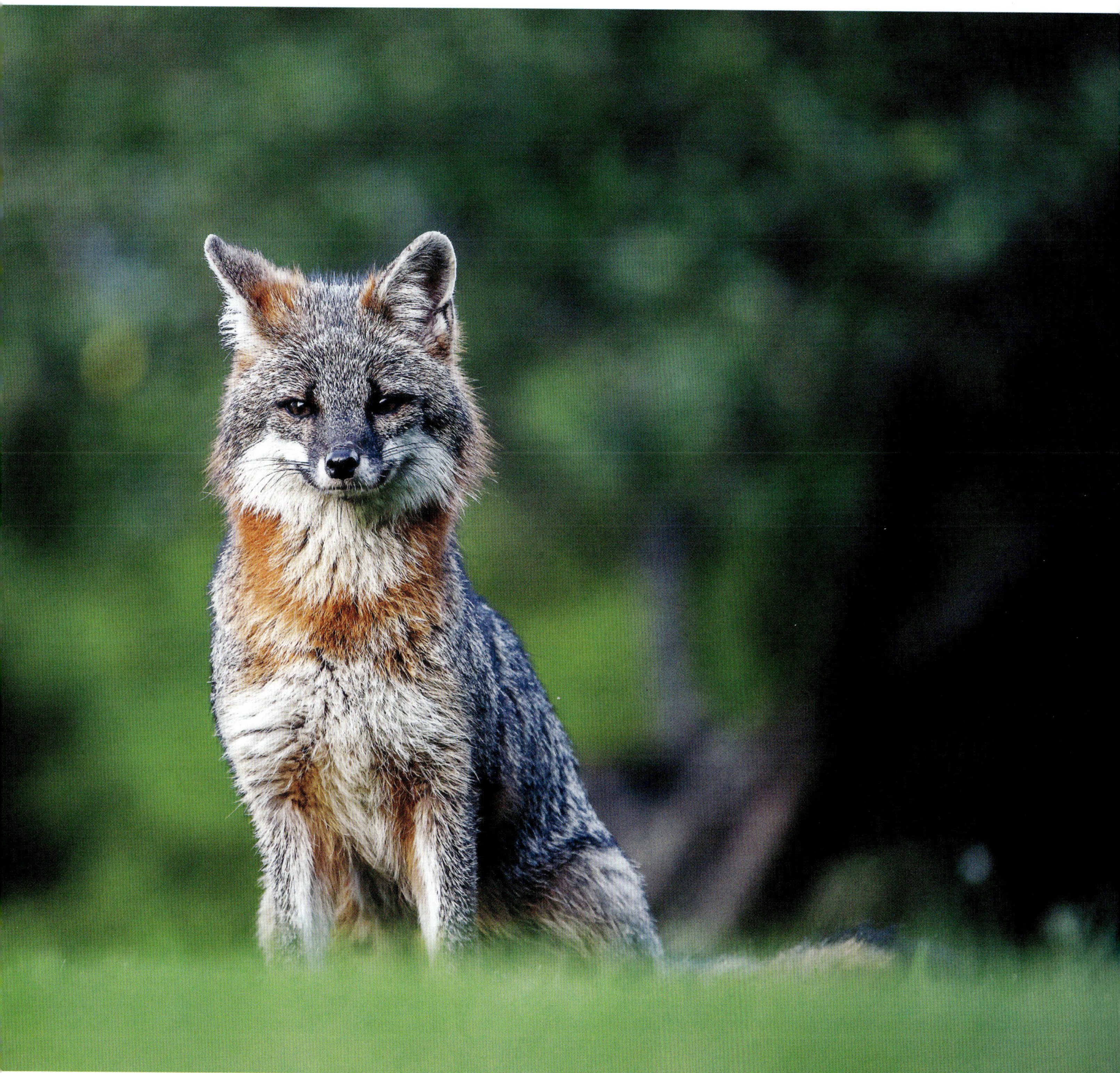

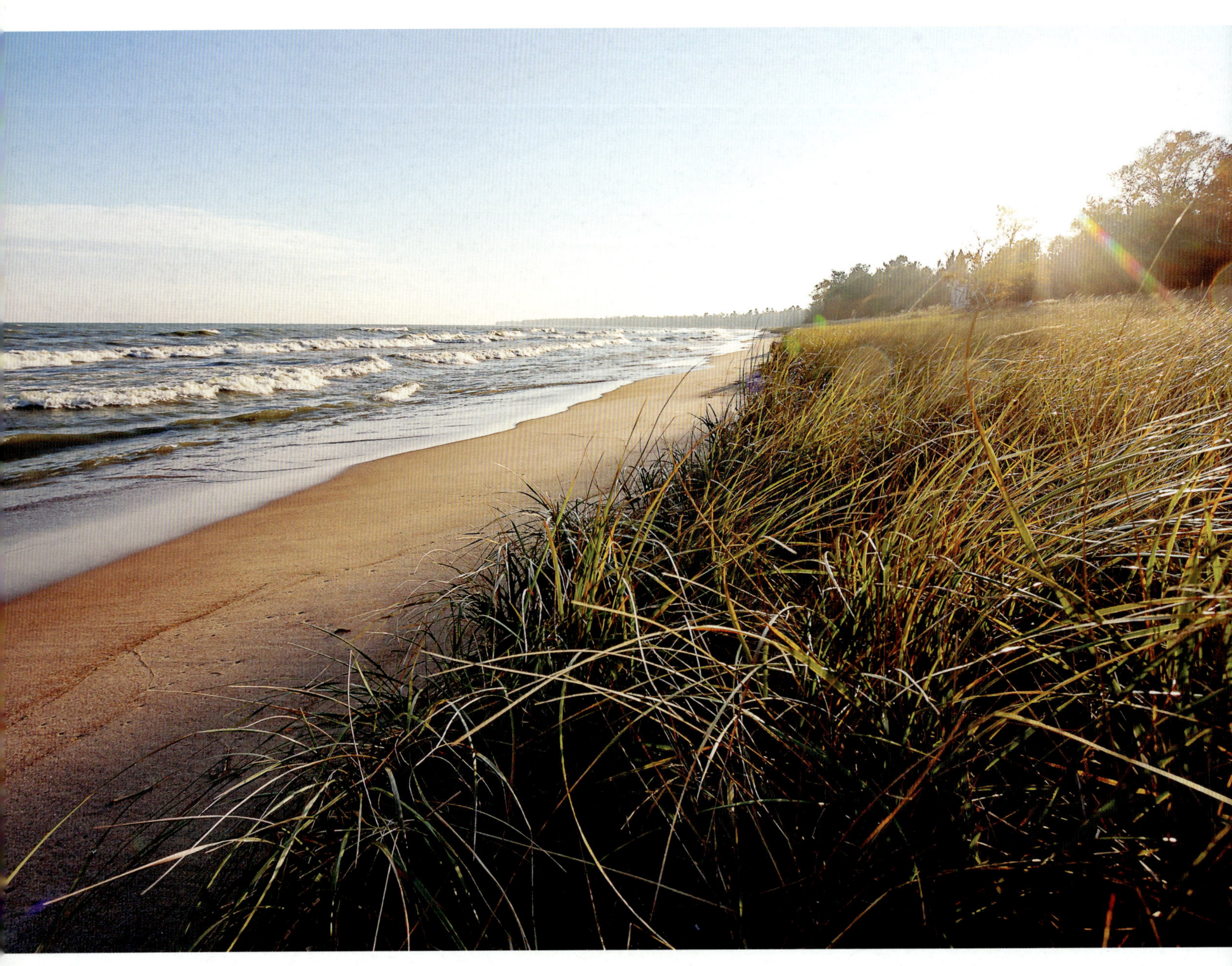

This page: Lake Michigan Shoreline, Glidden Drive – Heather.

Next page: Beach stones, Lake Michigan – Lucas.

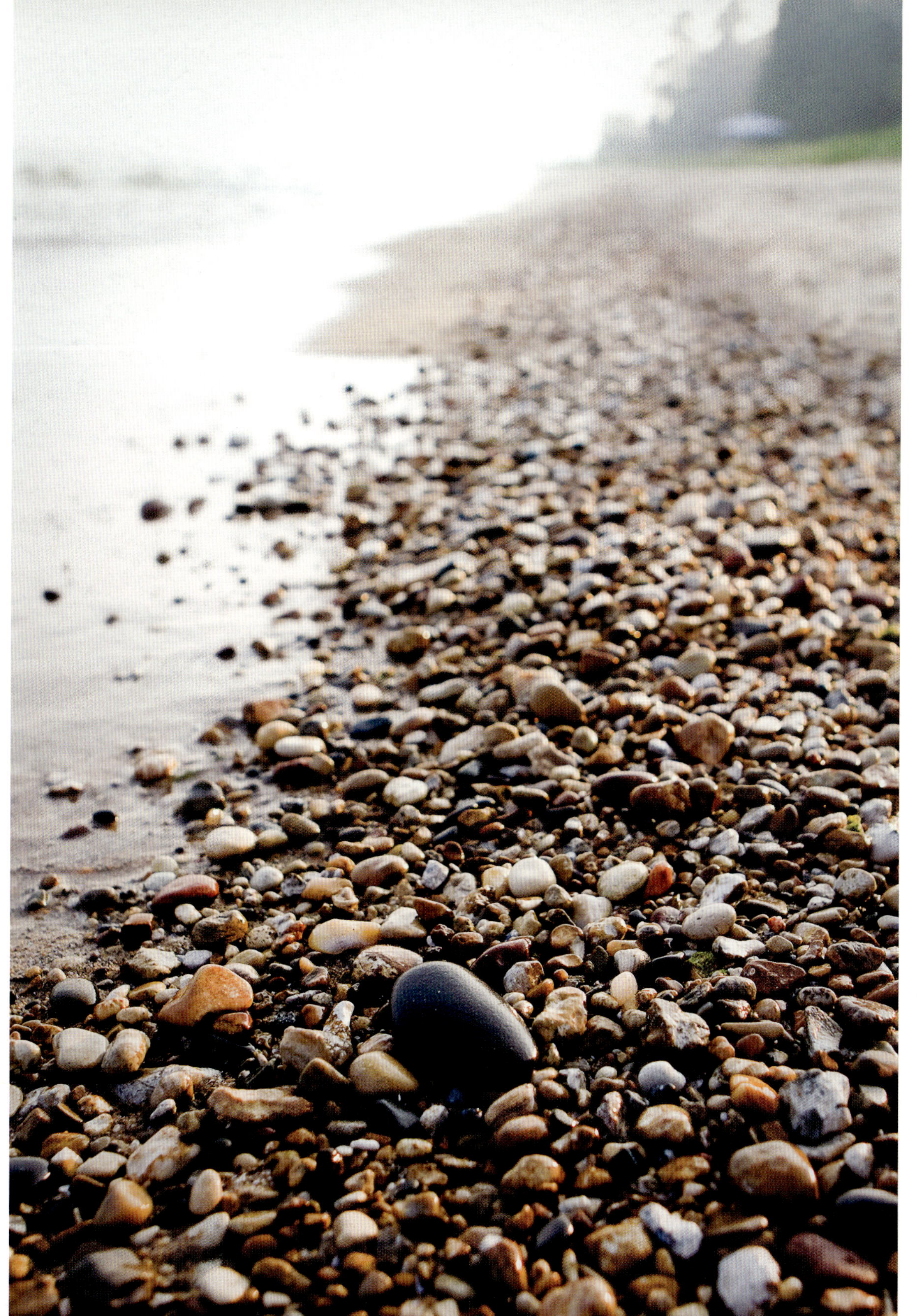

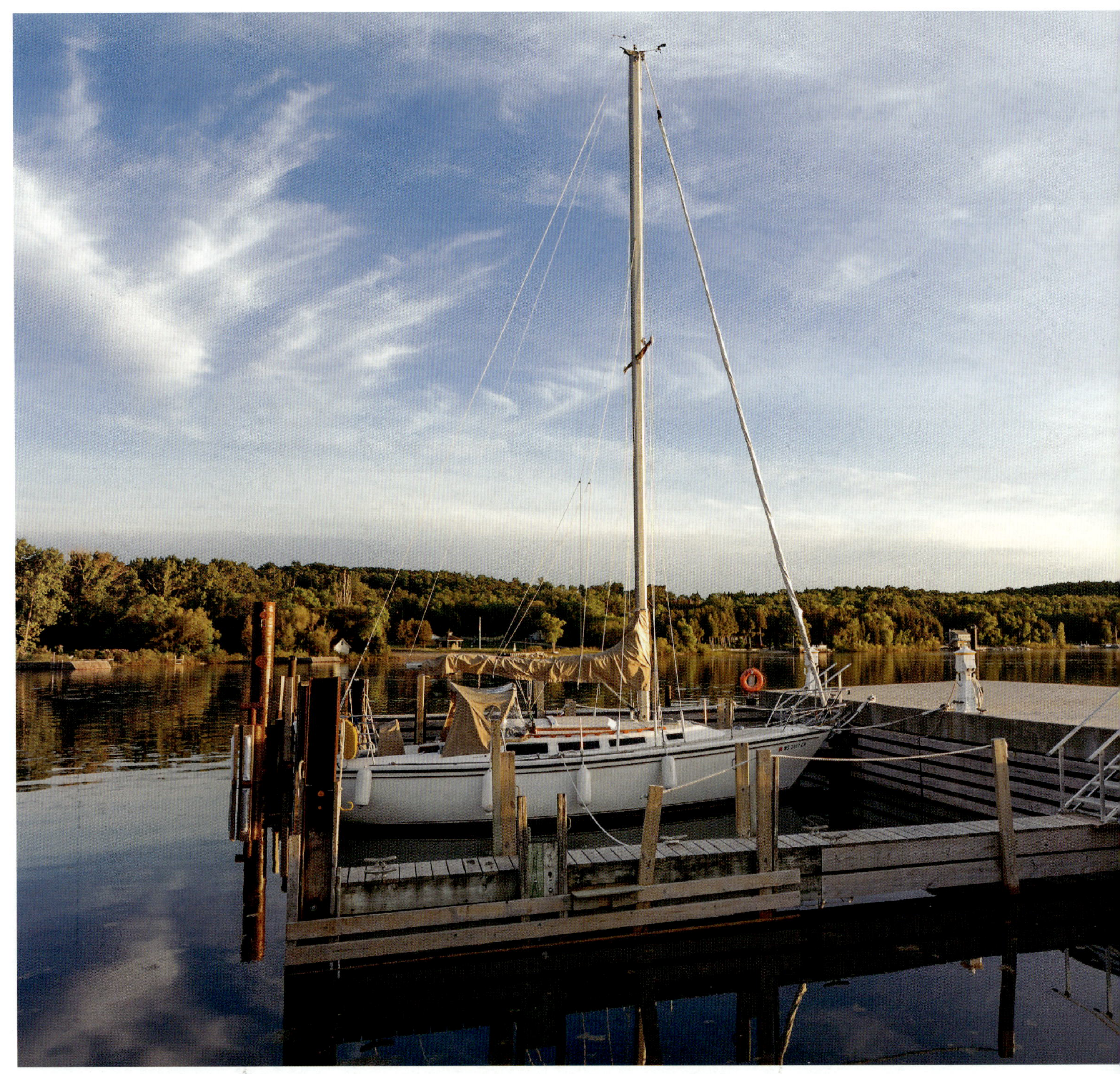

This page: Ellison Bay – Heather.

Next page: *Edith M. Becker*, Little Sister Bay – Heather.

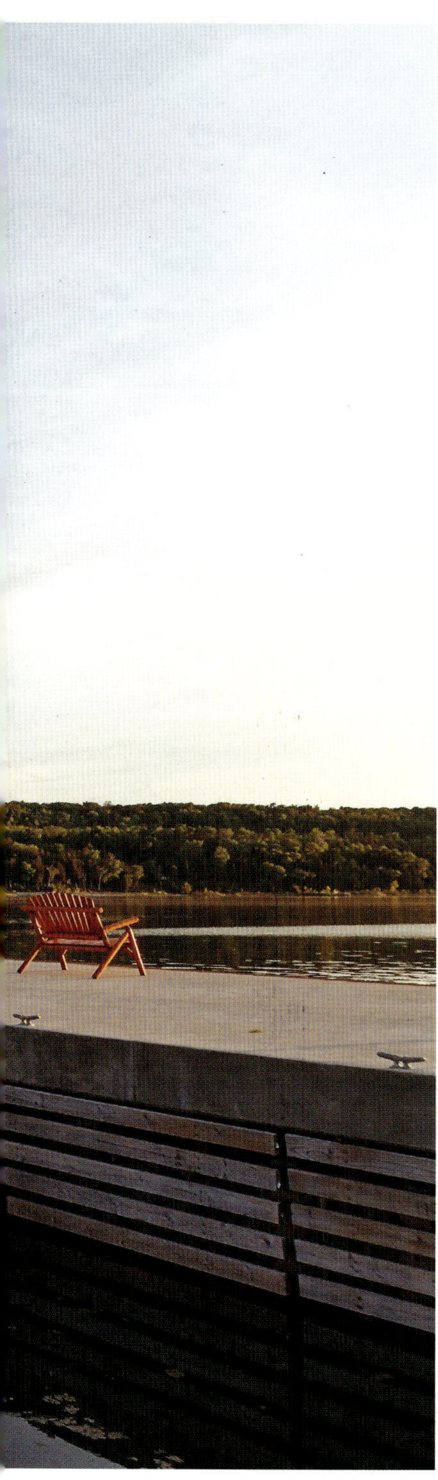

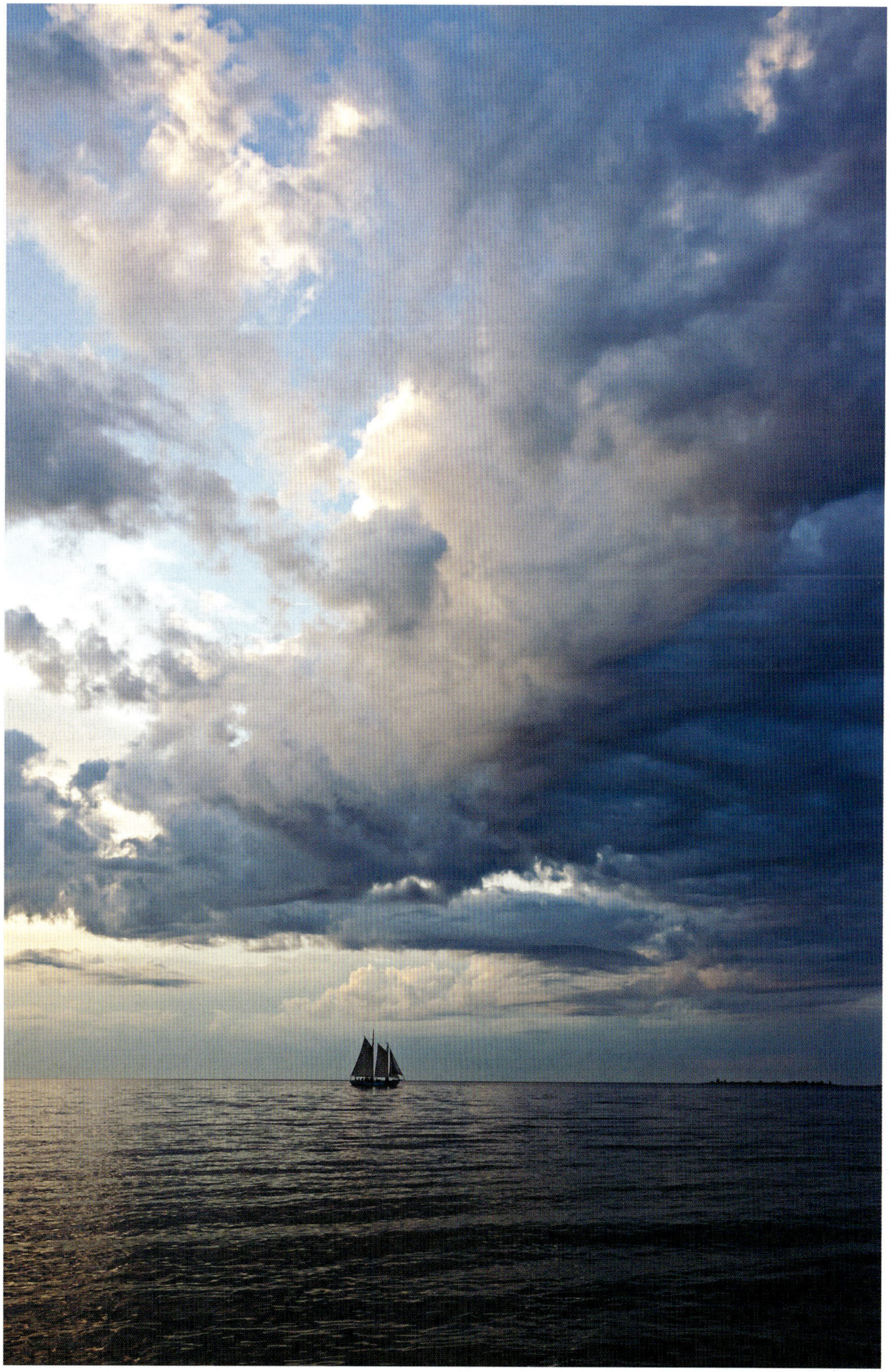

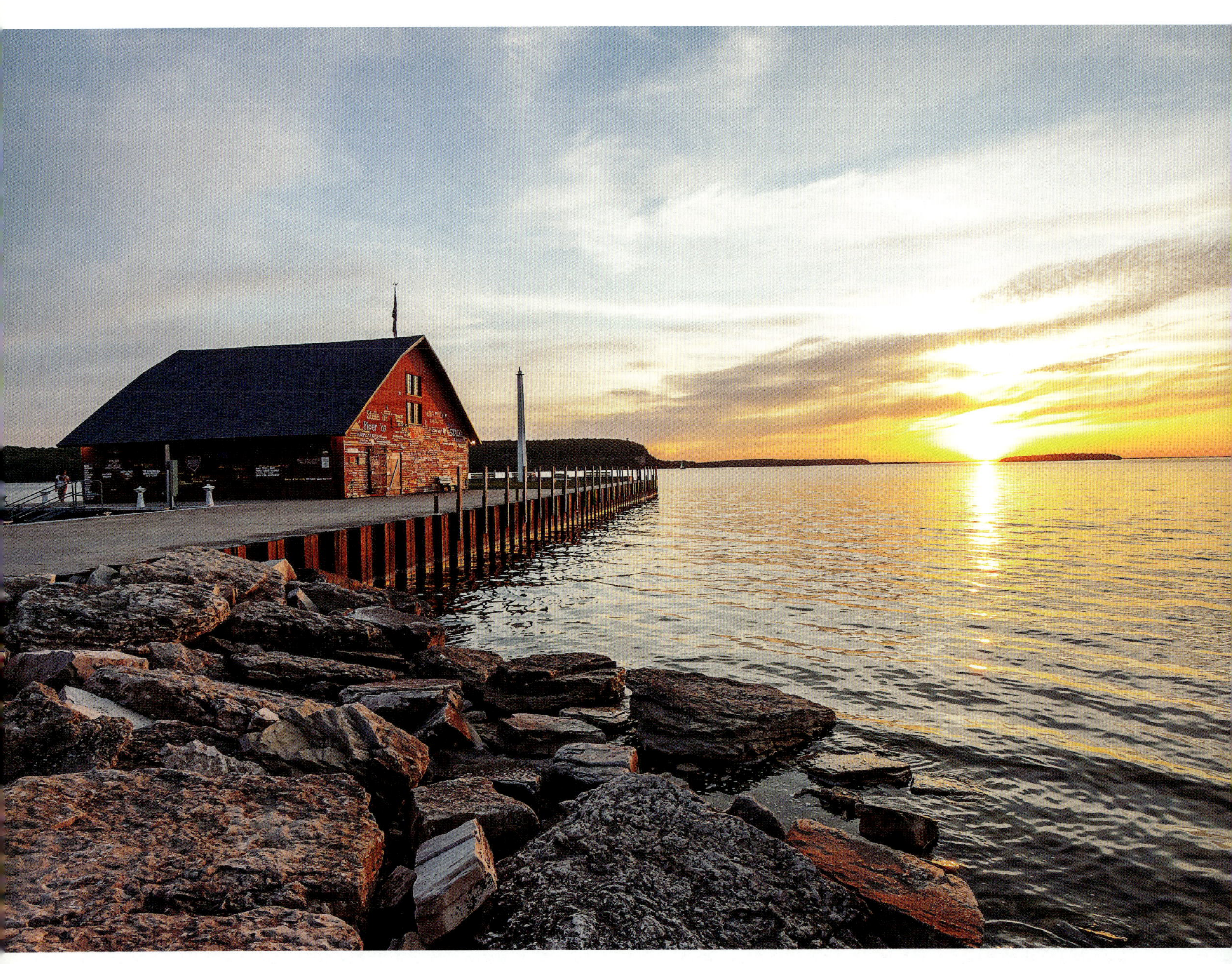

This page: Anderson Dock, Ephraim – Heather.

Next page: Sturgeon Bay Ship Canal Pierhead – Lucas.

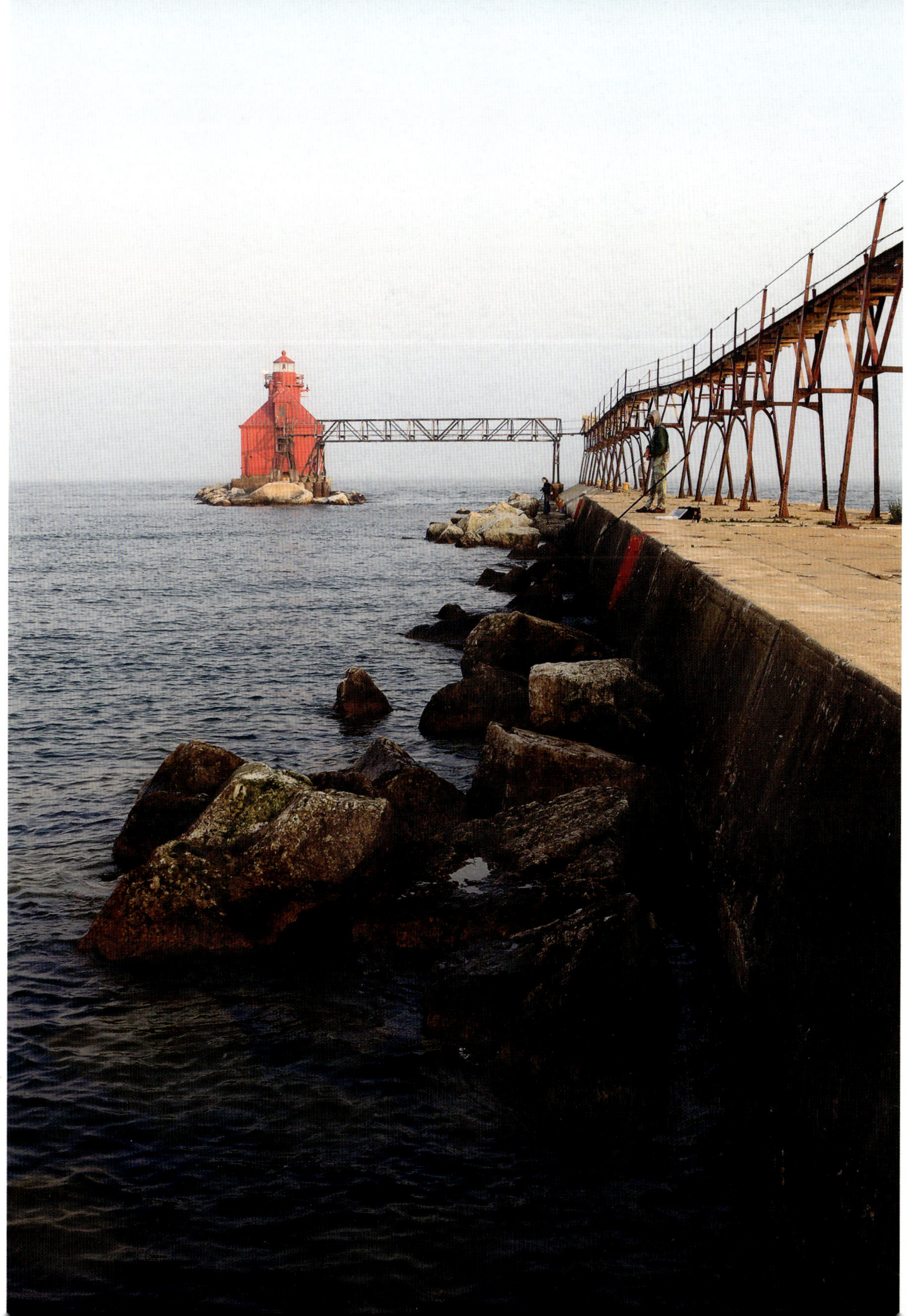

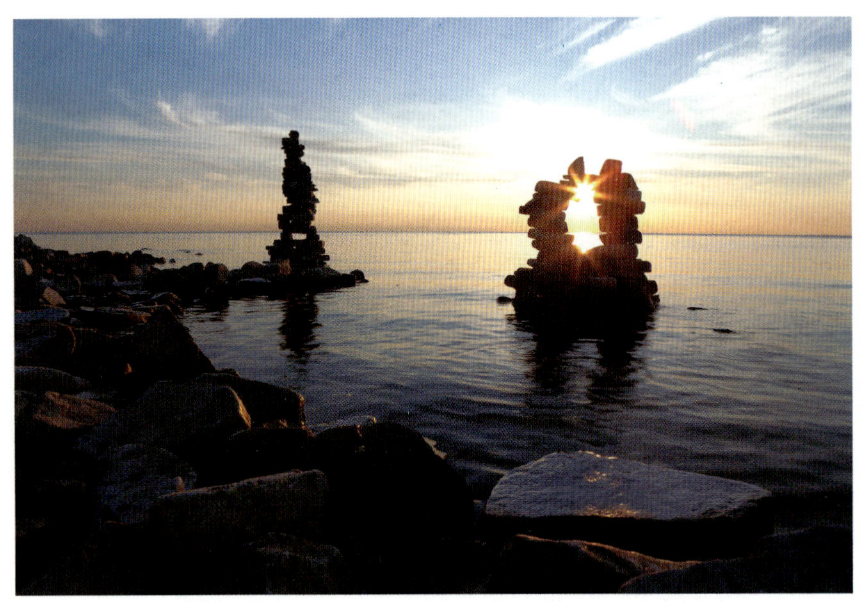

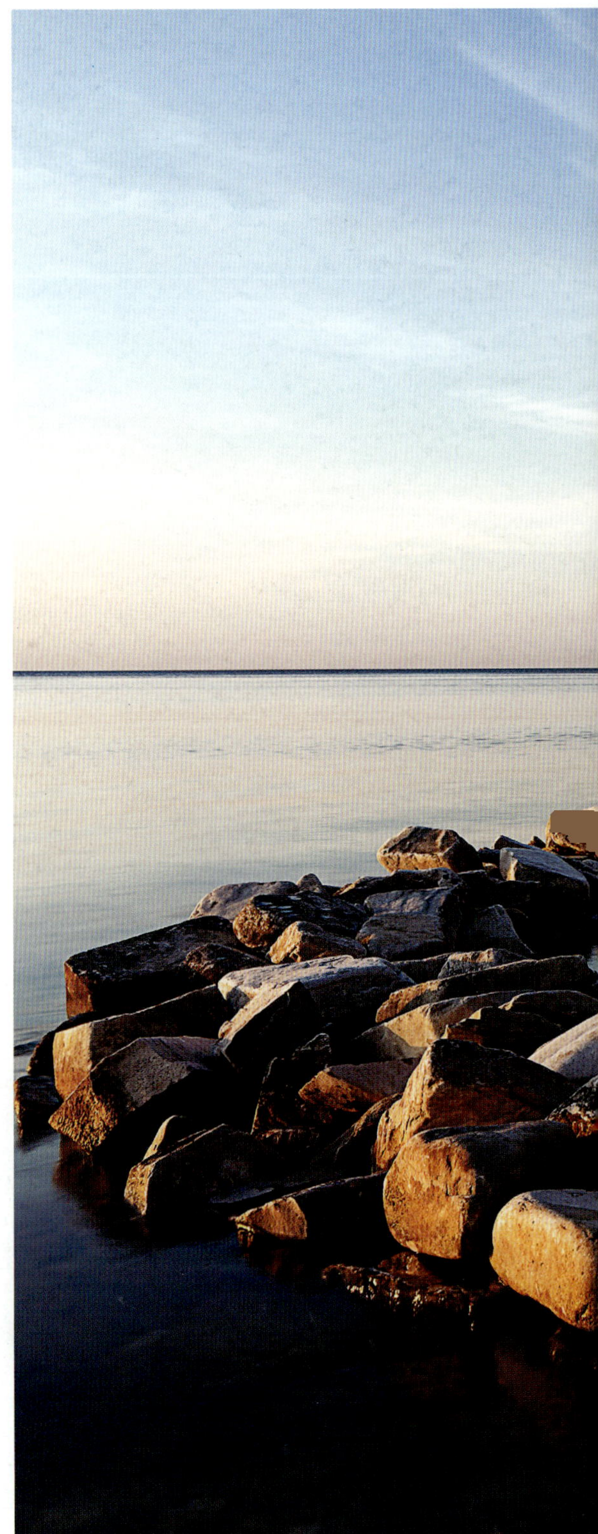

This page and the next: Cairns, Door Bluff Headlands County Park – Heather.

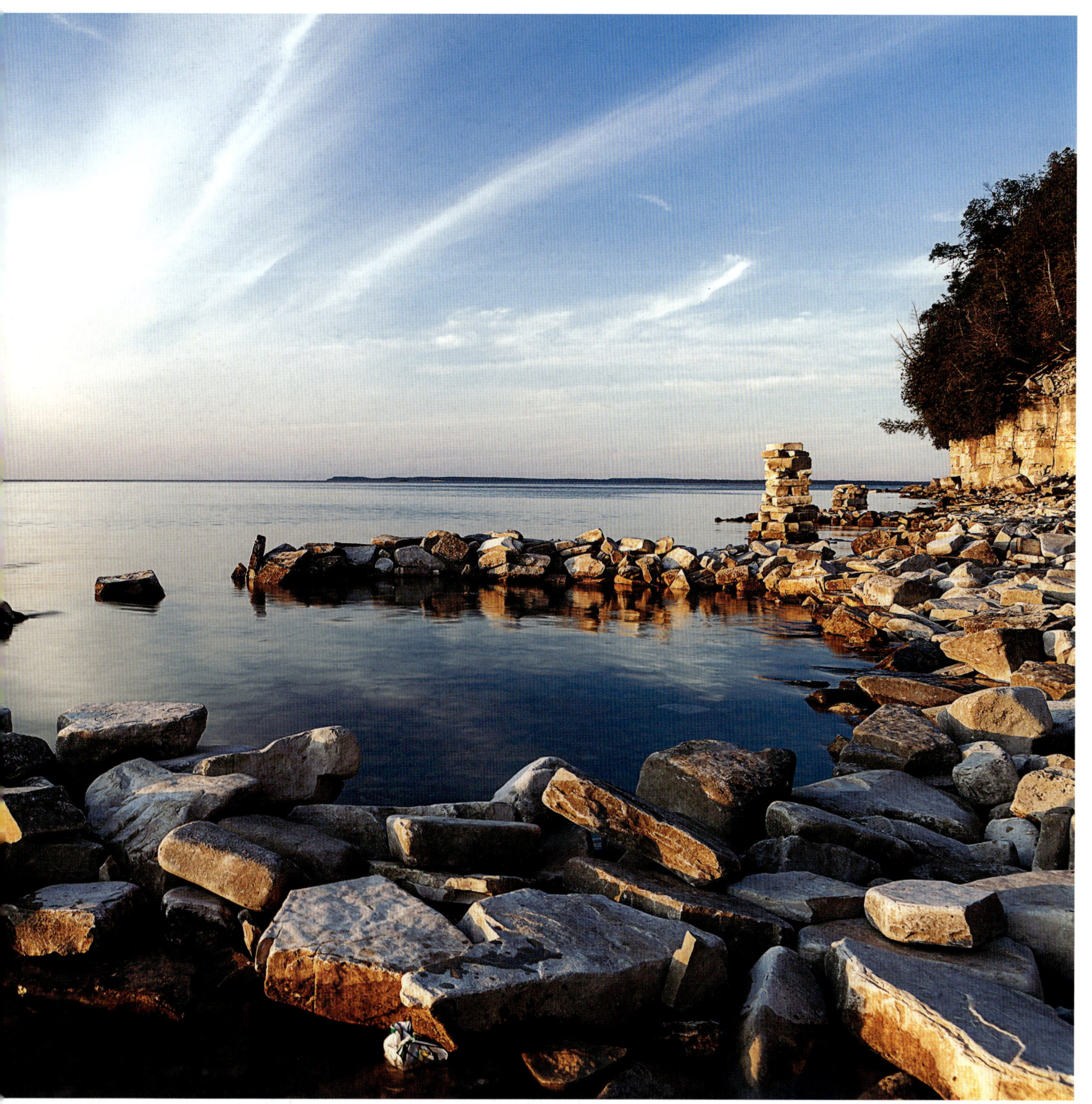

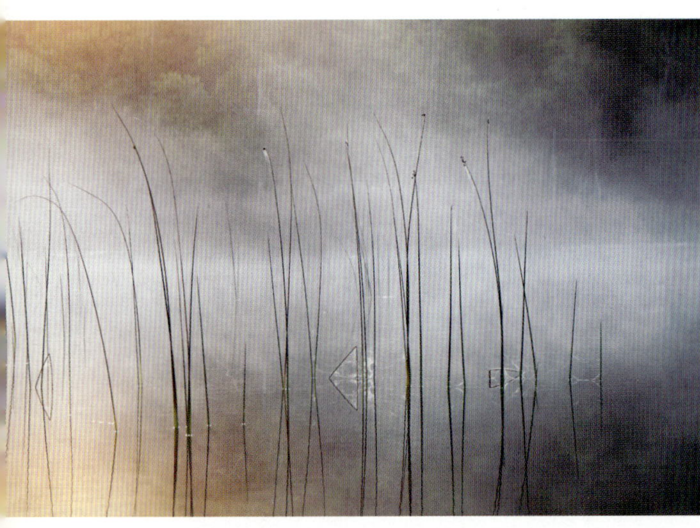

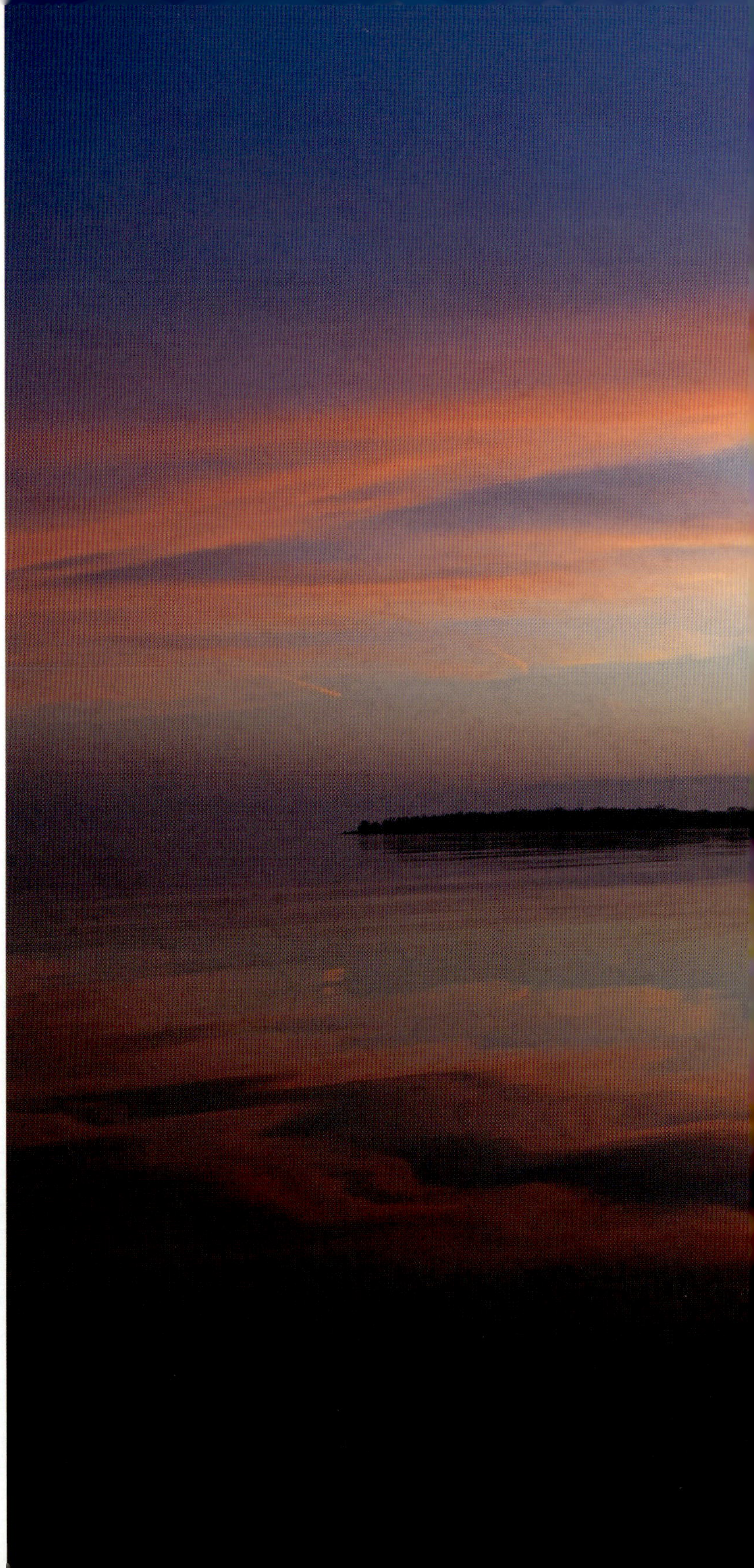

This page: Europe Lake, Ellison Bay – Heather.

Next page: Eye level from a kayak, Green Bay – Heather.

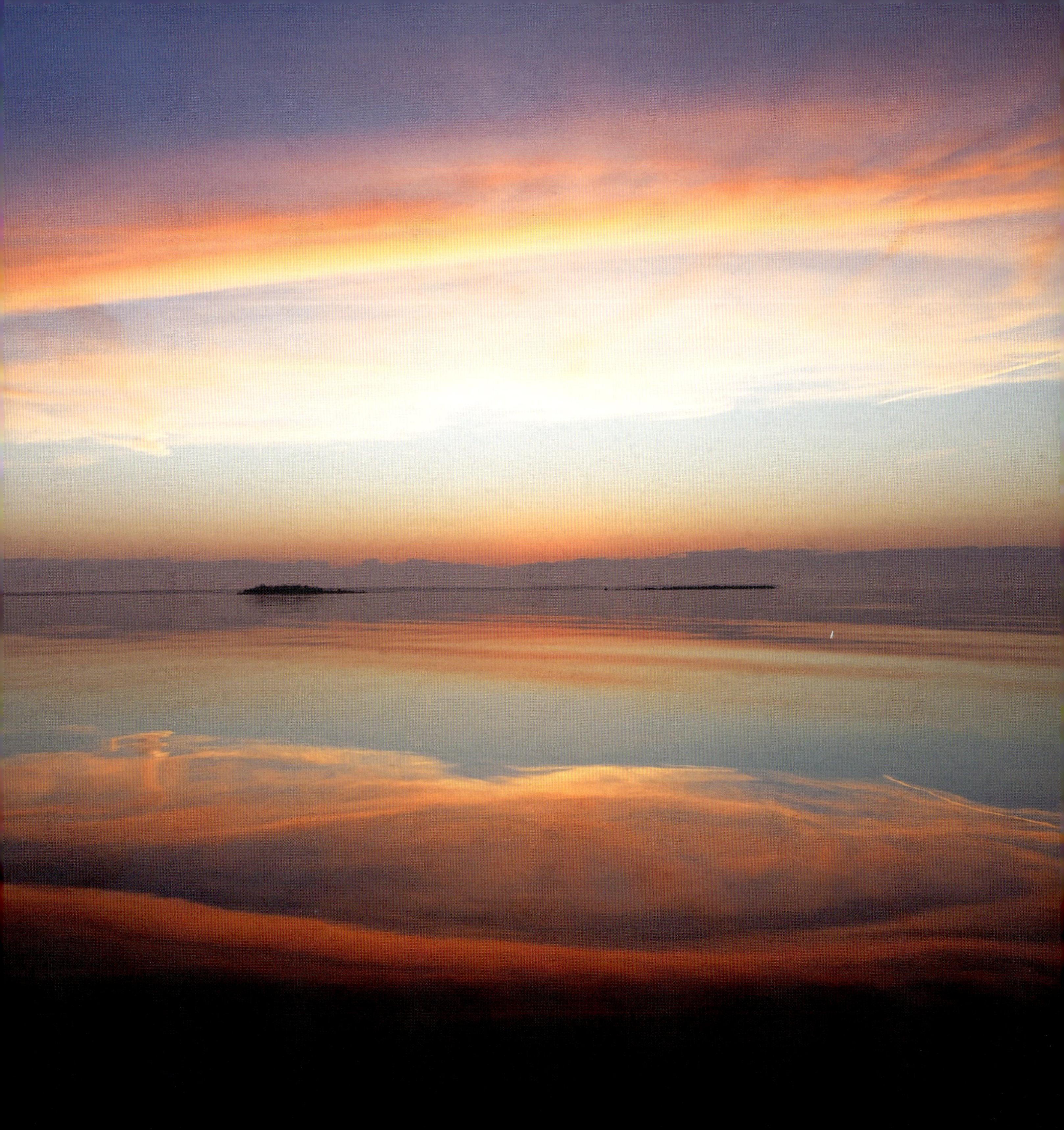

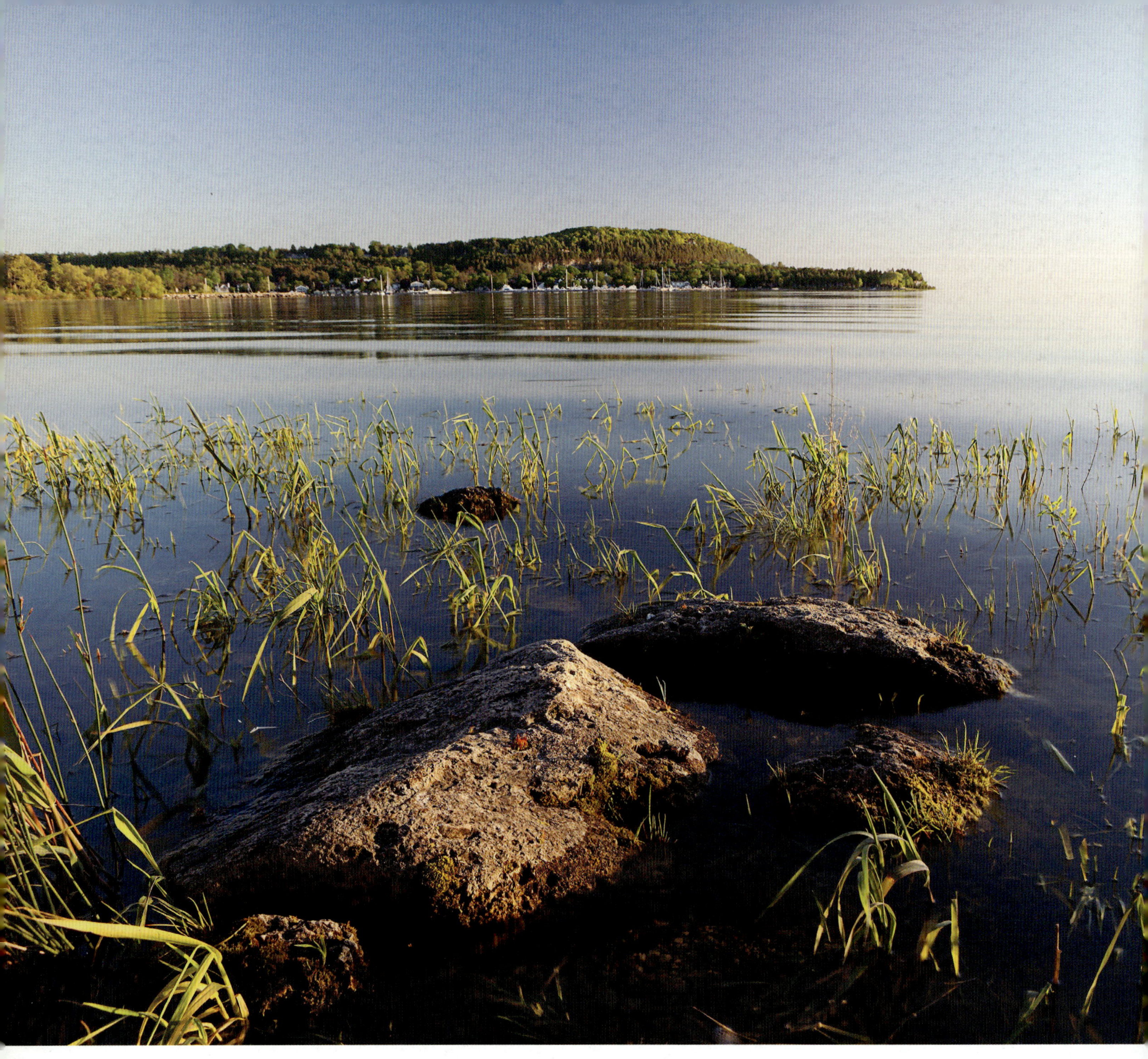

This page: Fish Creek from Nelson Point, Peninsula State Park – Heather.

Next page: Sunrise, Cana Island Lighthouse, Baileys Harbor – Heather.

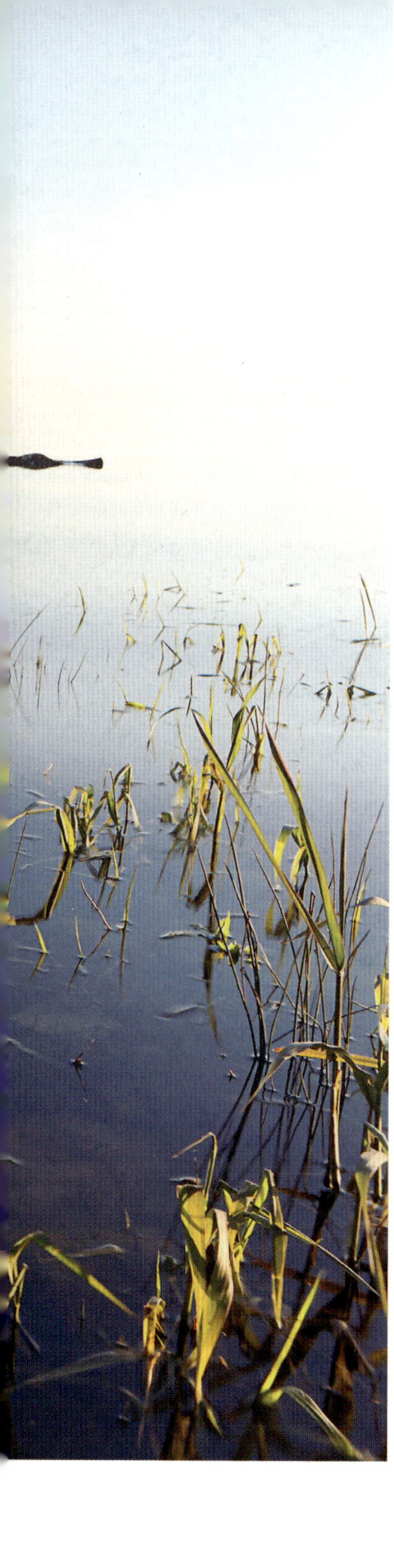

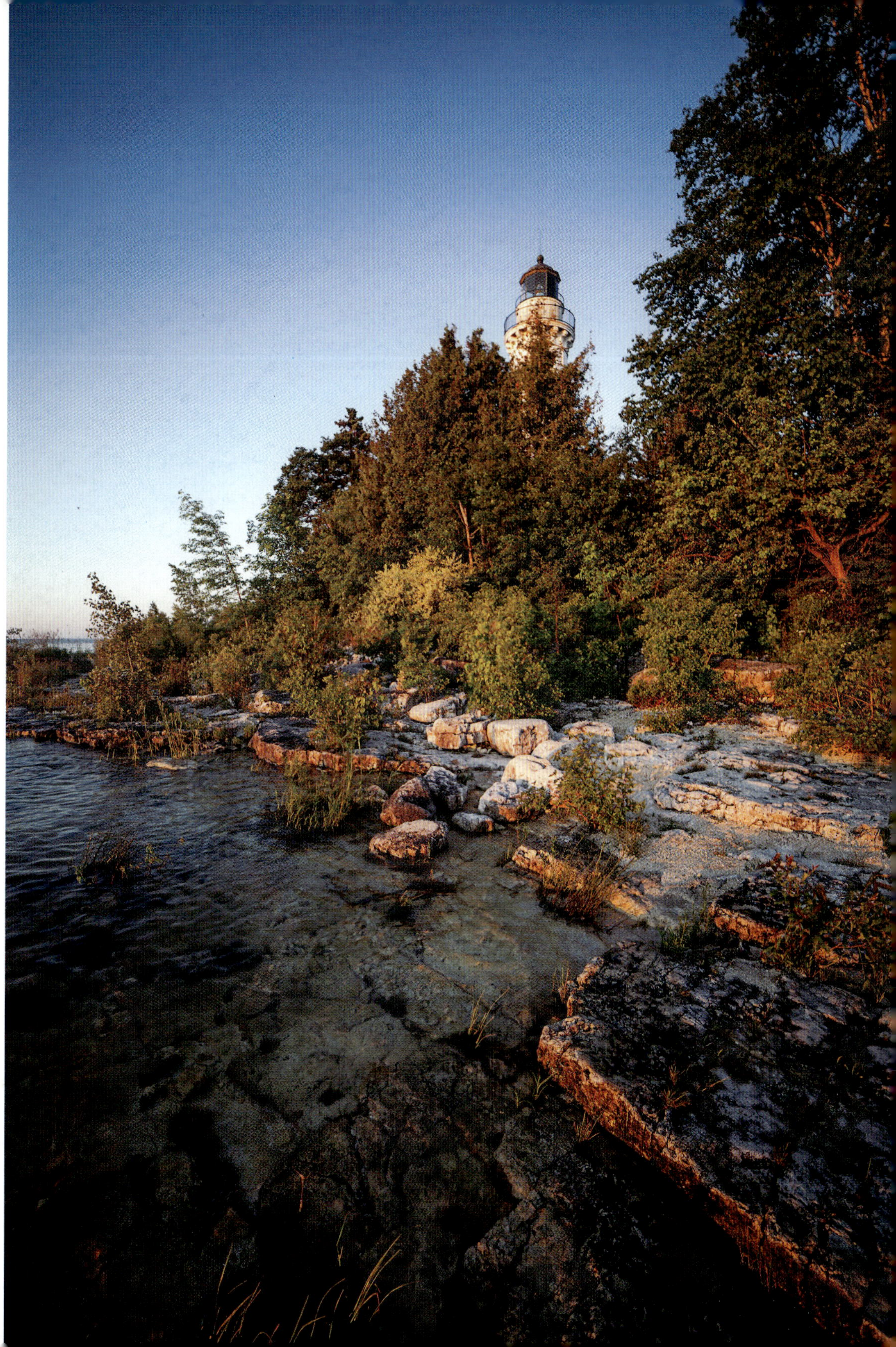

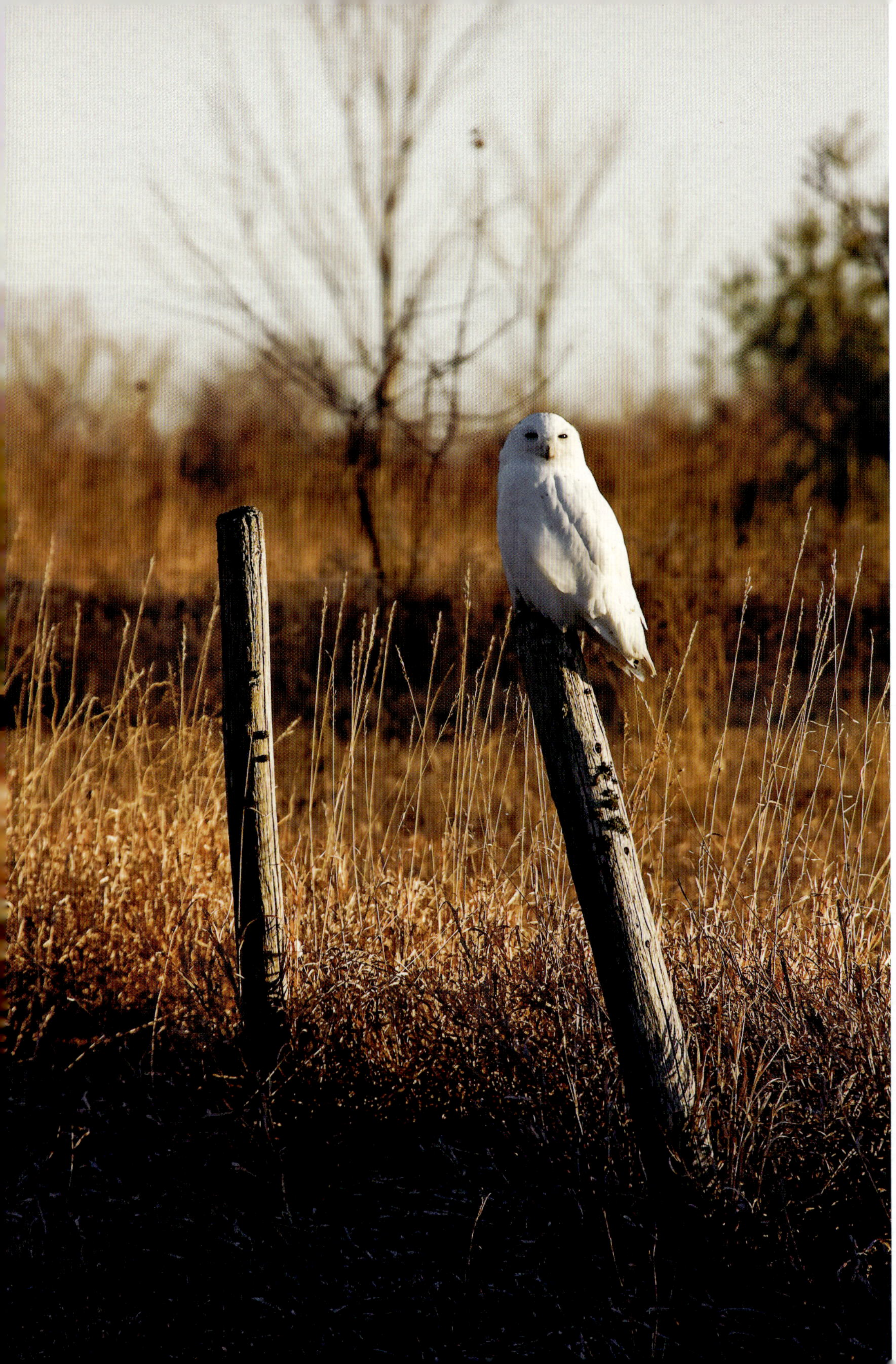

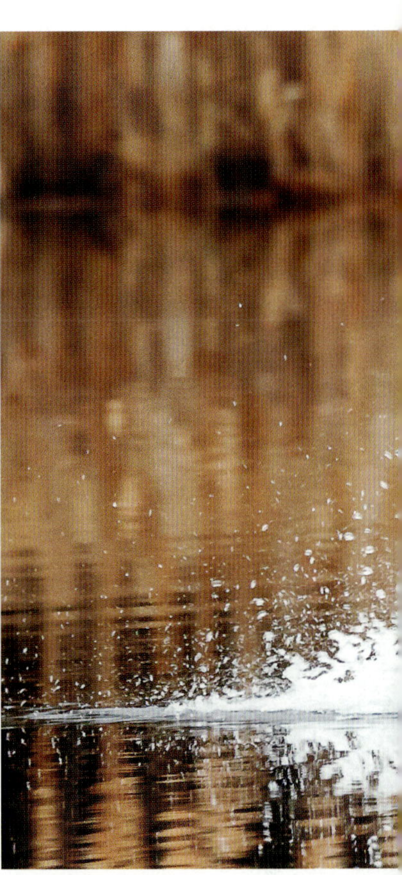

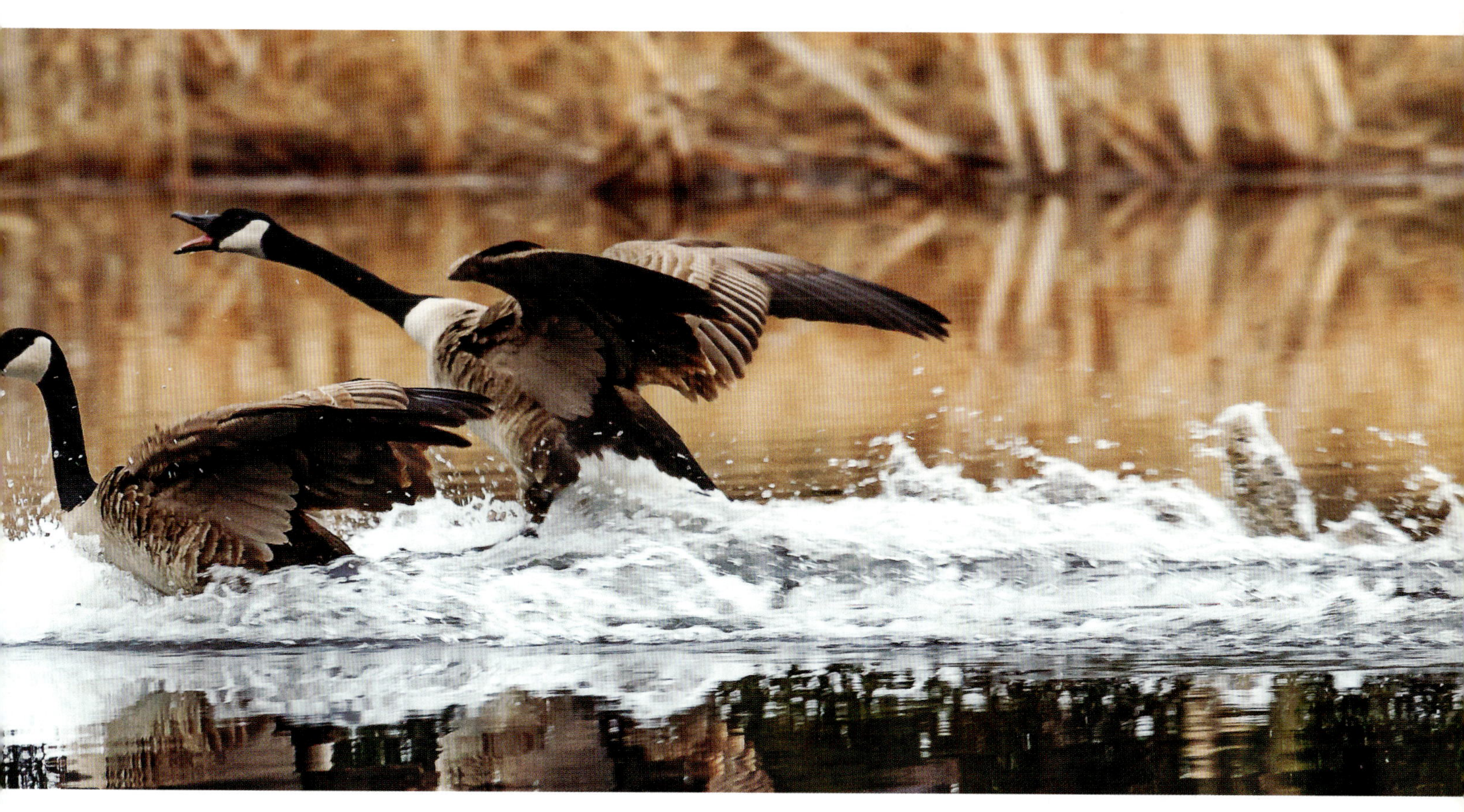

Previous page: Snowy Owl, Ellison Bay – Lucas.

This page: Canada Geese, Mink River, Ellison Bay – Lucas.

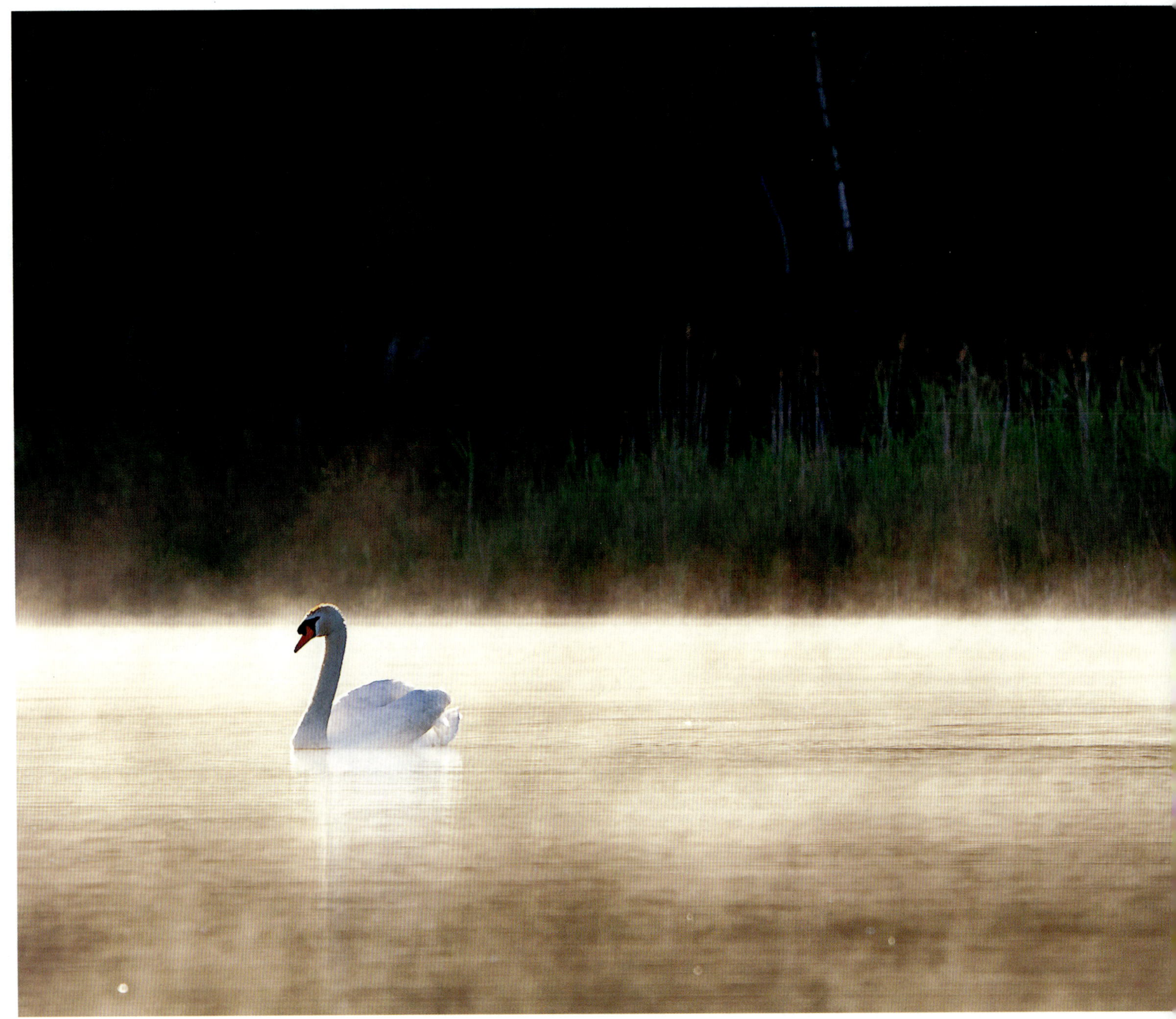

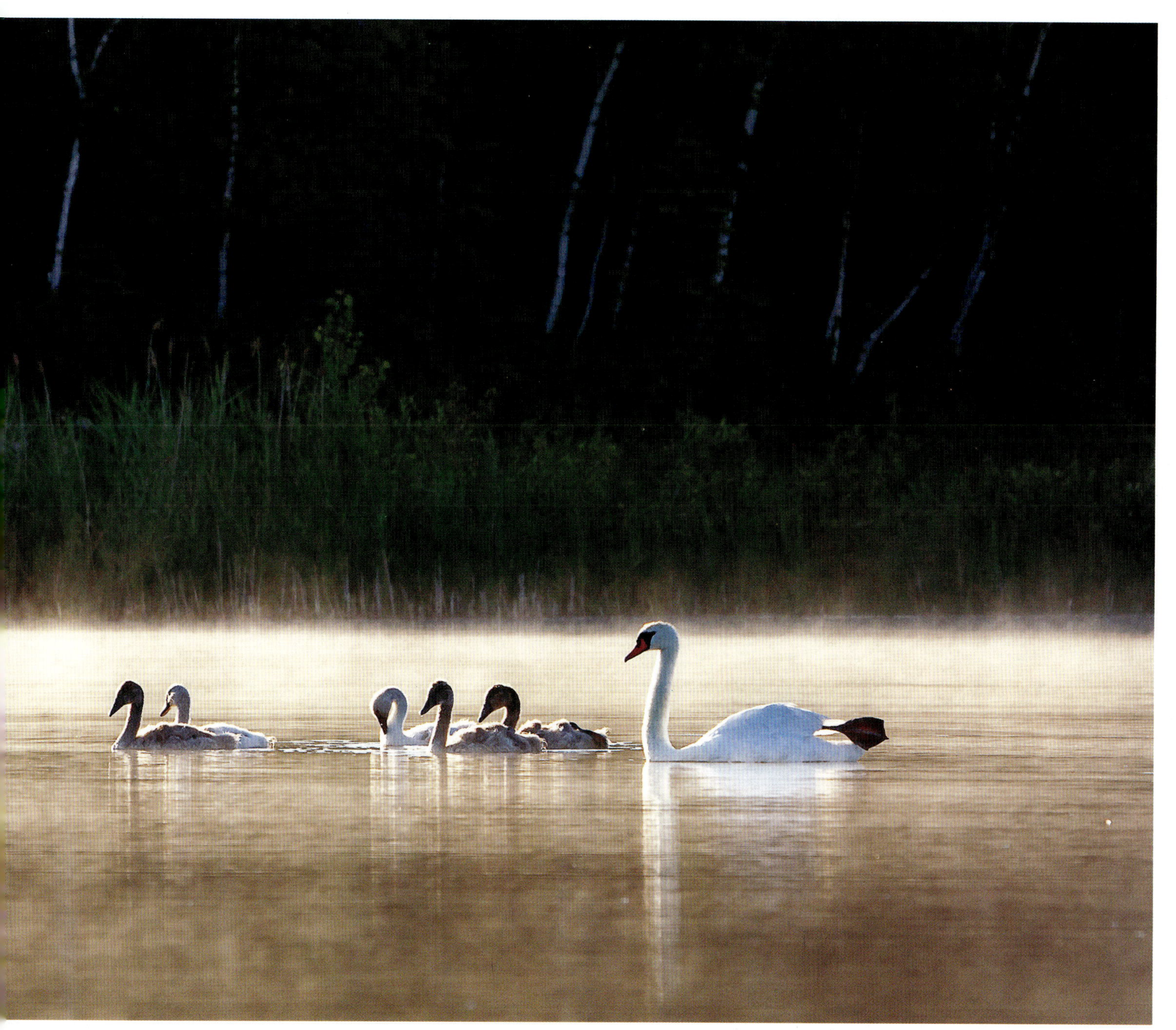

Swans, Washington Island – Heather and Lucas.

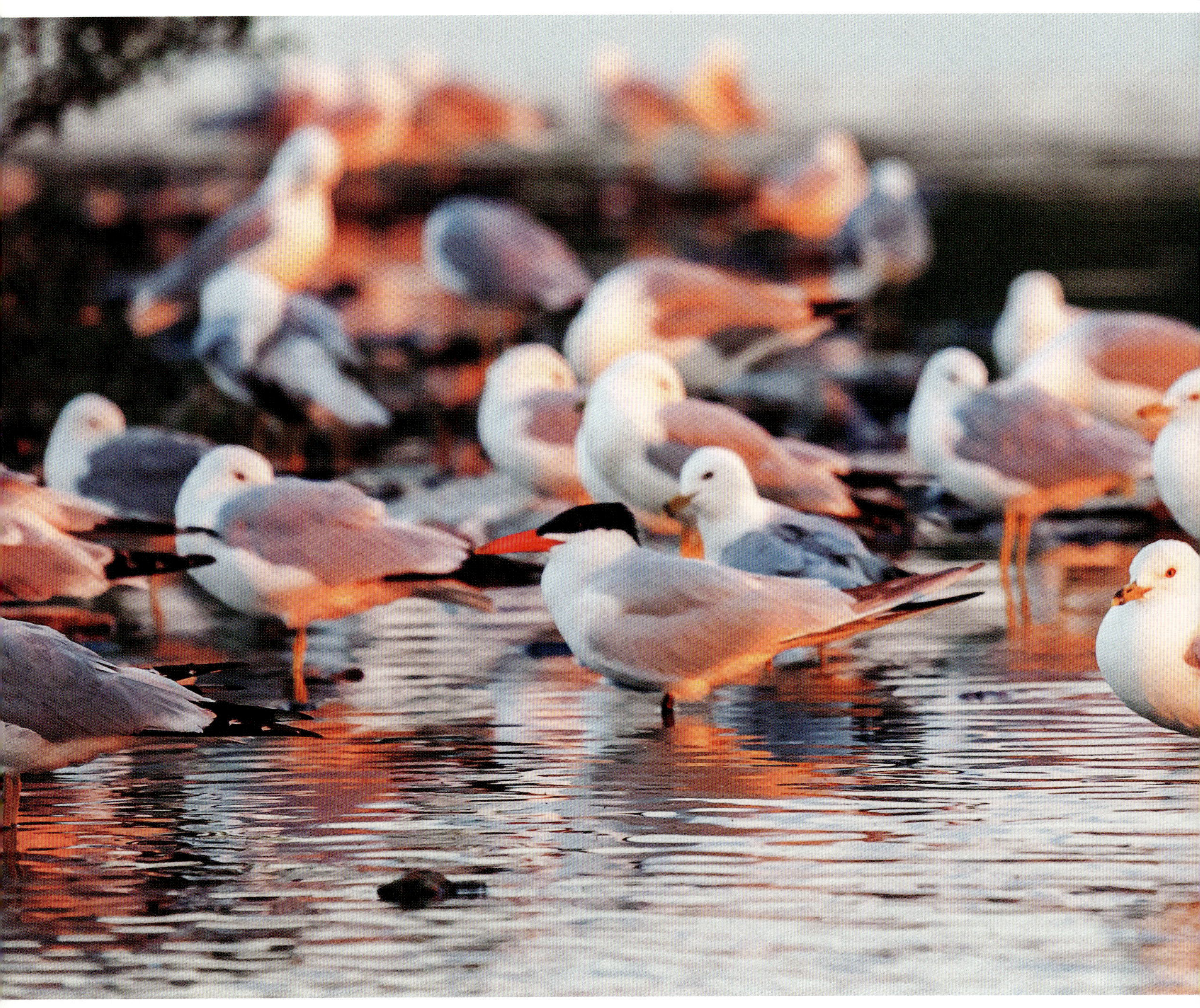

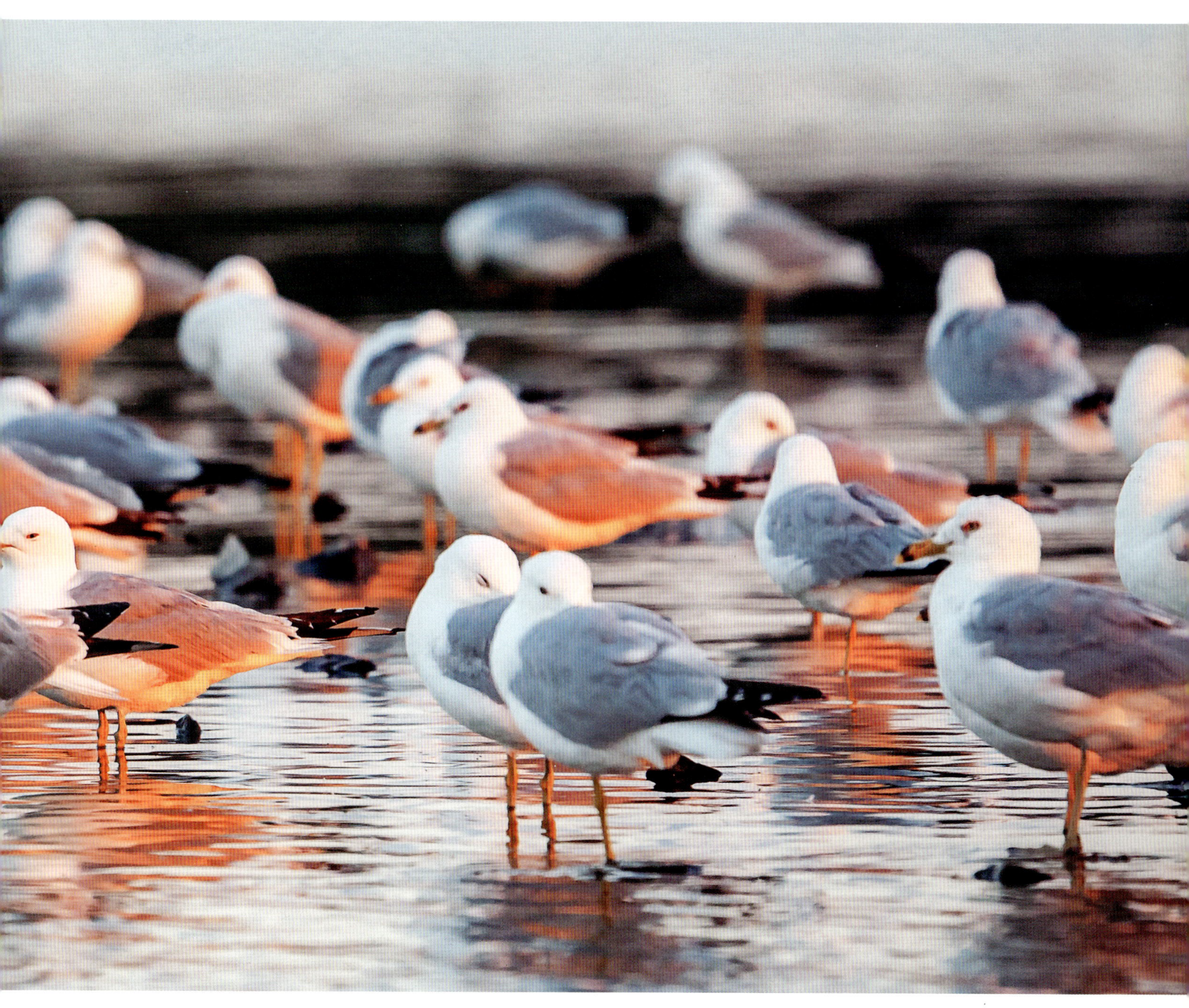

This page: *One Wrong Tern*, Washington Island – Heather and Lucas.

Following pages: White Pelicans, Strawberry Islands, near Peninsula State Park – Heather and Lucas.

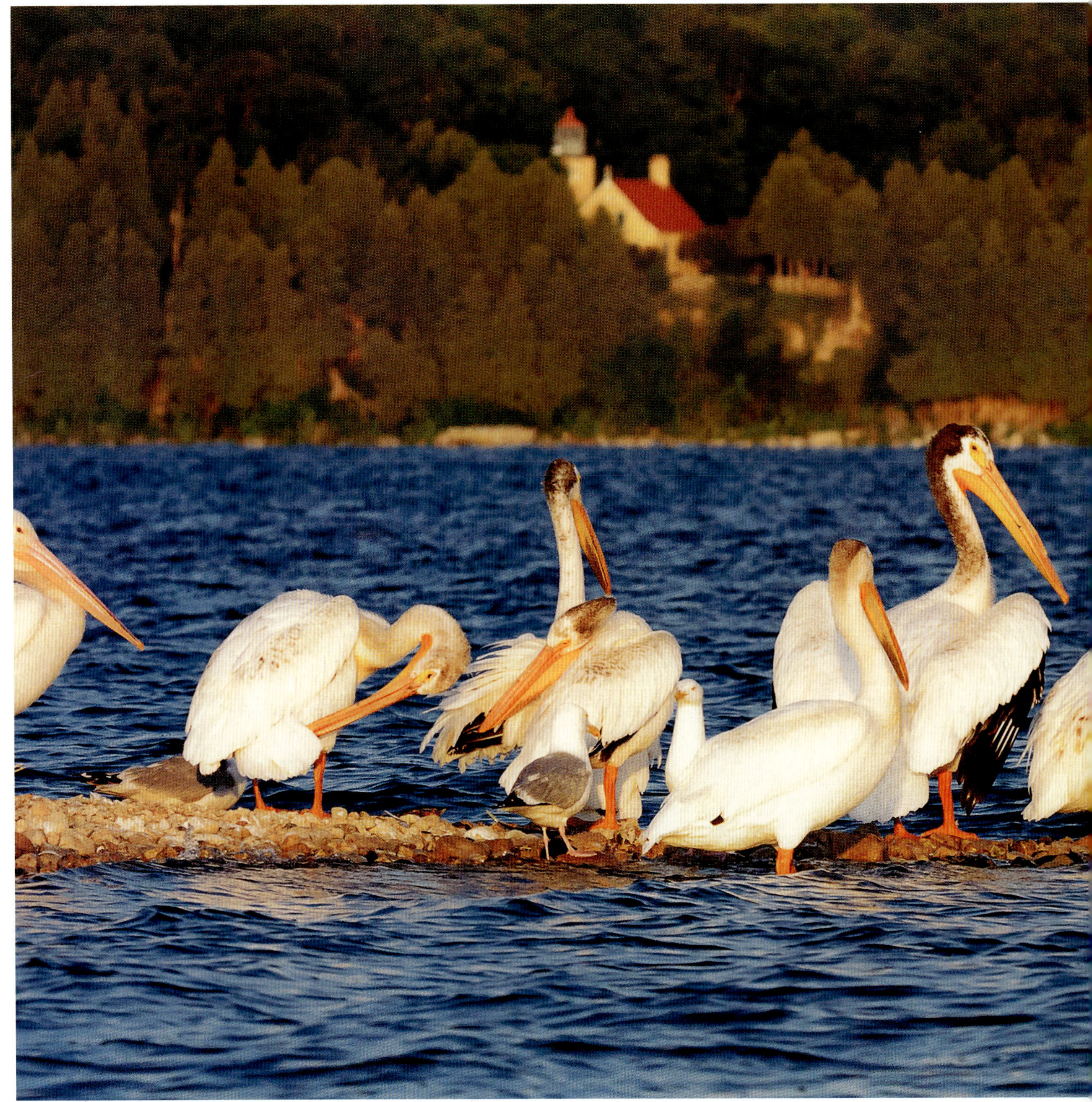

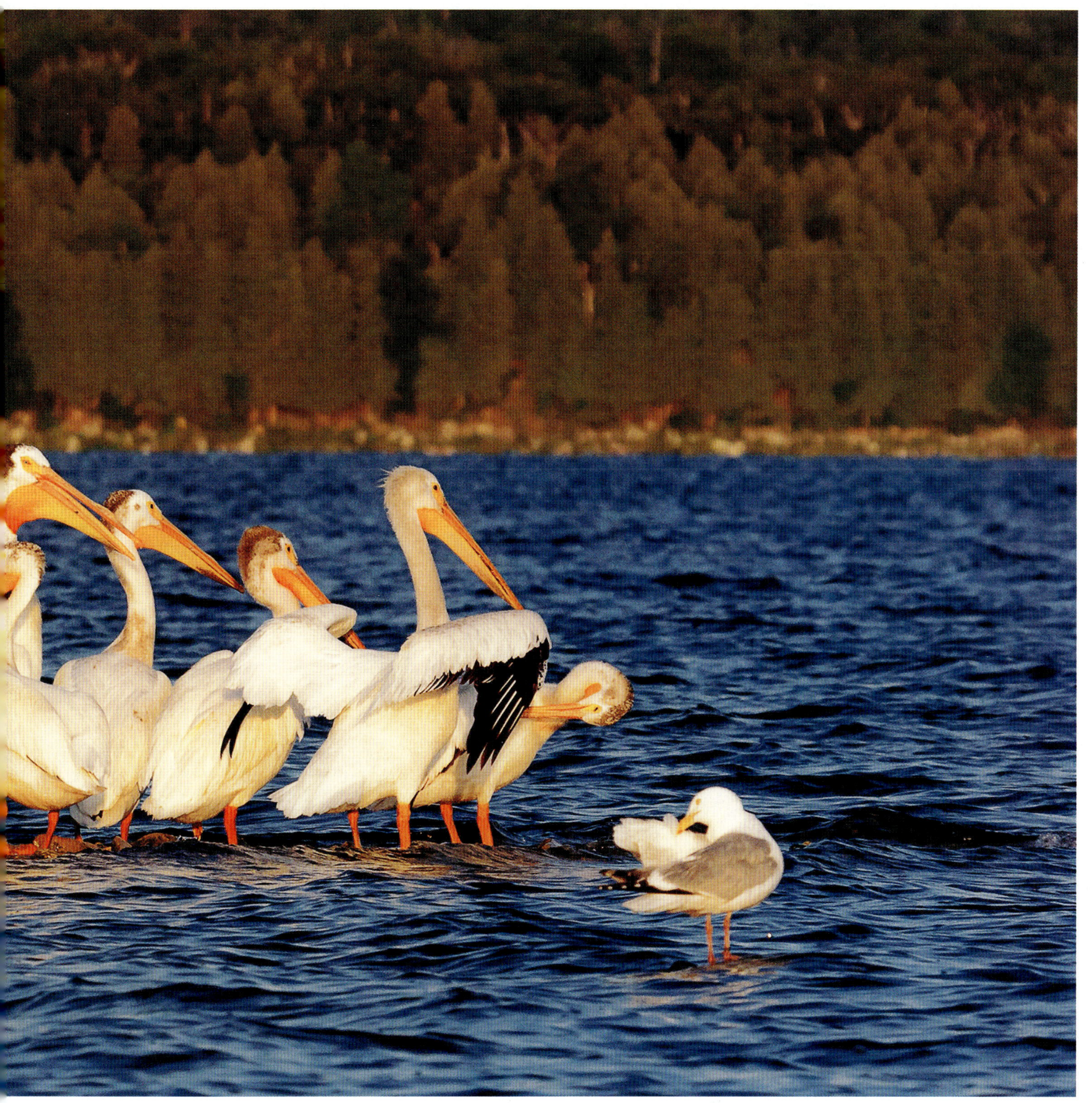

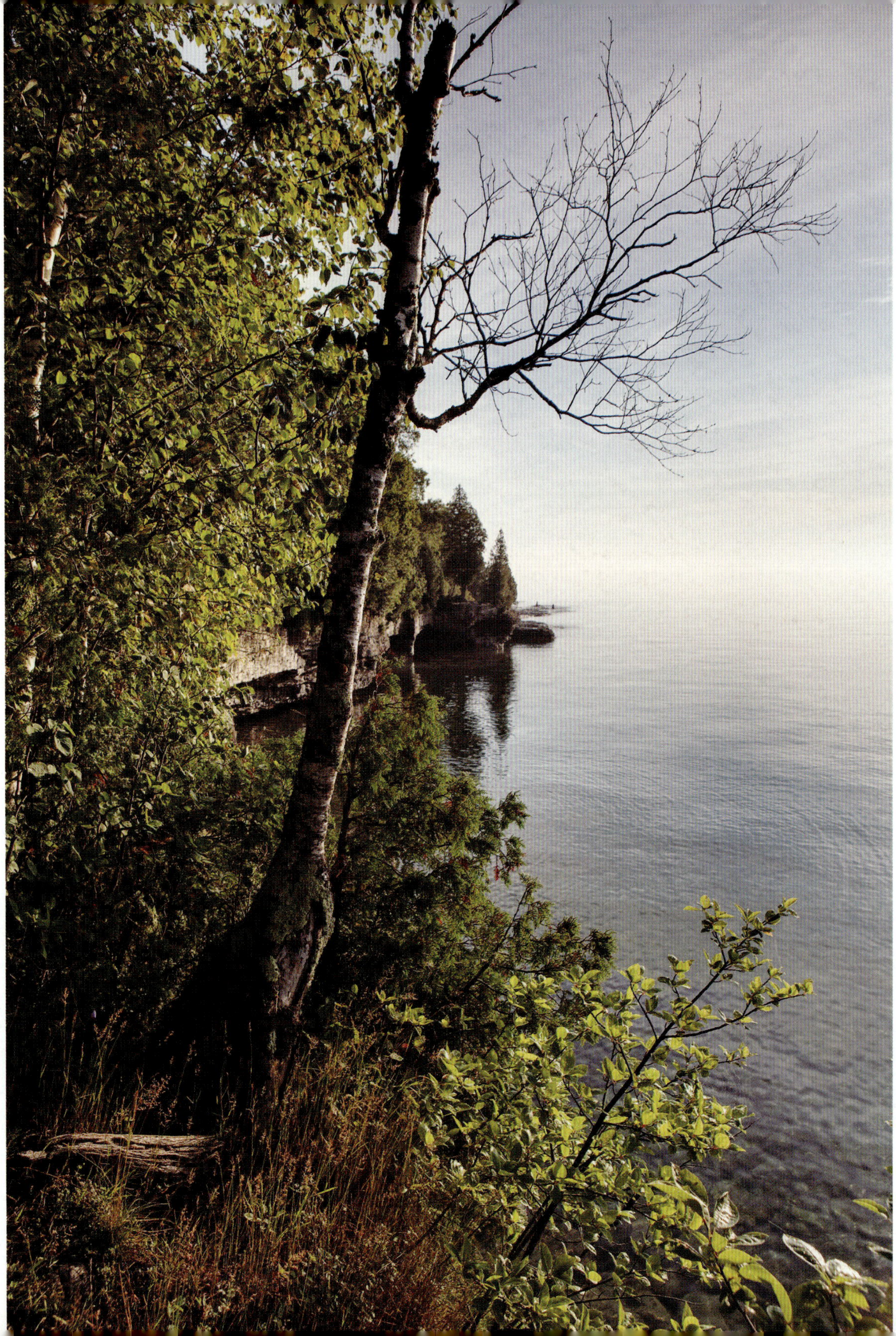

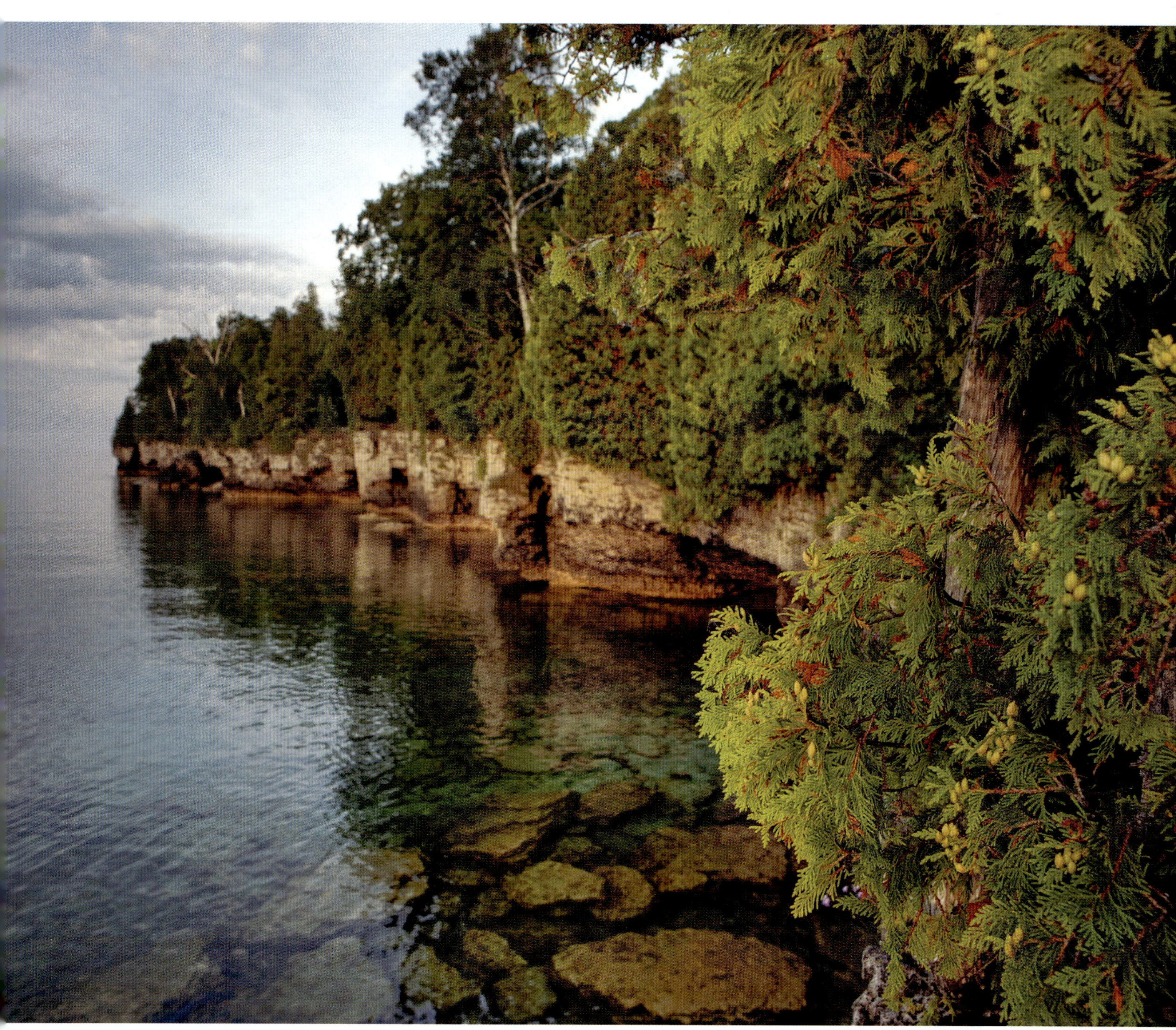

This page and the previous page: Cave Point County Park, Jacksonport – Lucas.

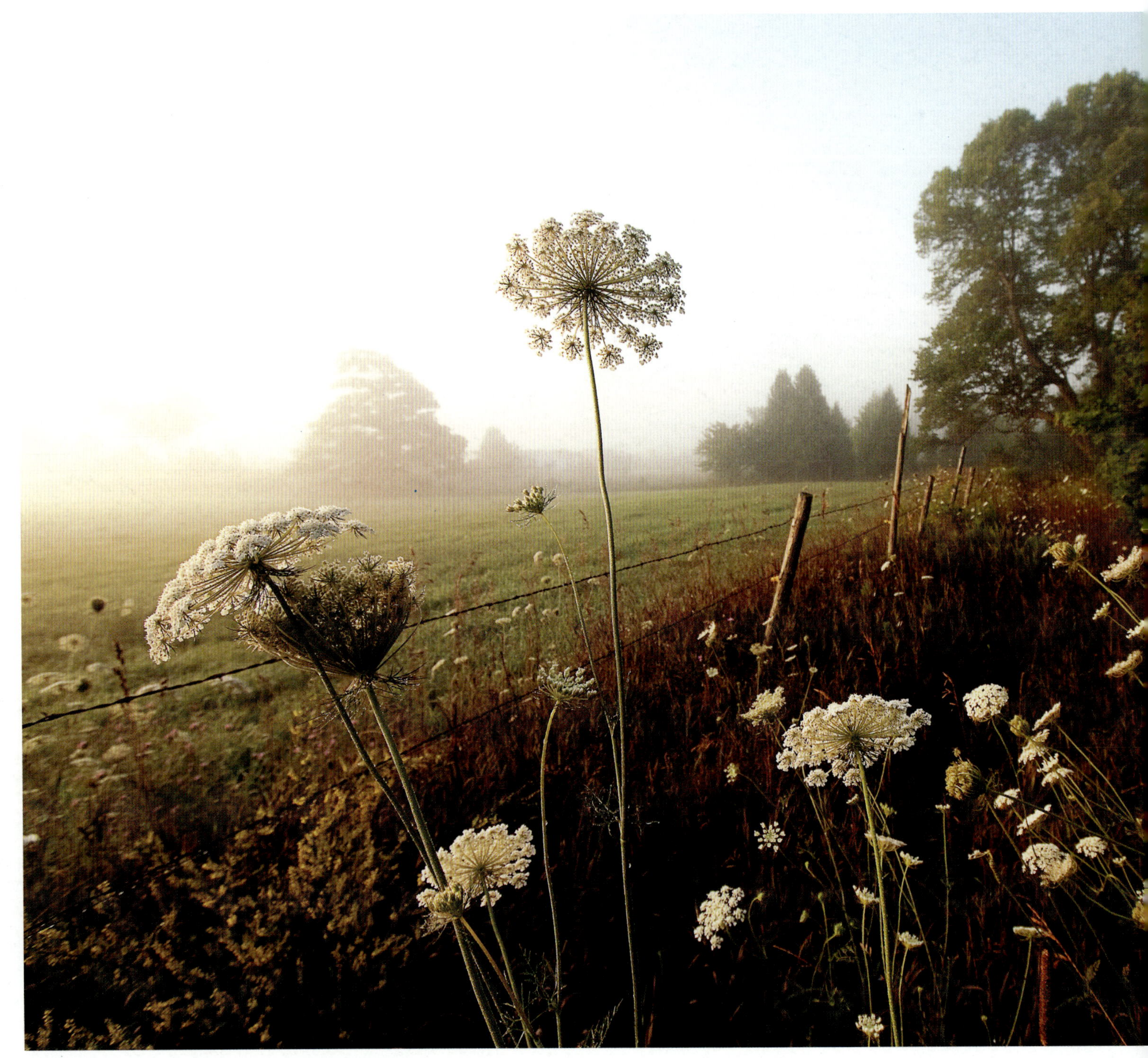

This page: Queen Anne's Lace, Sister Bay – Heather. **Next page:** Maple, Sister Bay – Lucas.

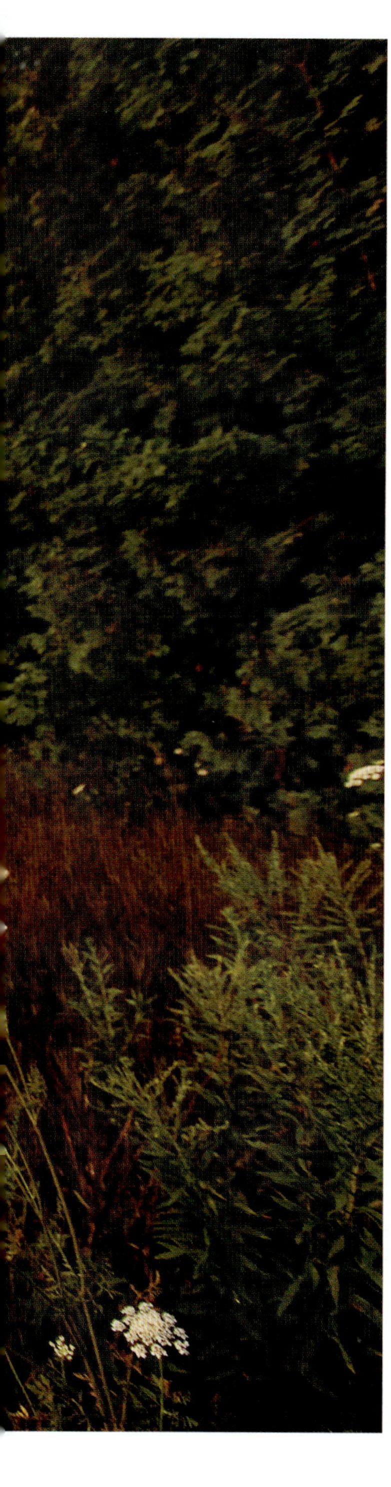

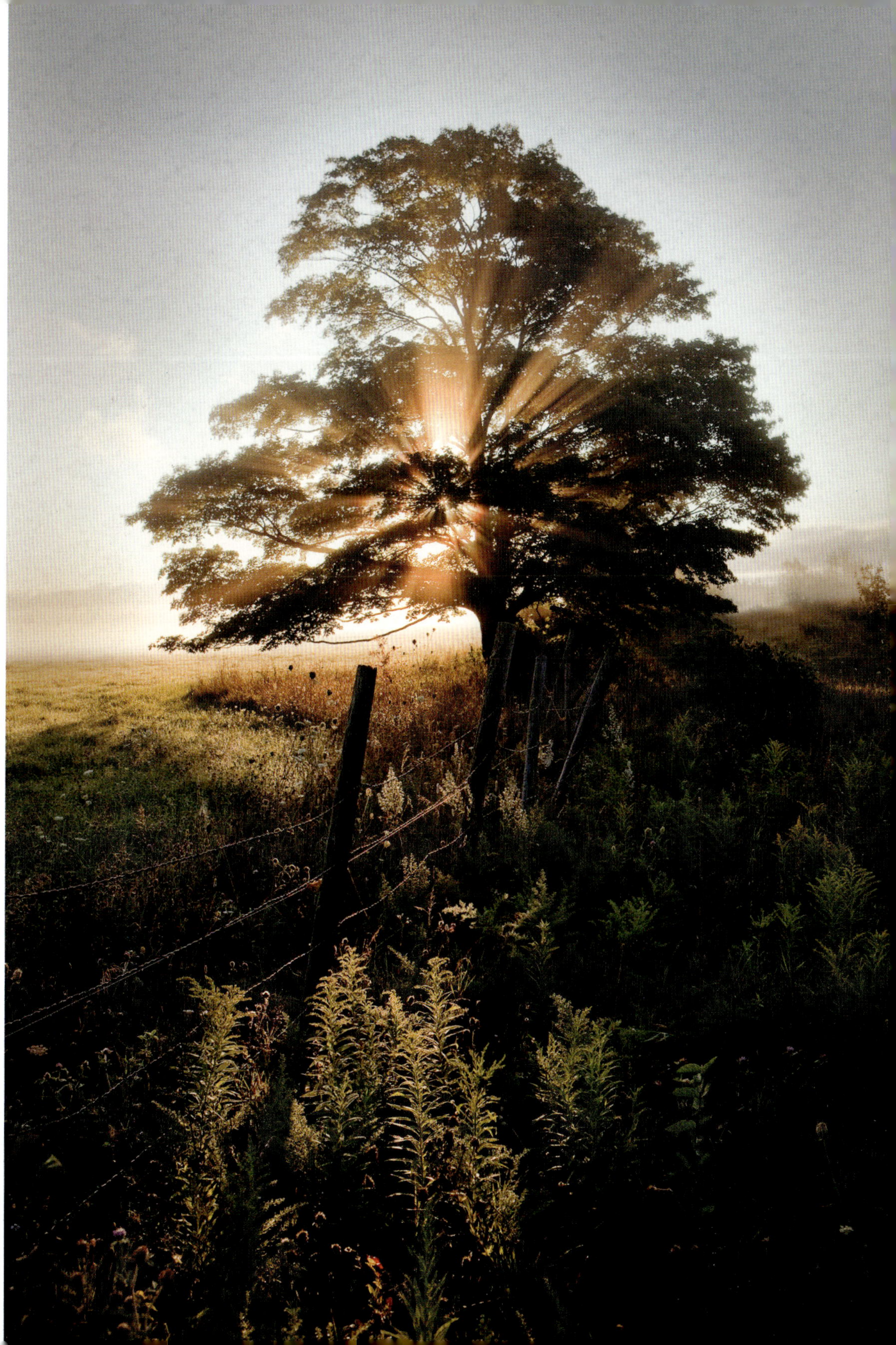

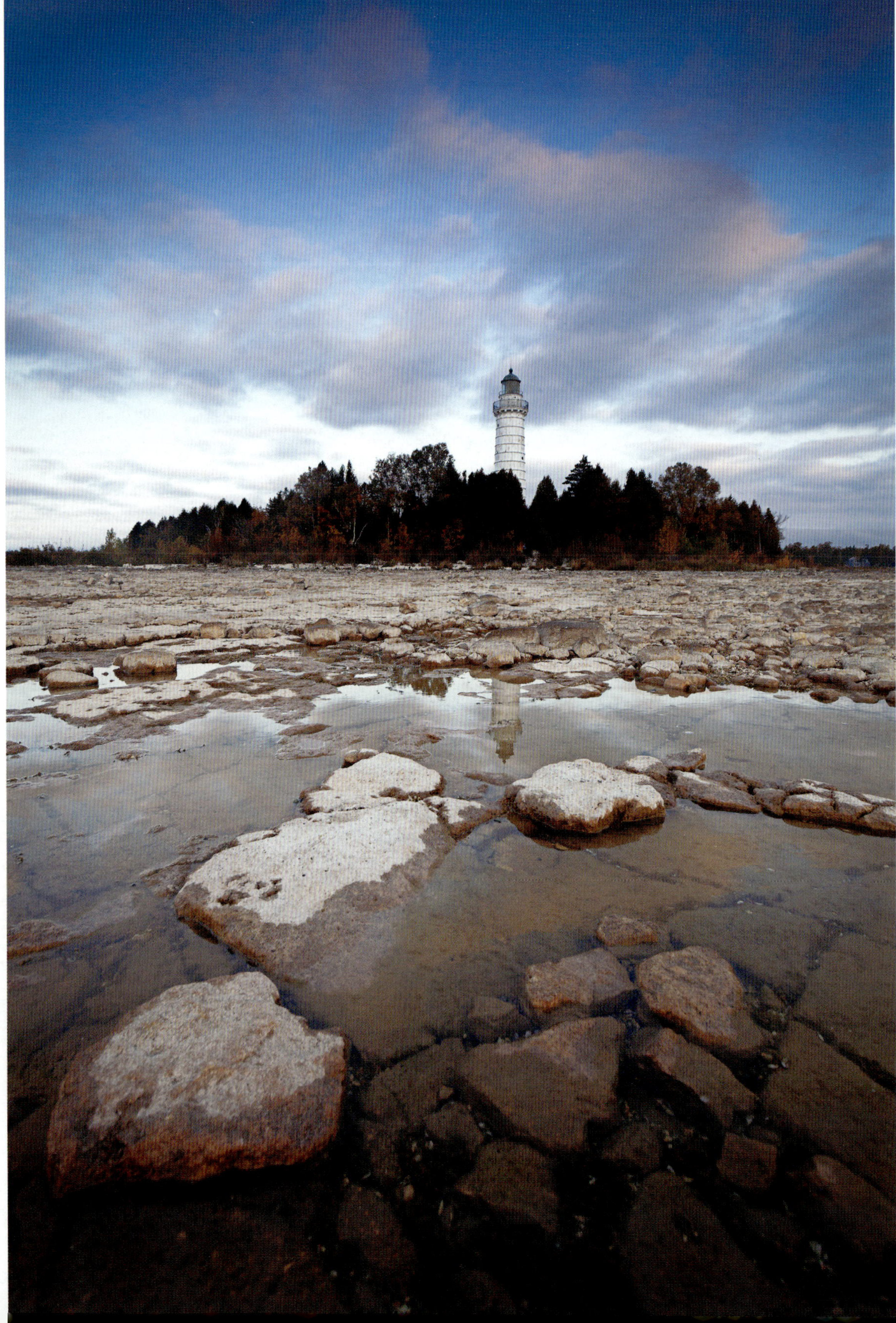

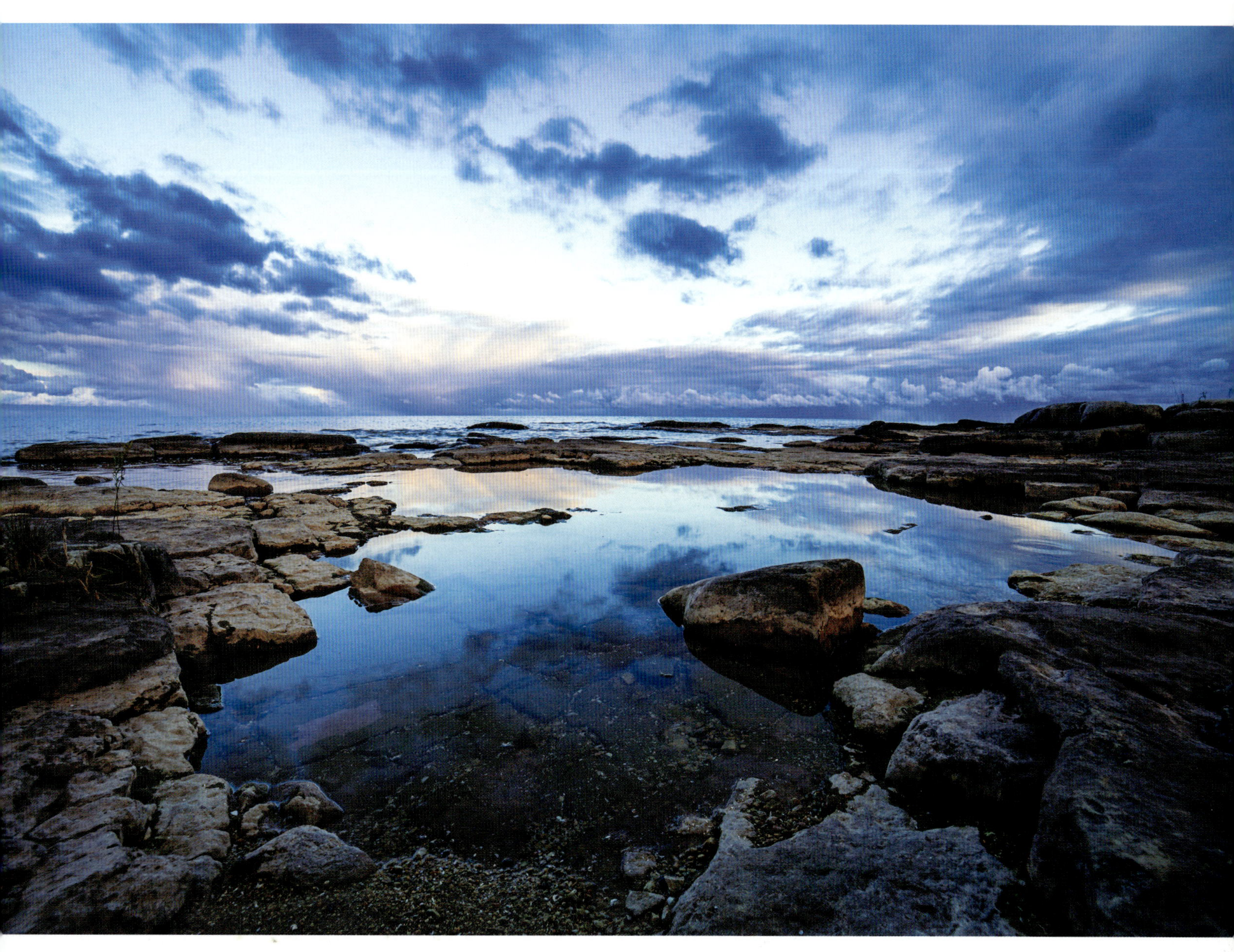

Previous page: Cana Island Lighthouse, Baileys Harbor – Heather.

This page: Sunset reflected, Toft Point – Lucas.

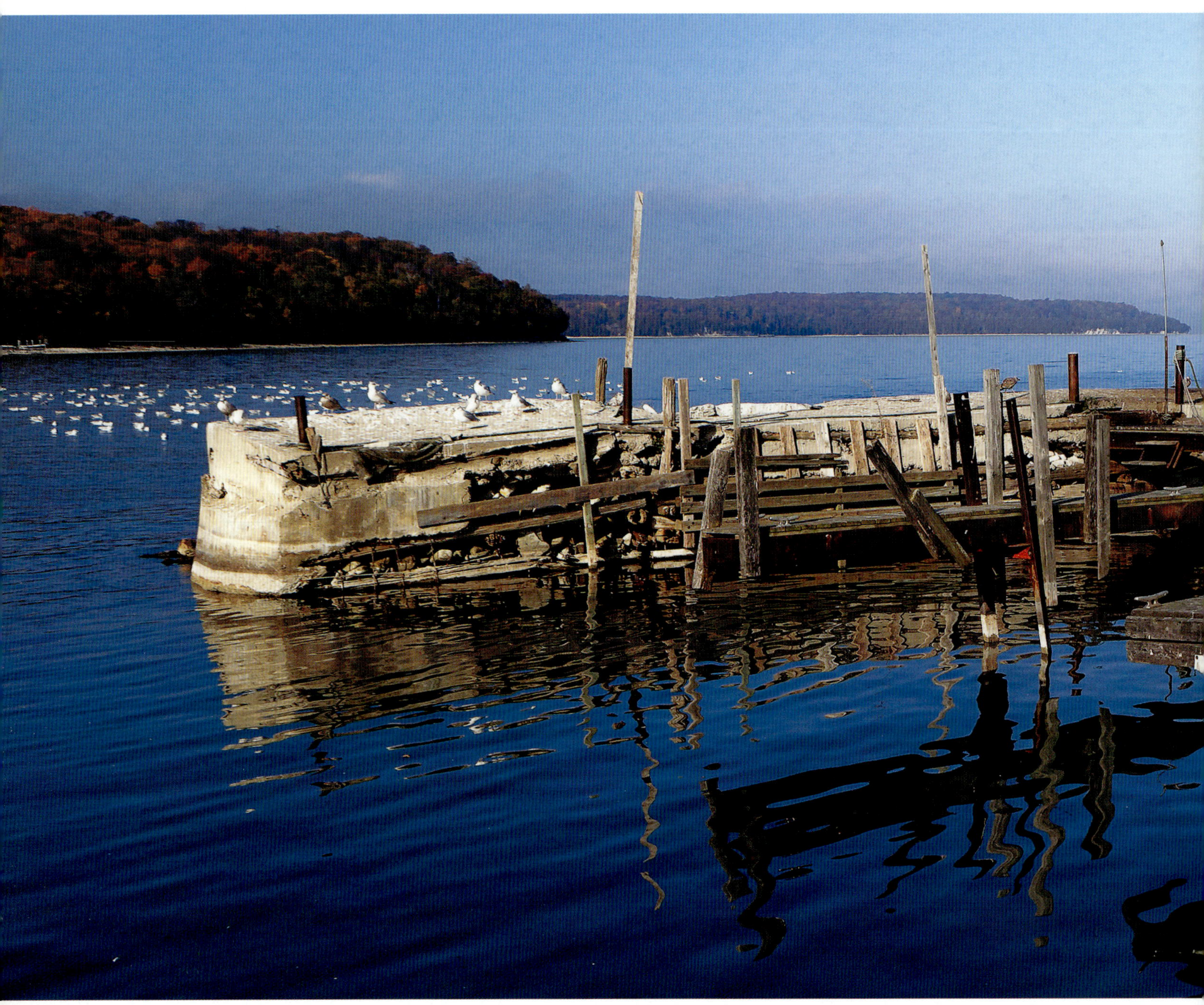

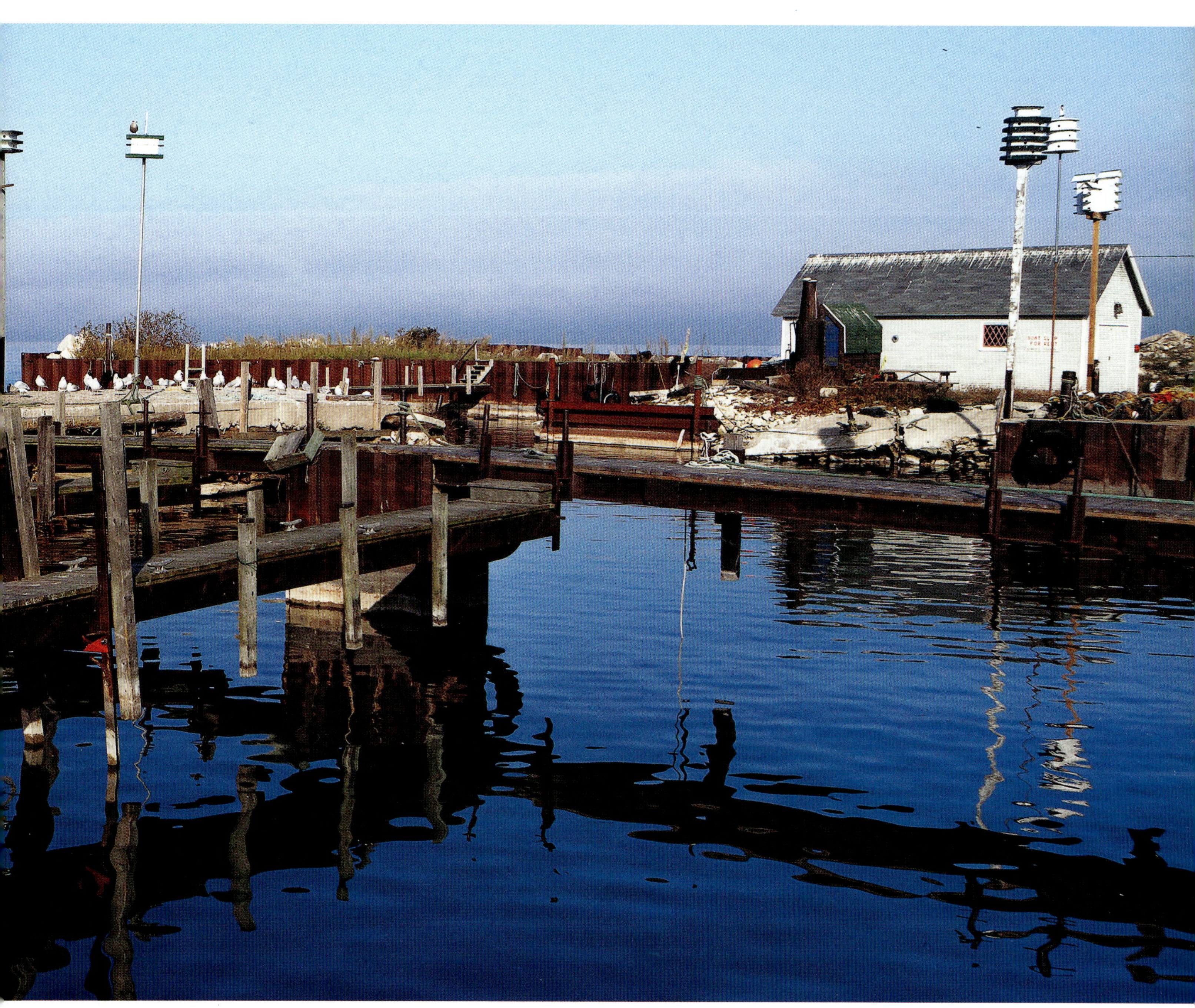

Gills Rock – Heather.

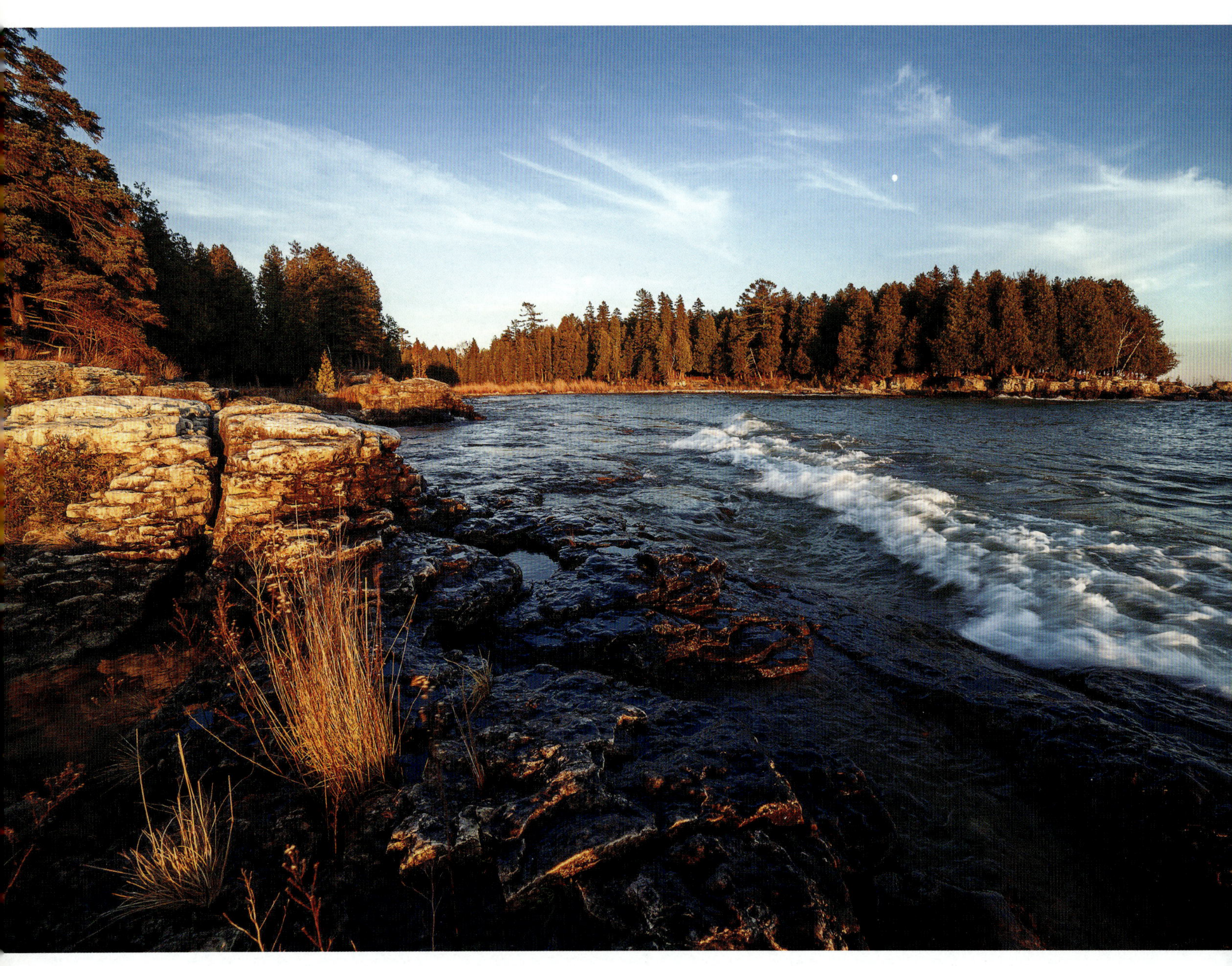

This page: Marshall's Point – Lucas.

Next page: North Bay – Heather.

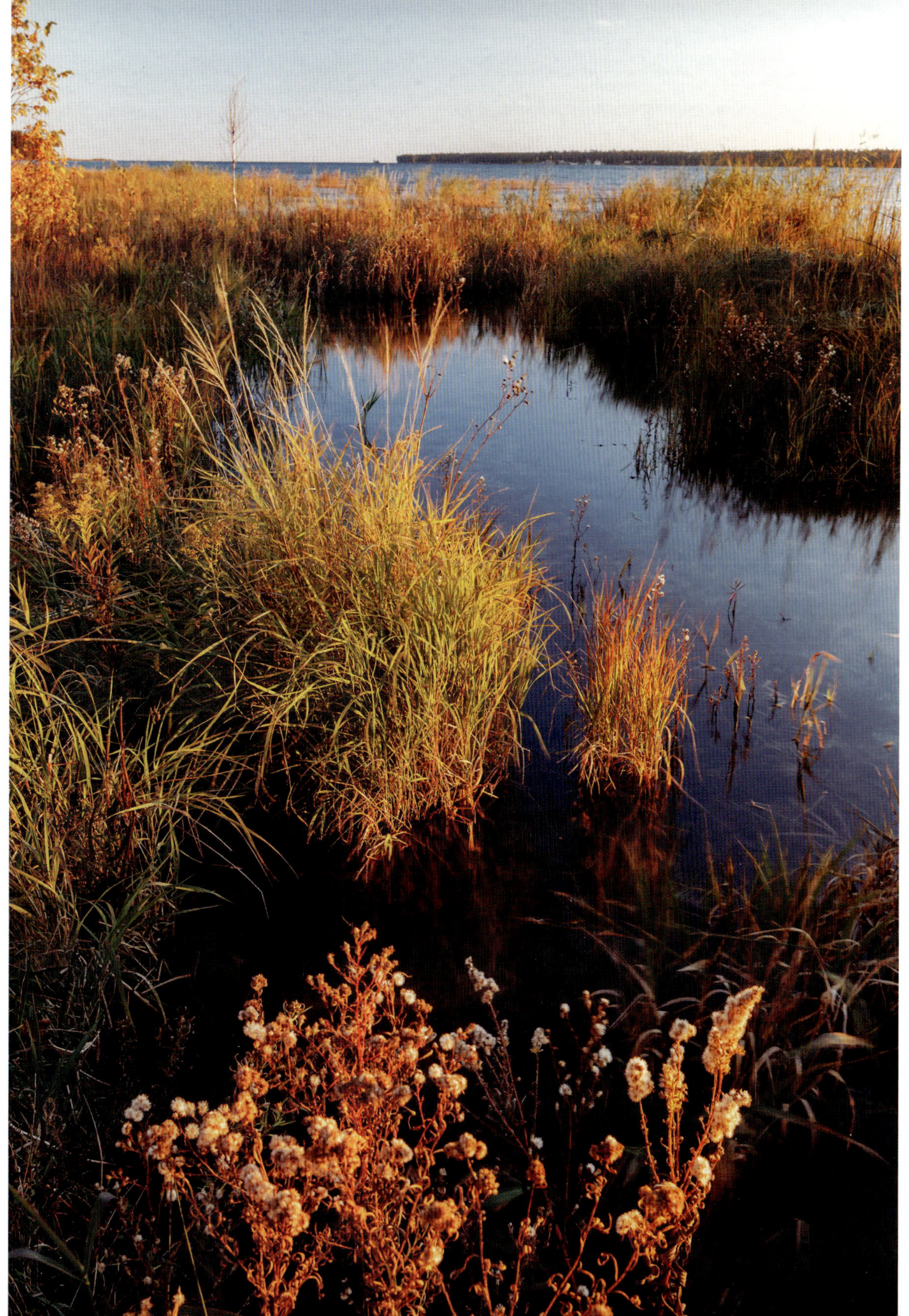

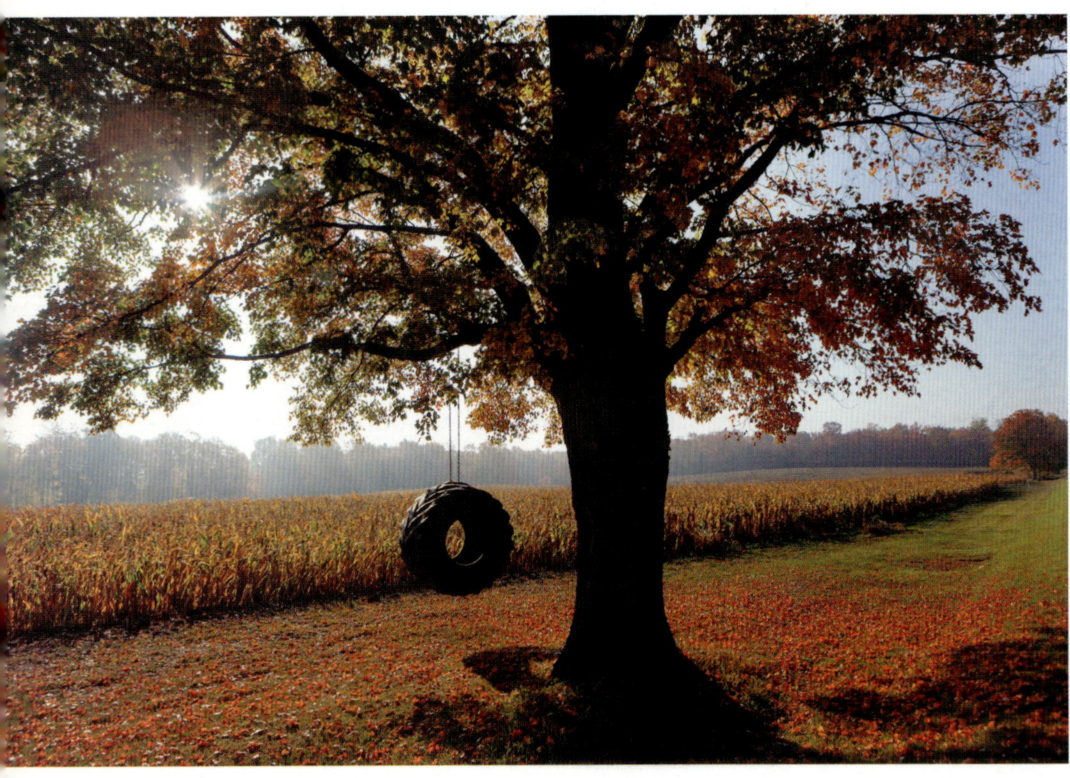

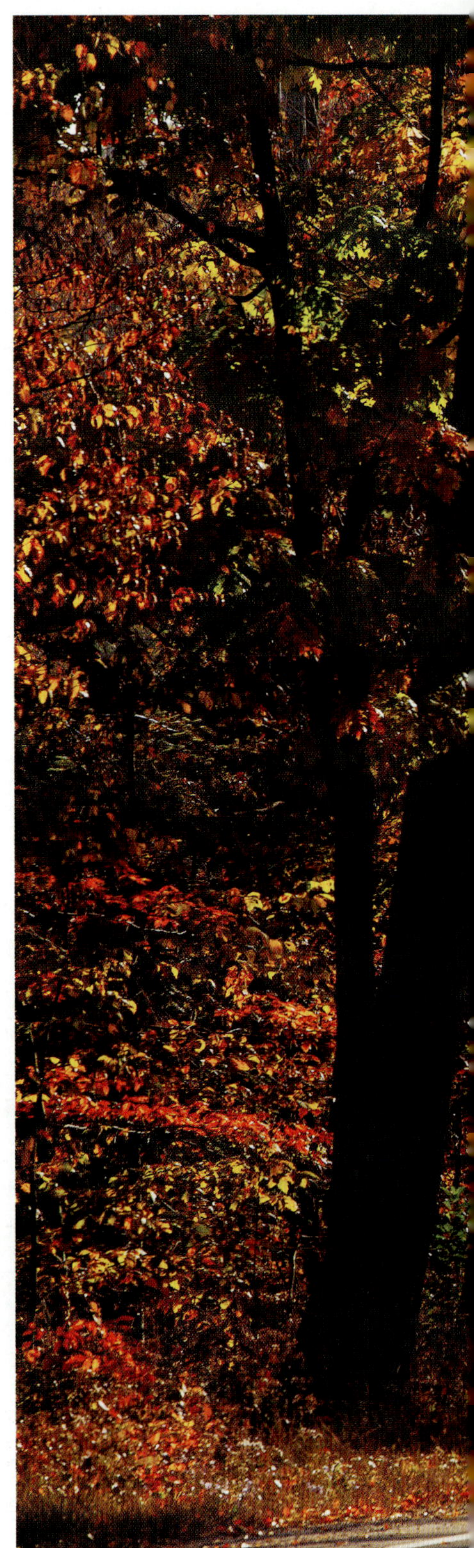

This page: Tire swing, Sister Bay – Heather.

Next page: Road to Northport – Heather.

Following pages: Eagle Bluff, Ephraim; Maple, Sister Bay – Lucas.

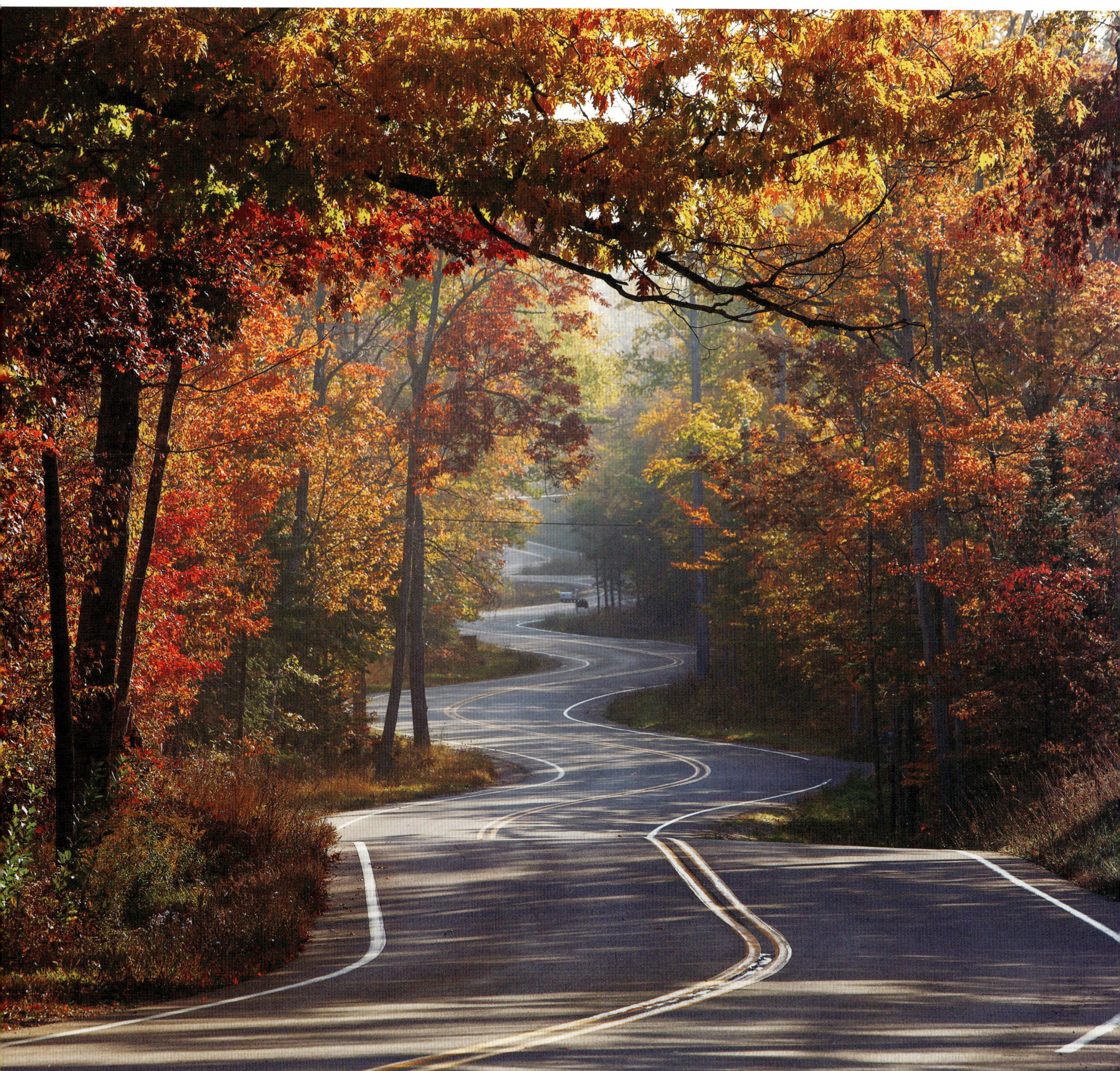

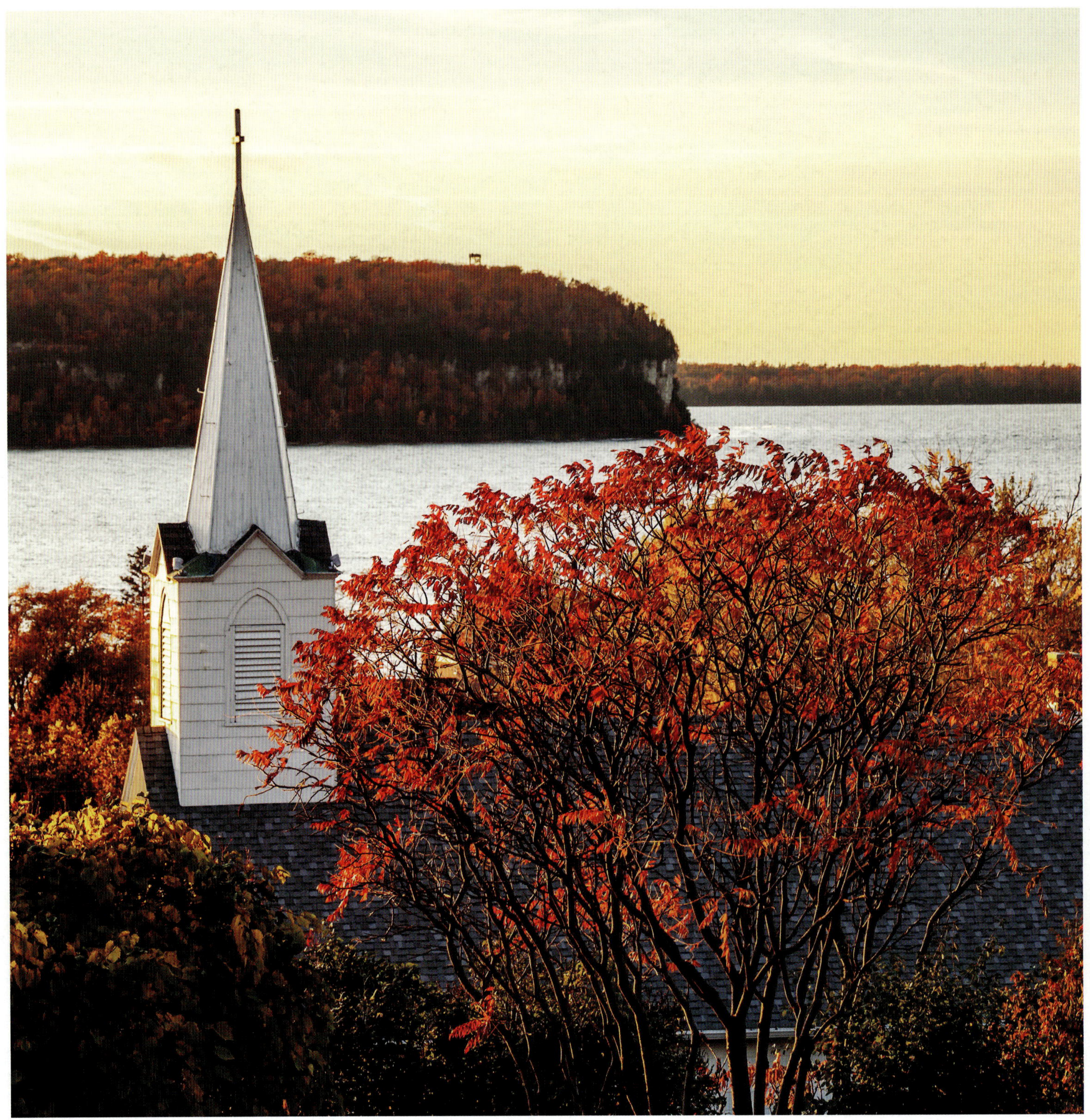

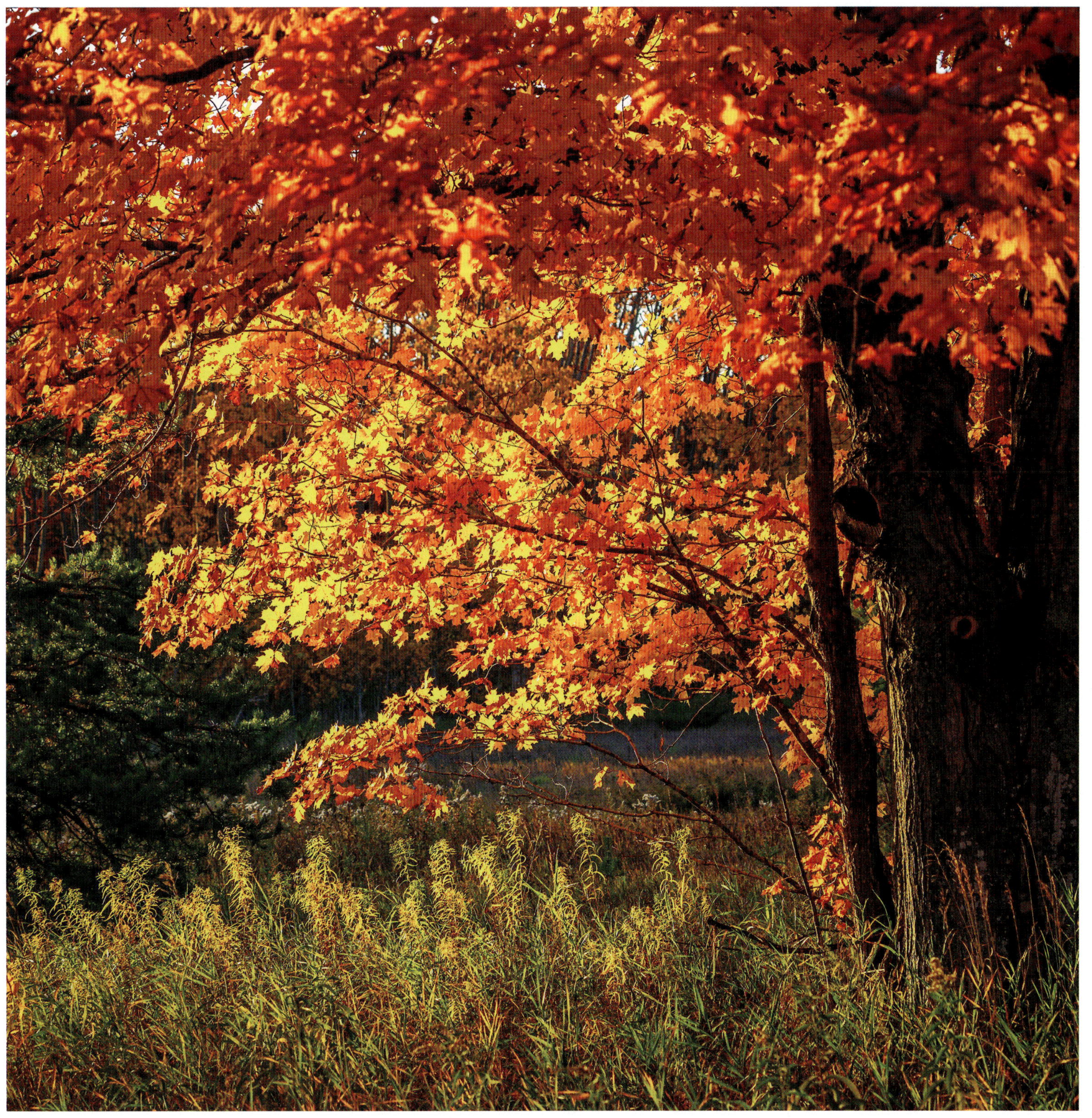

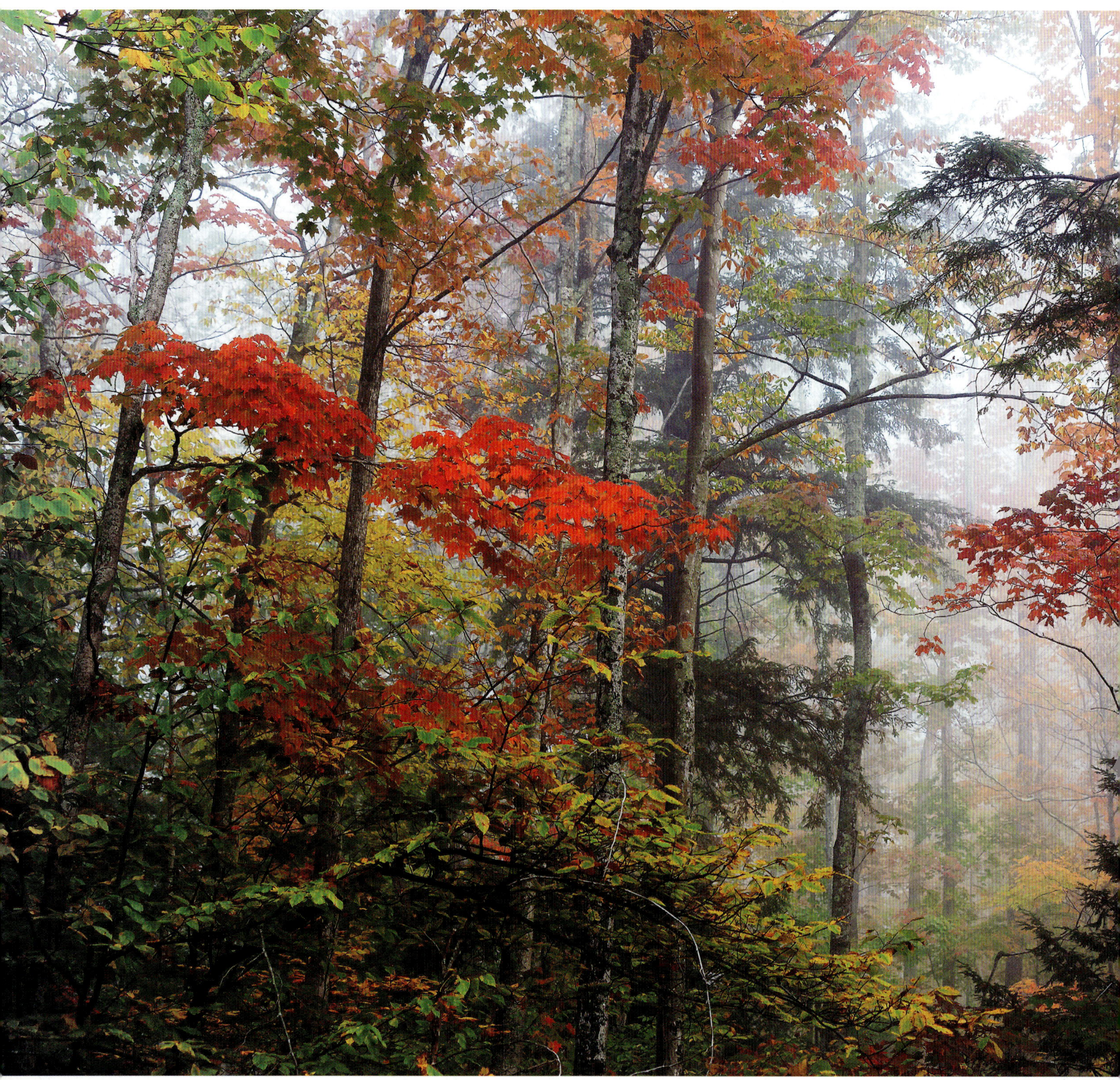

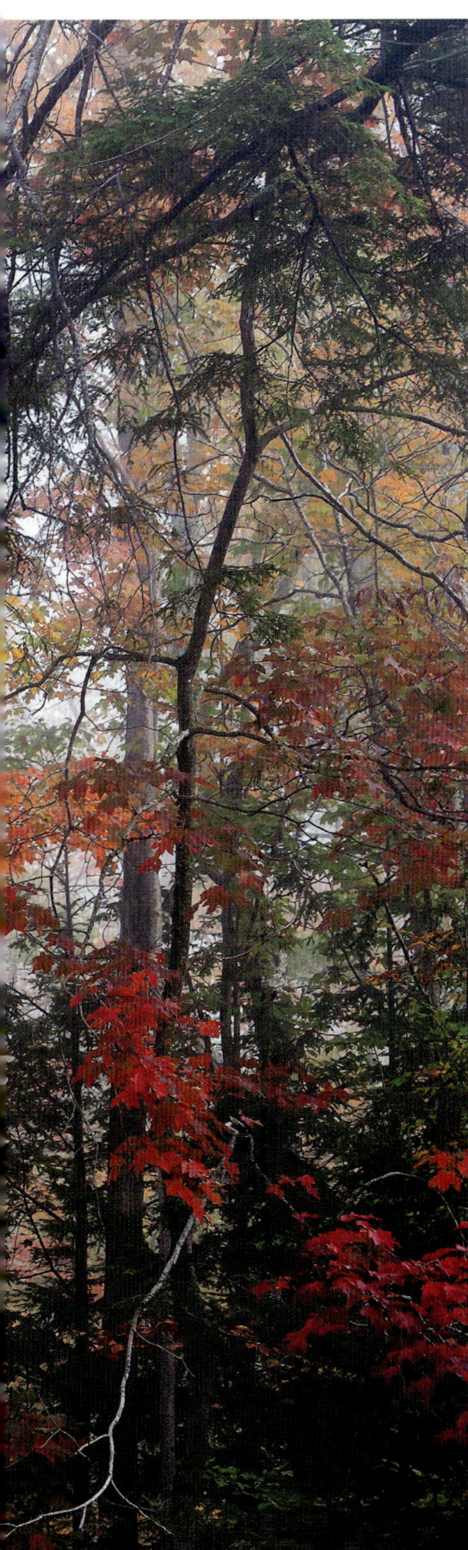

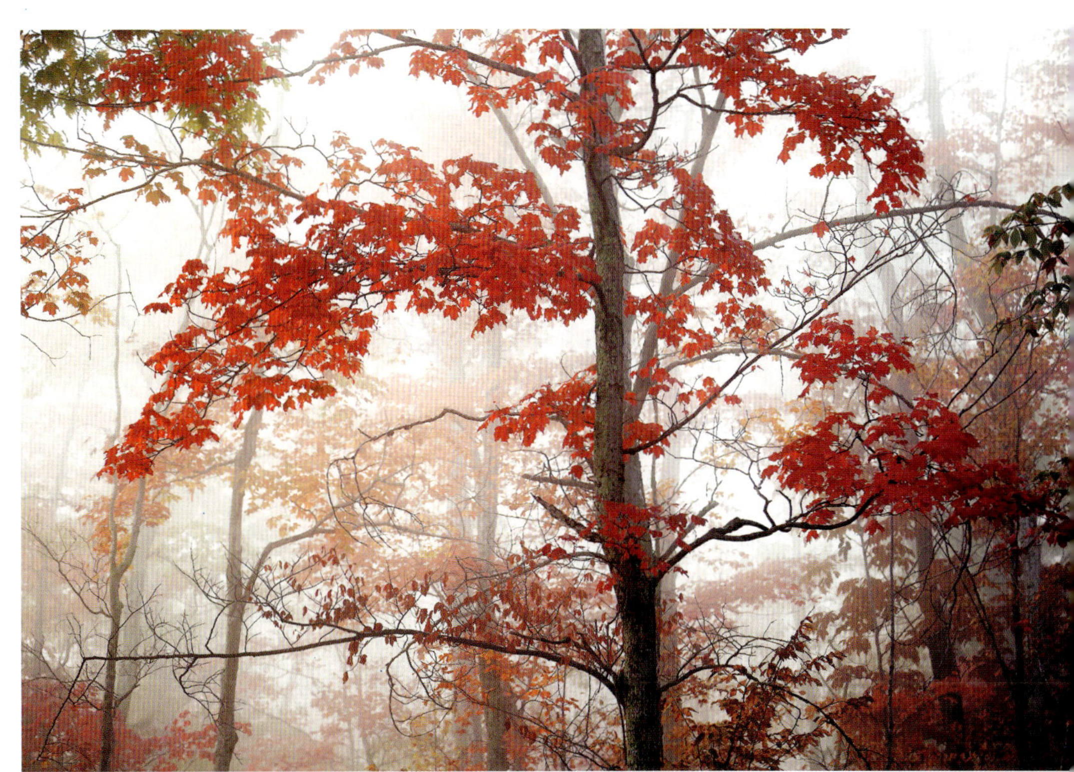

Previous page and this page: Northport – Heather.

Following pages: Fish Creek Harbor – Heather and Lucas.

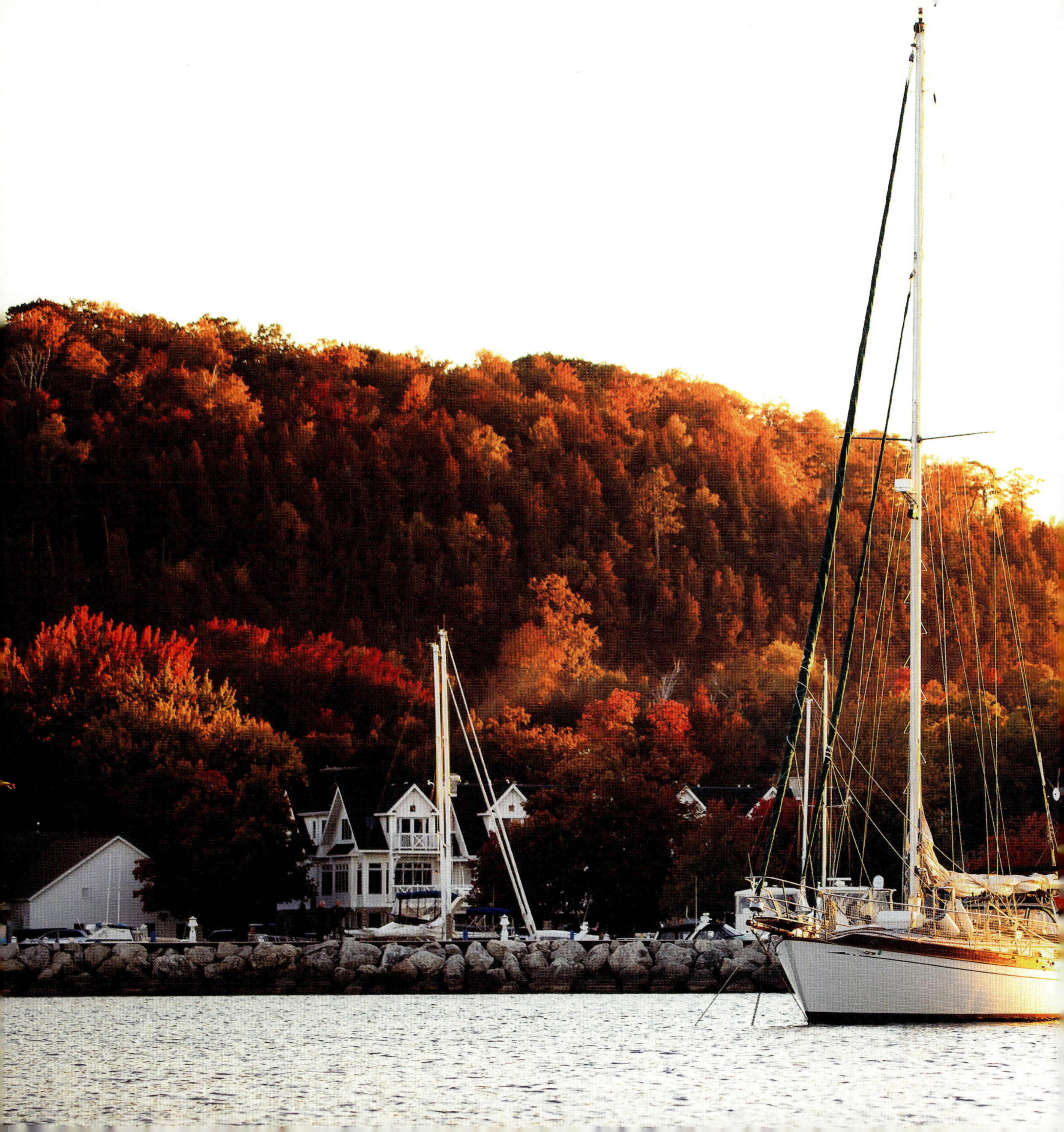

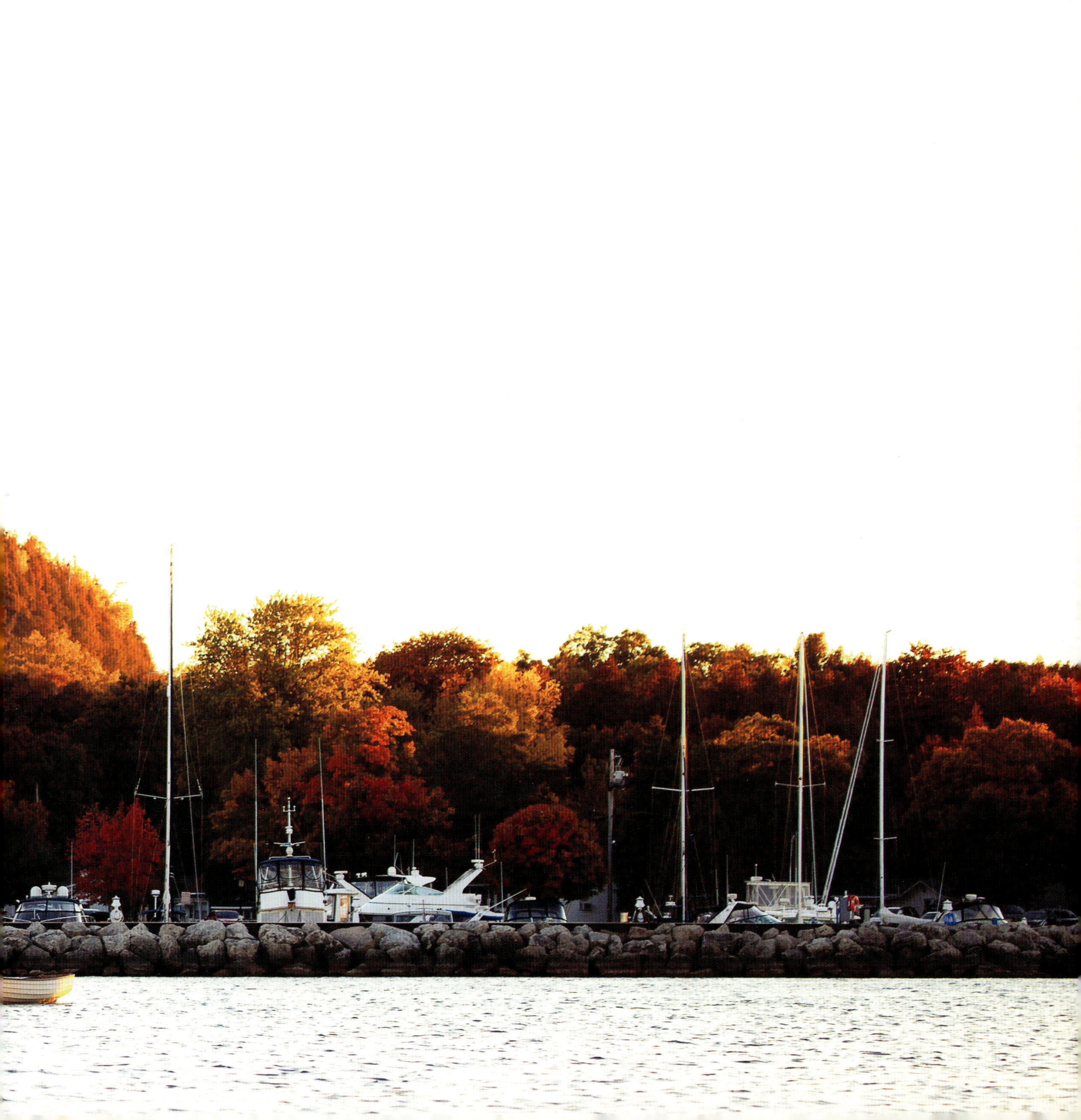

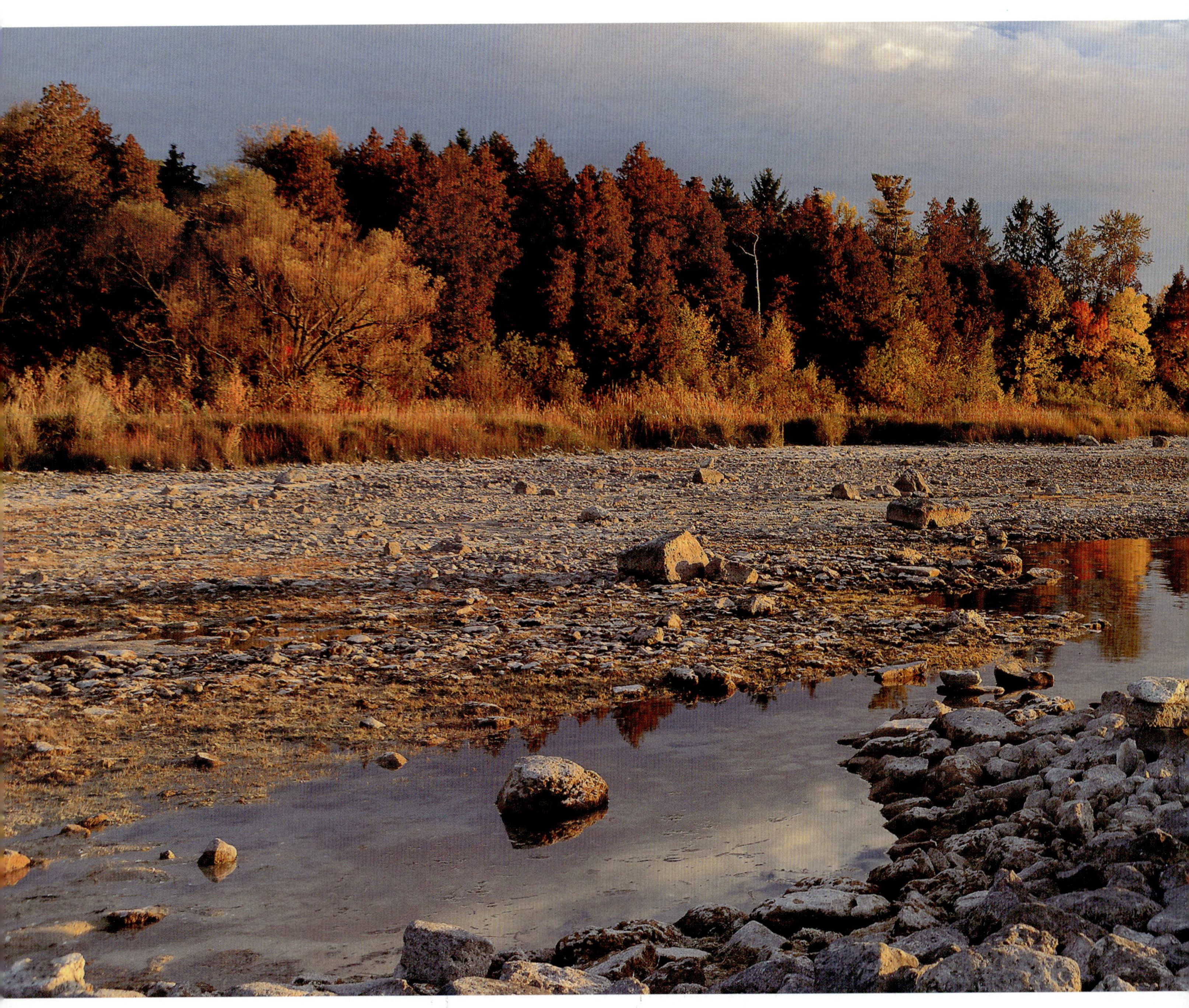

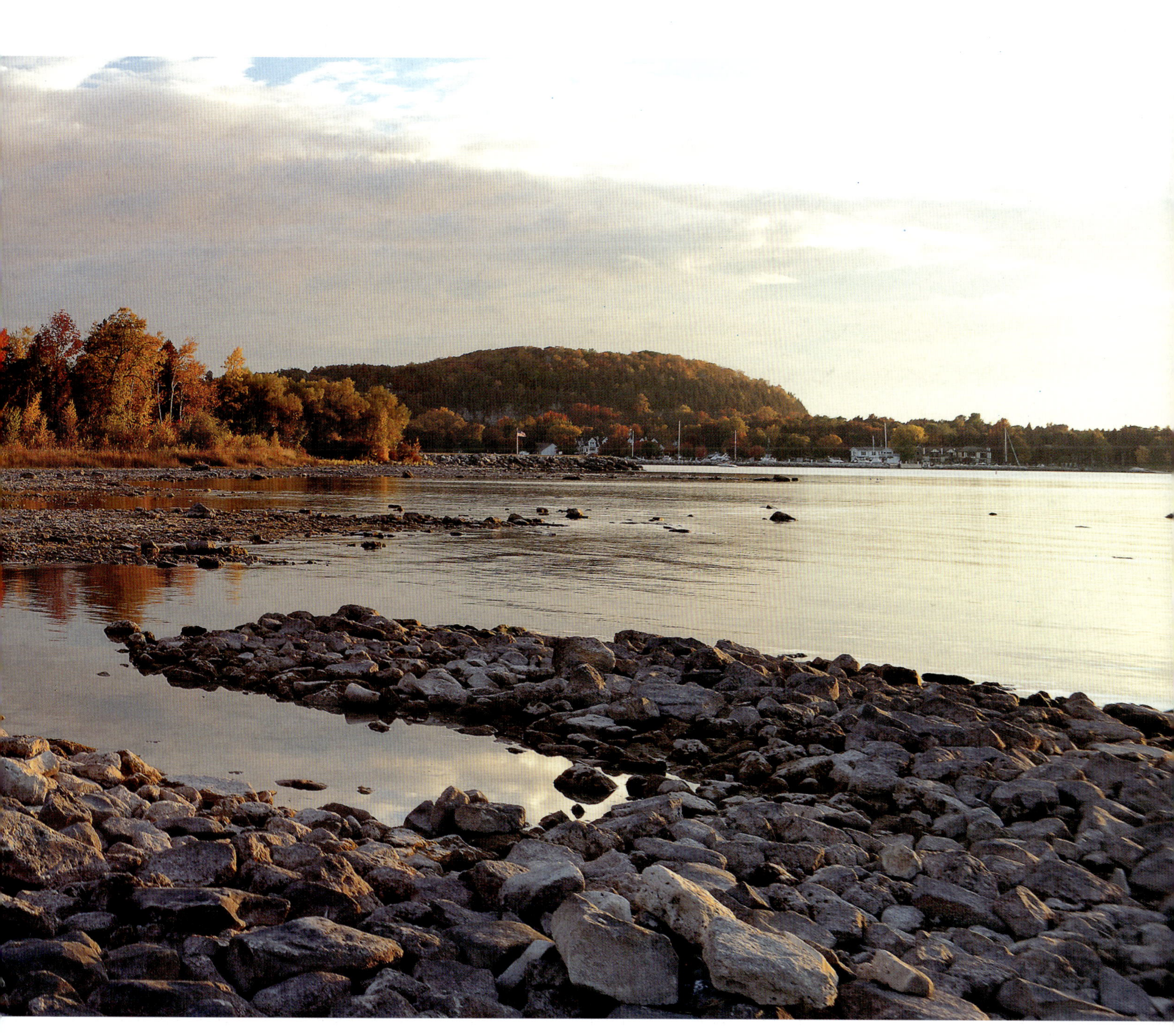

Peninsula State Park – Heather.

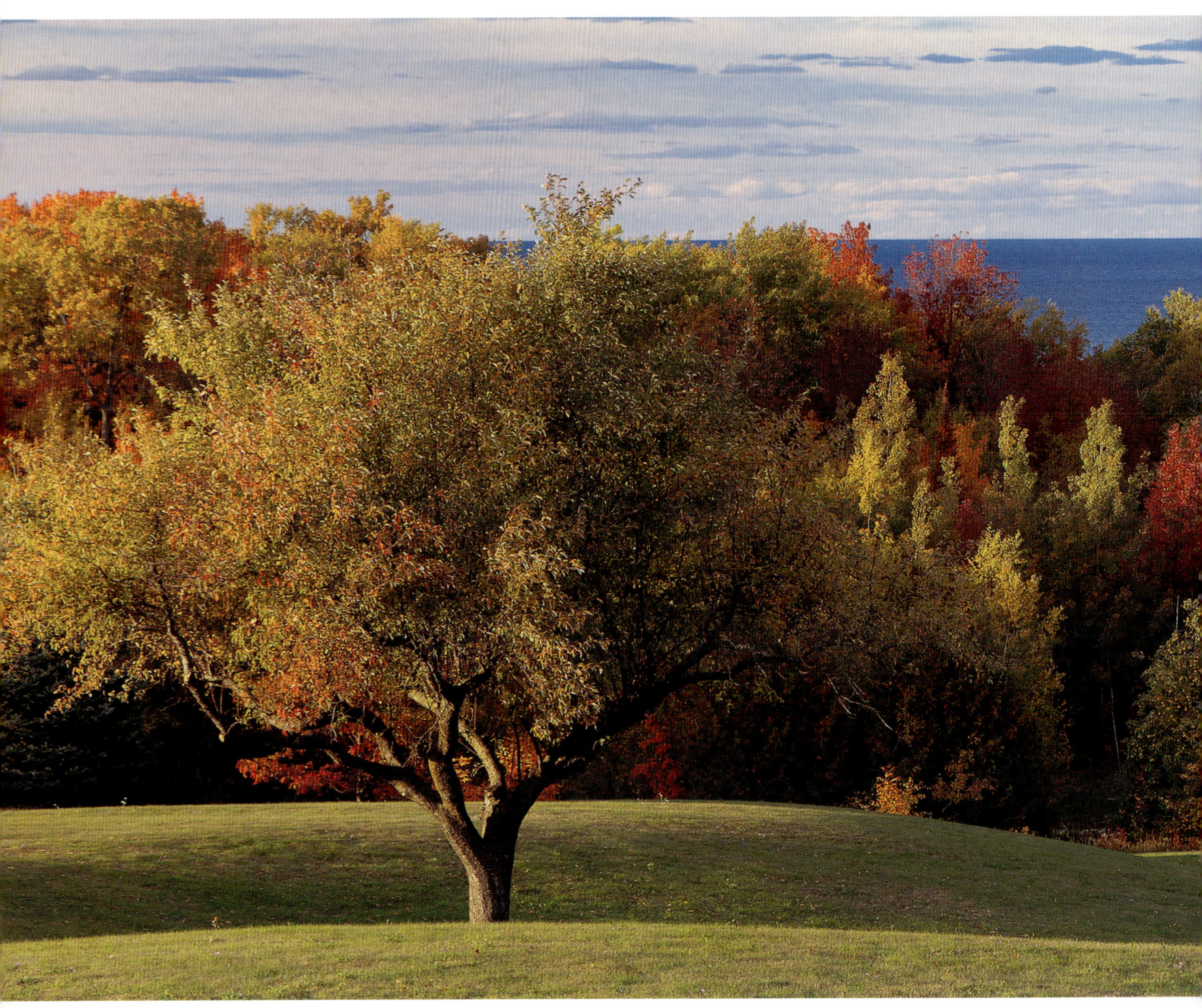

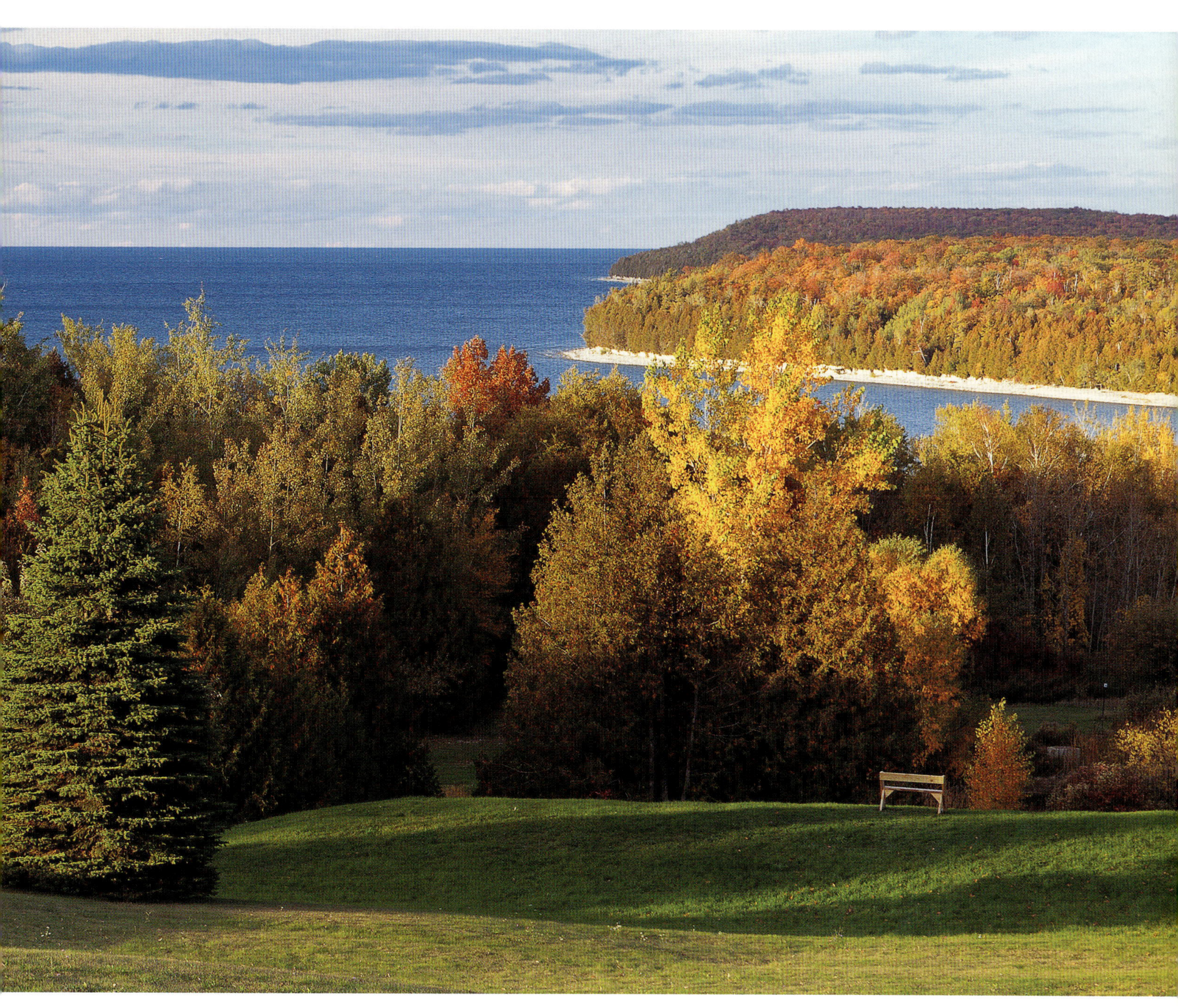

The Grand View, Ellison Bay – Heather.

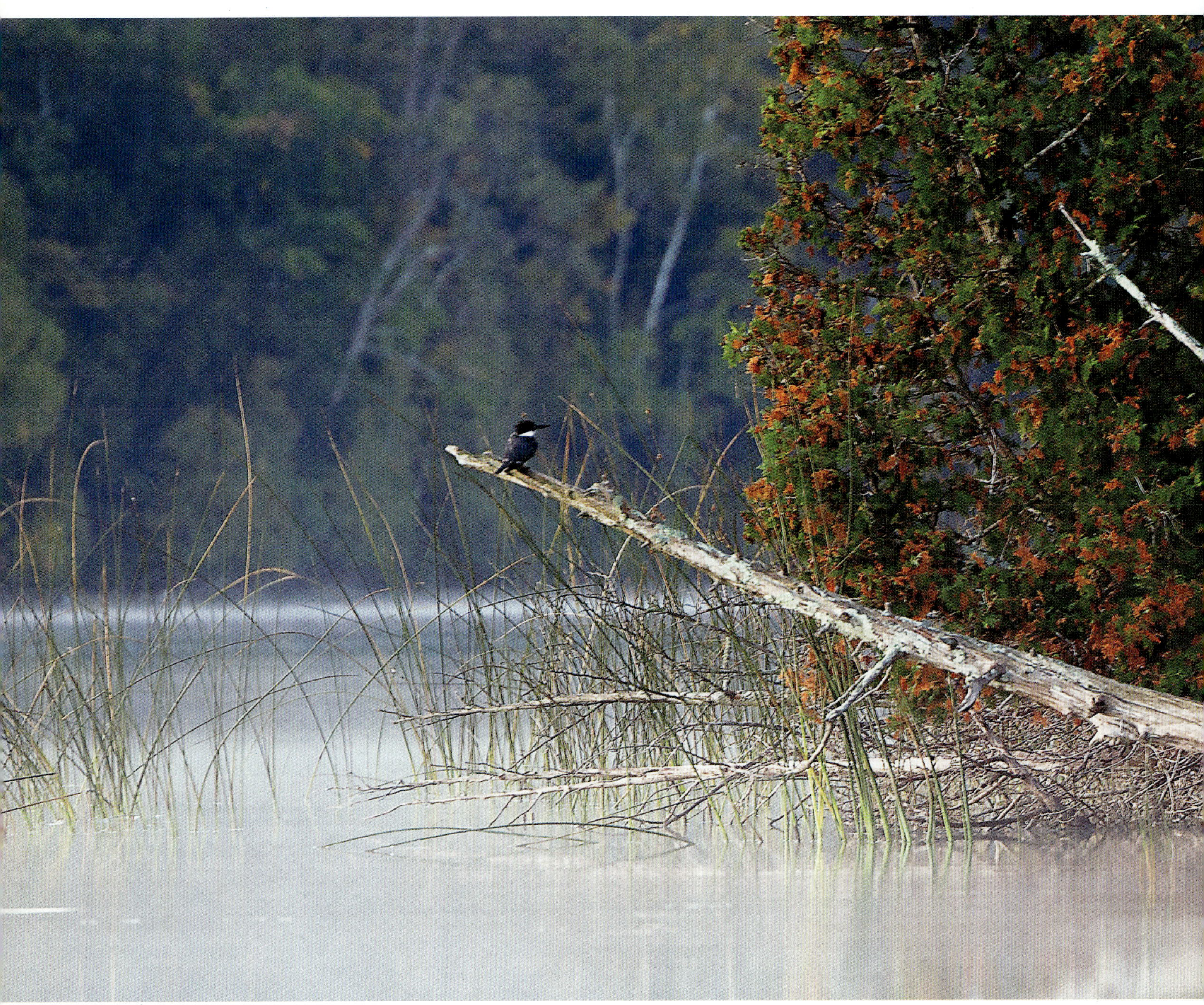

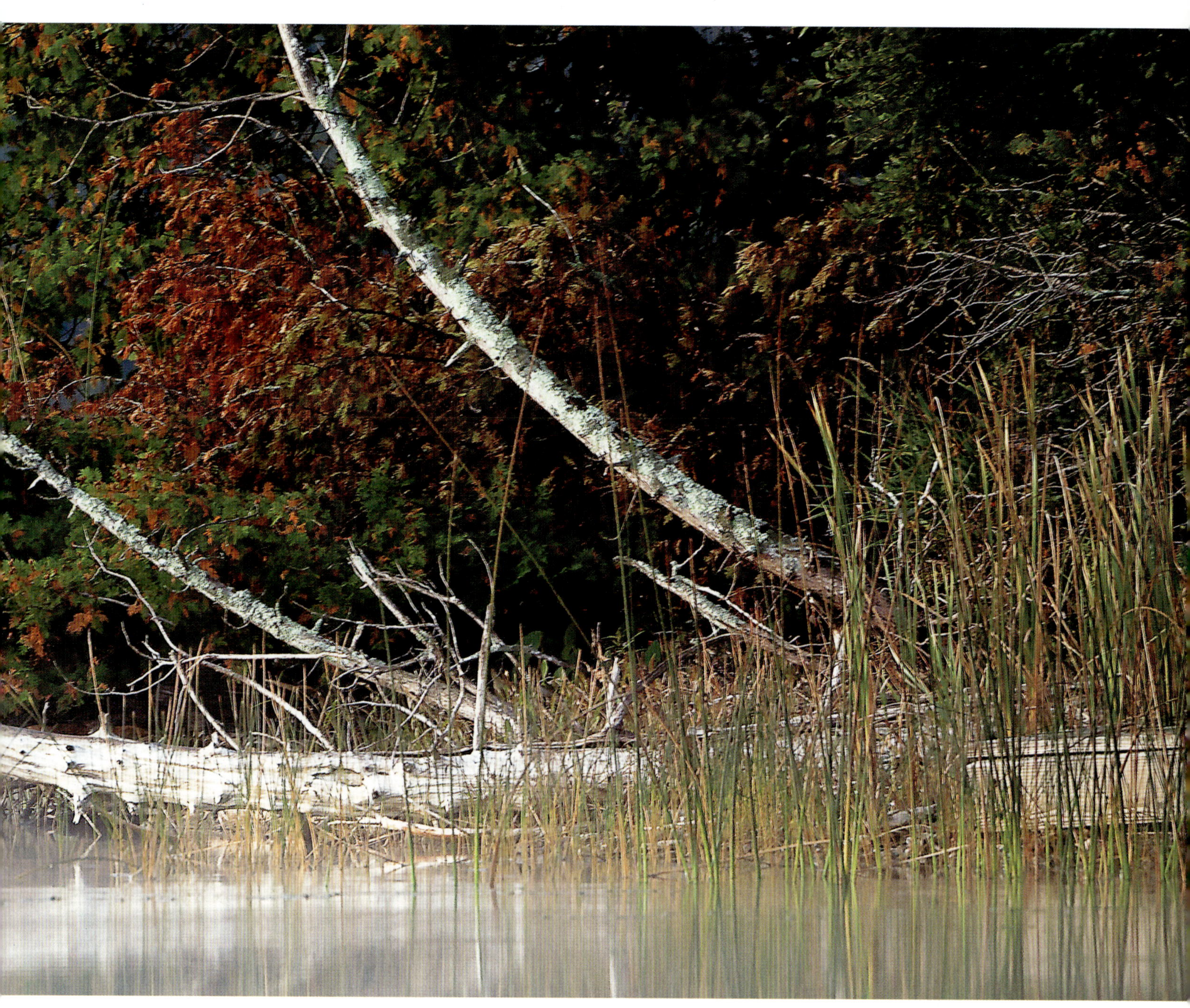

Belted Kingfisher, Europe Lake – Heather and Lucas.

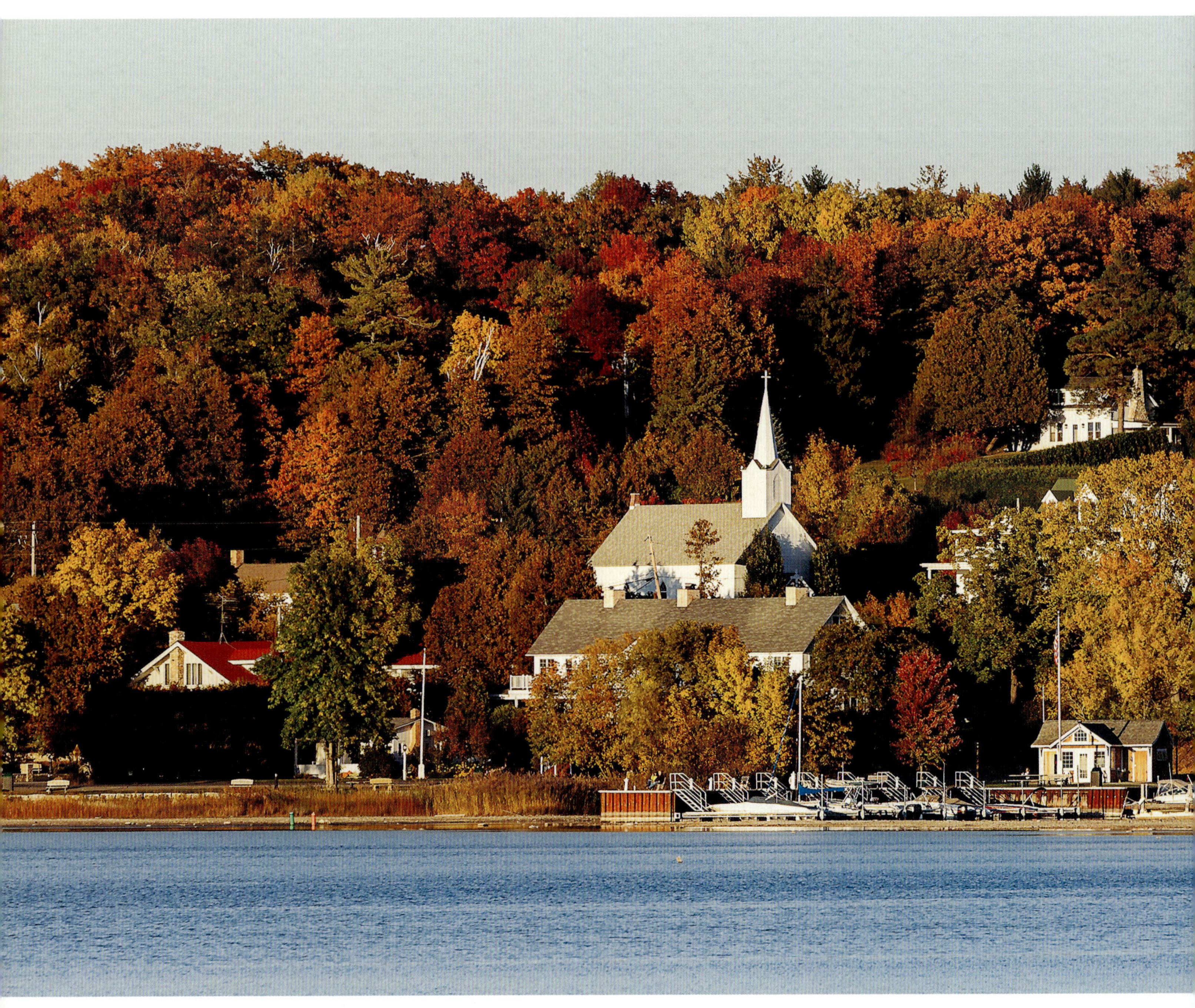

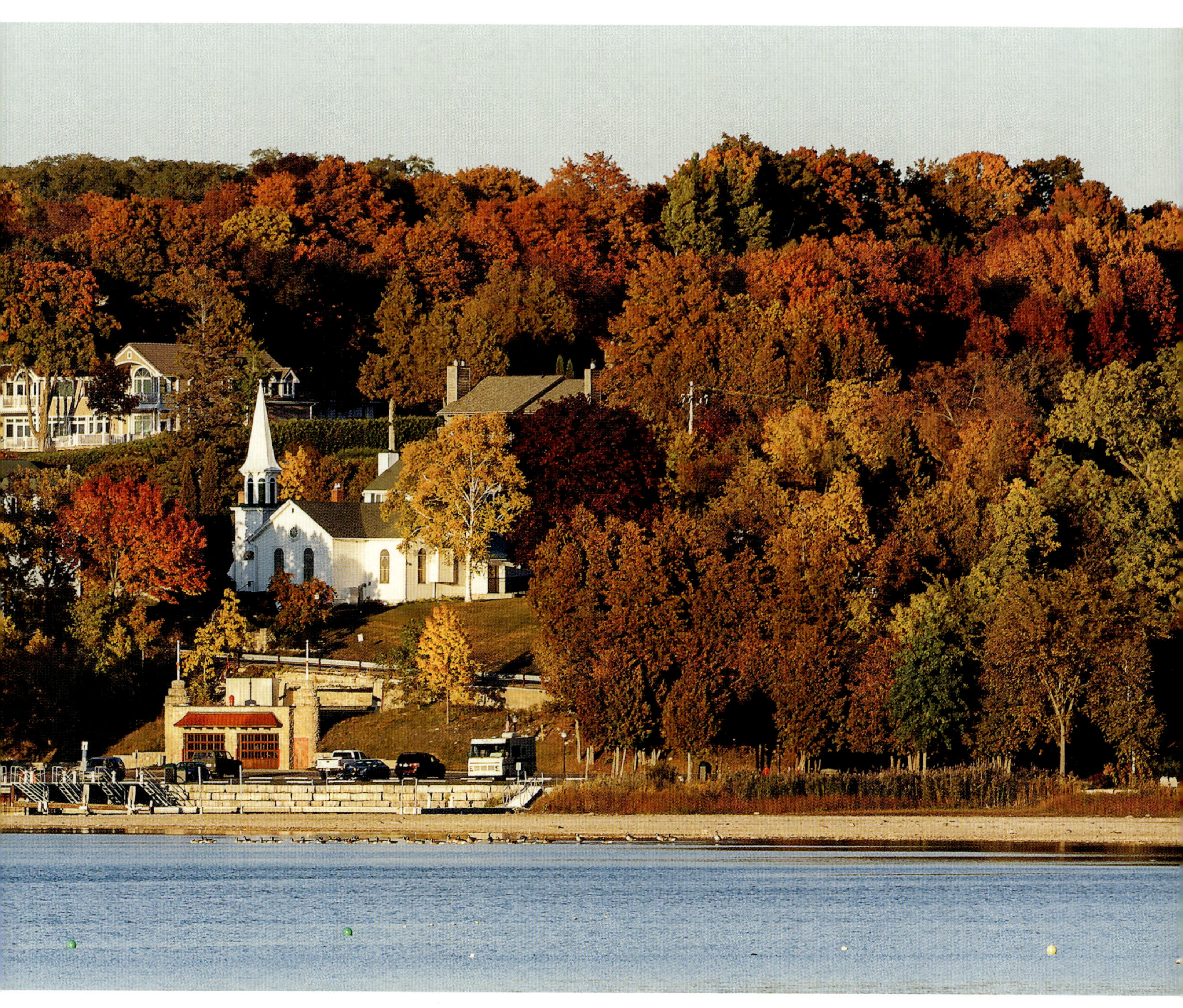

Ephraim – Lucas.

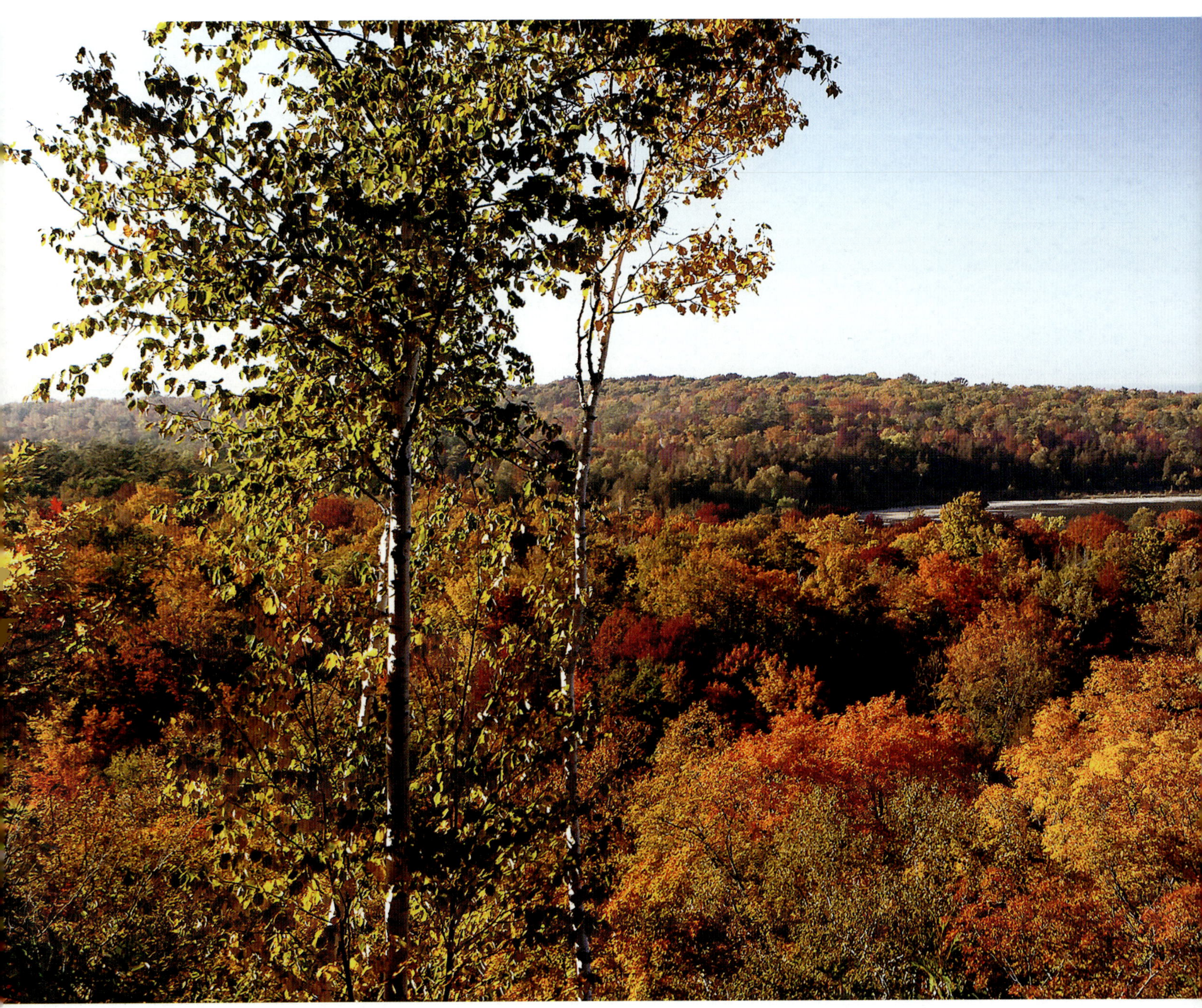

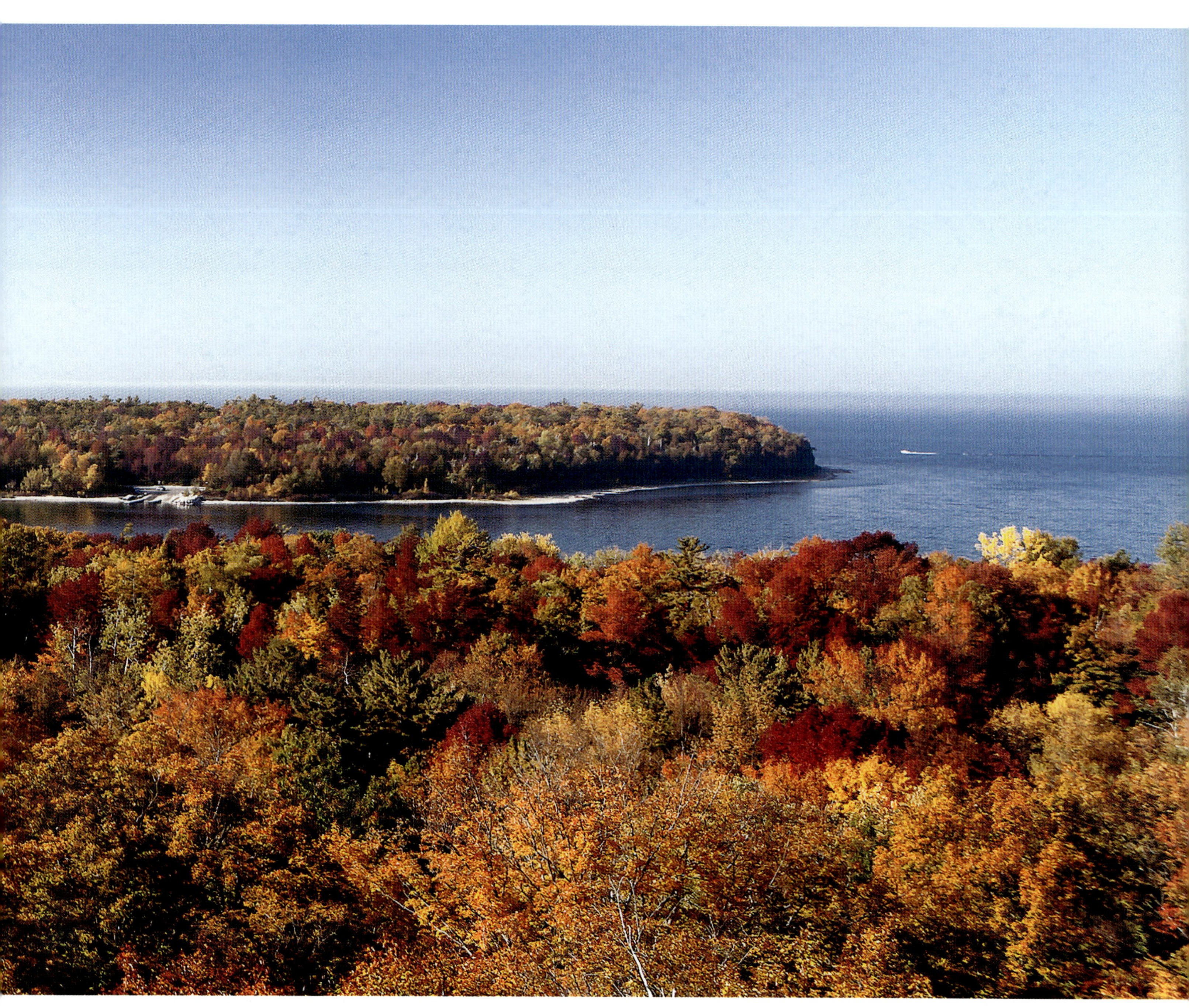

Nicolet Bay, Peninsula State Park – Heather.

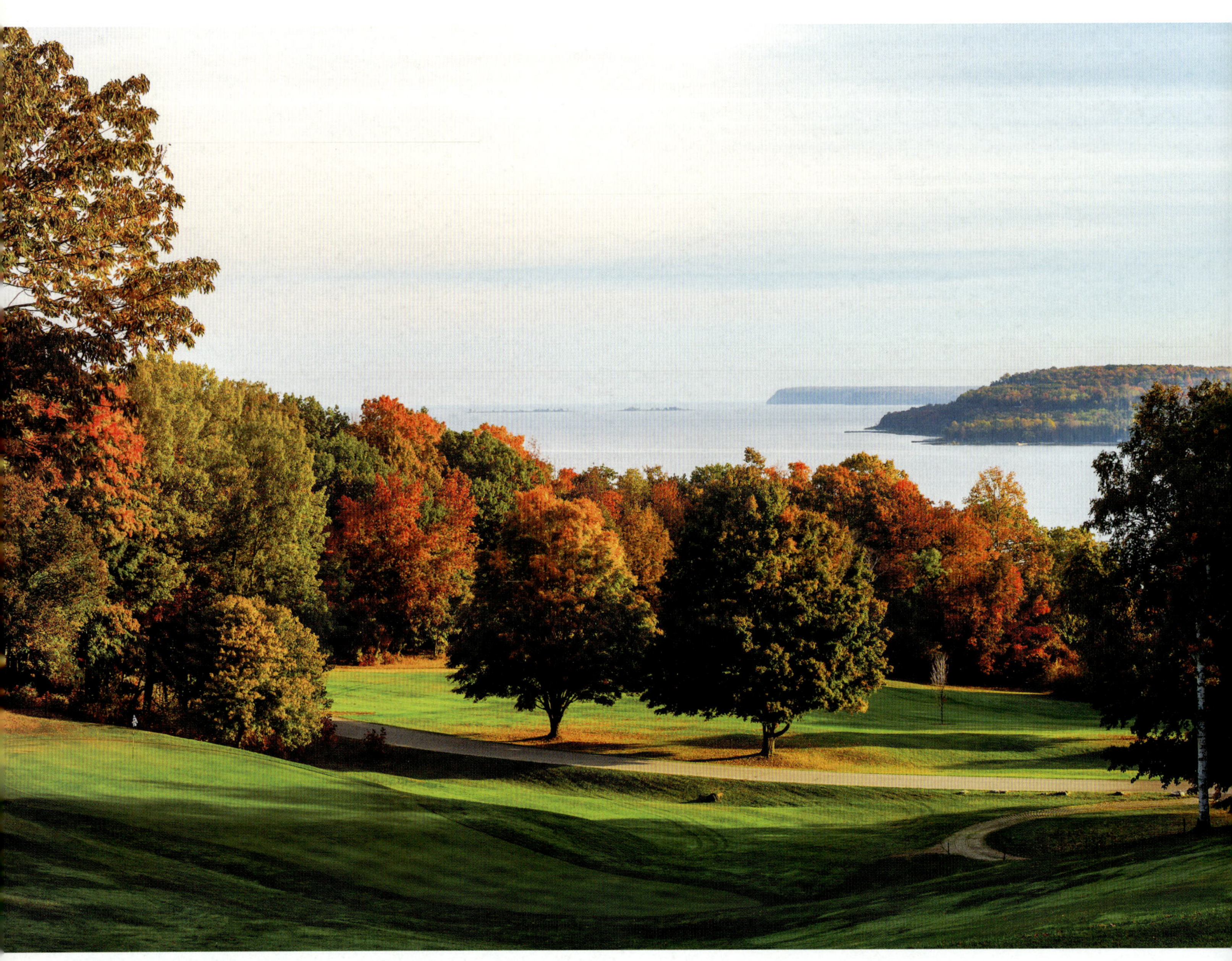

This page: Hill 17, Peninsula State Park Golf Course – Lucas.

Next page: Sister Bay – Lucas.

Following pages: Ice formations, Lake Michigan – Heather.

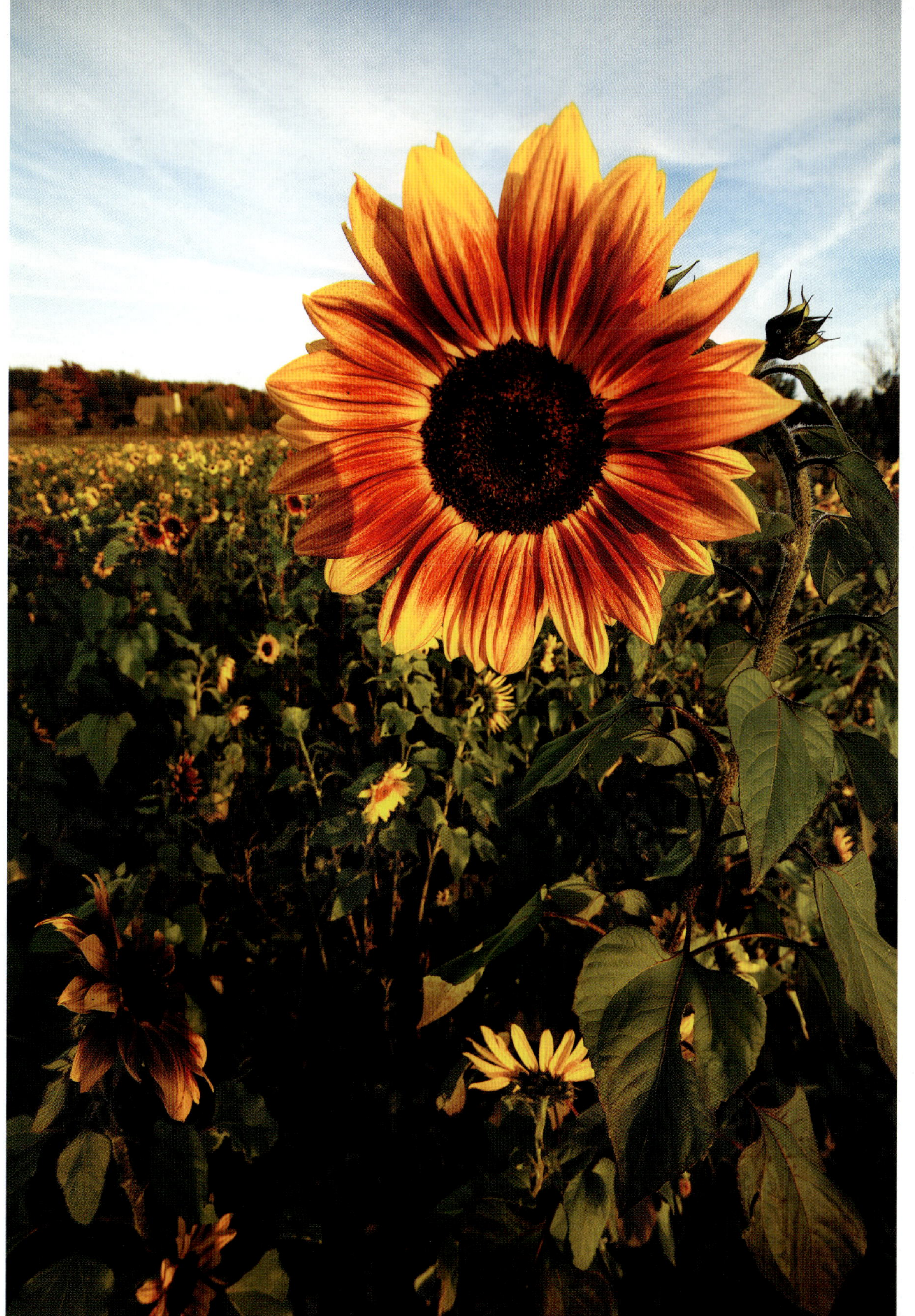

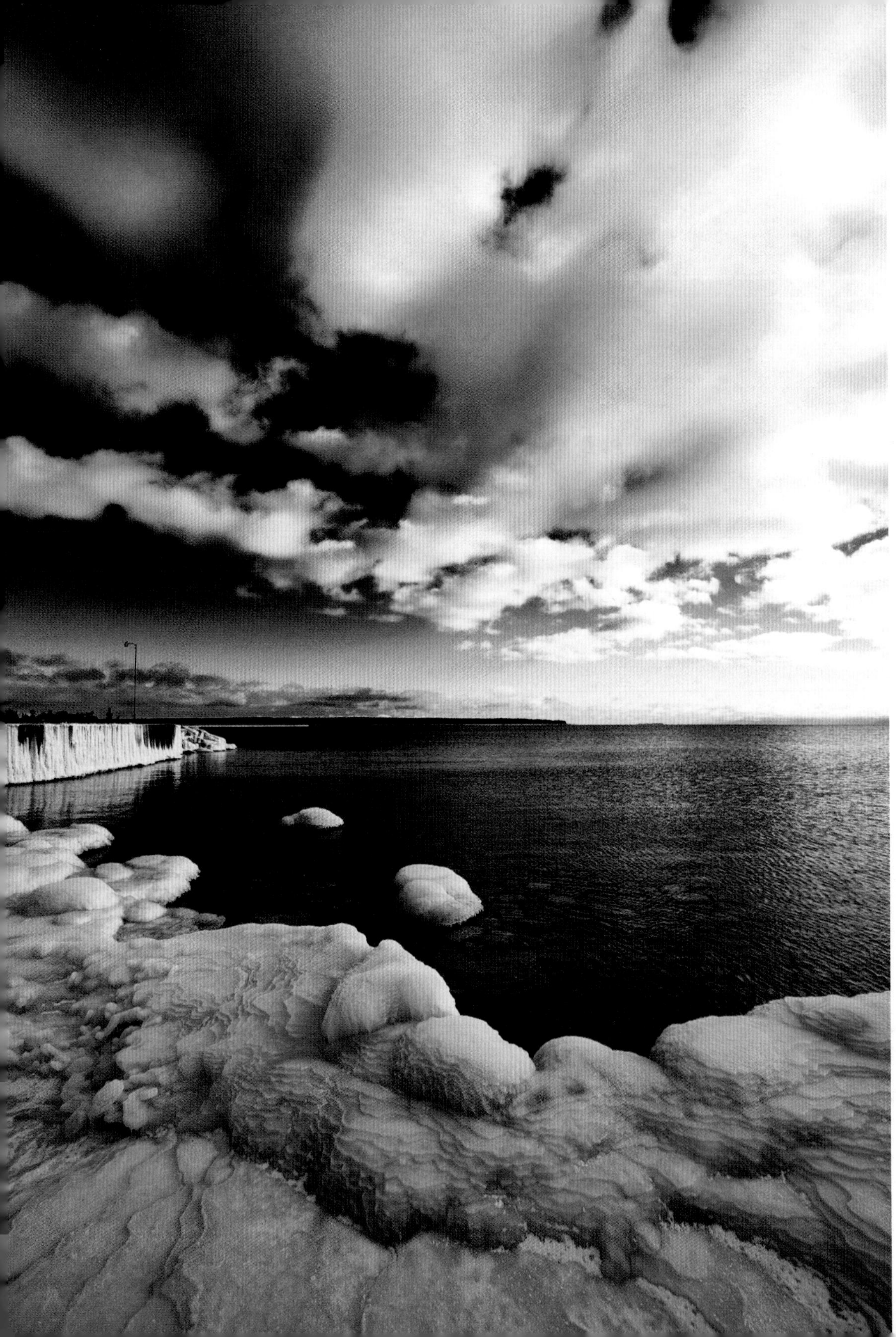

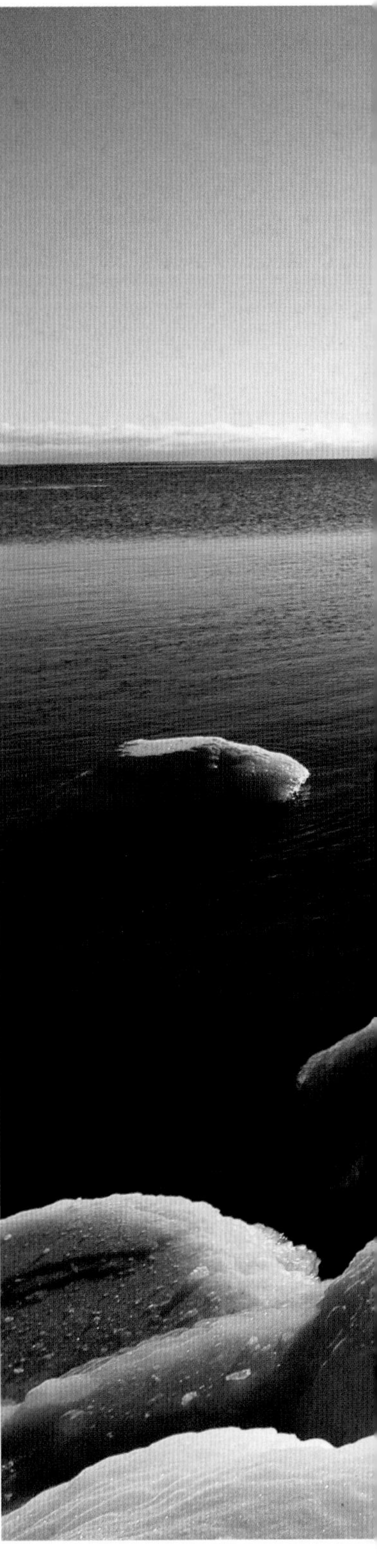

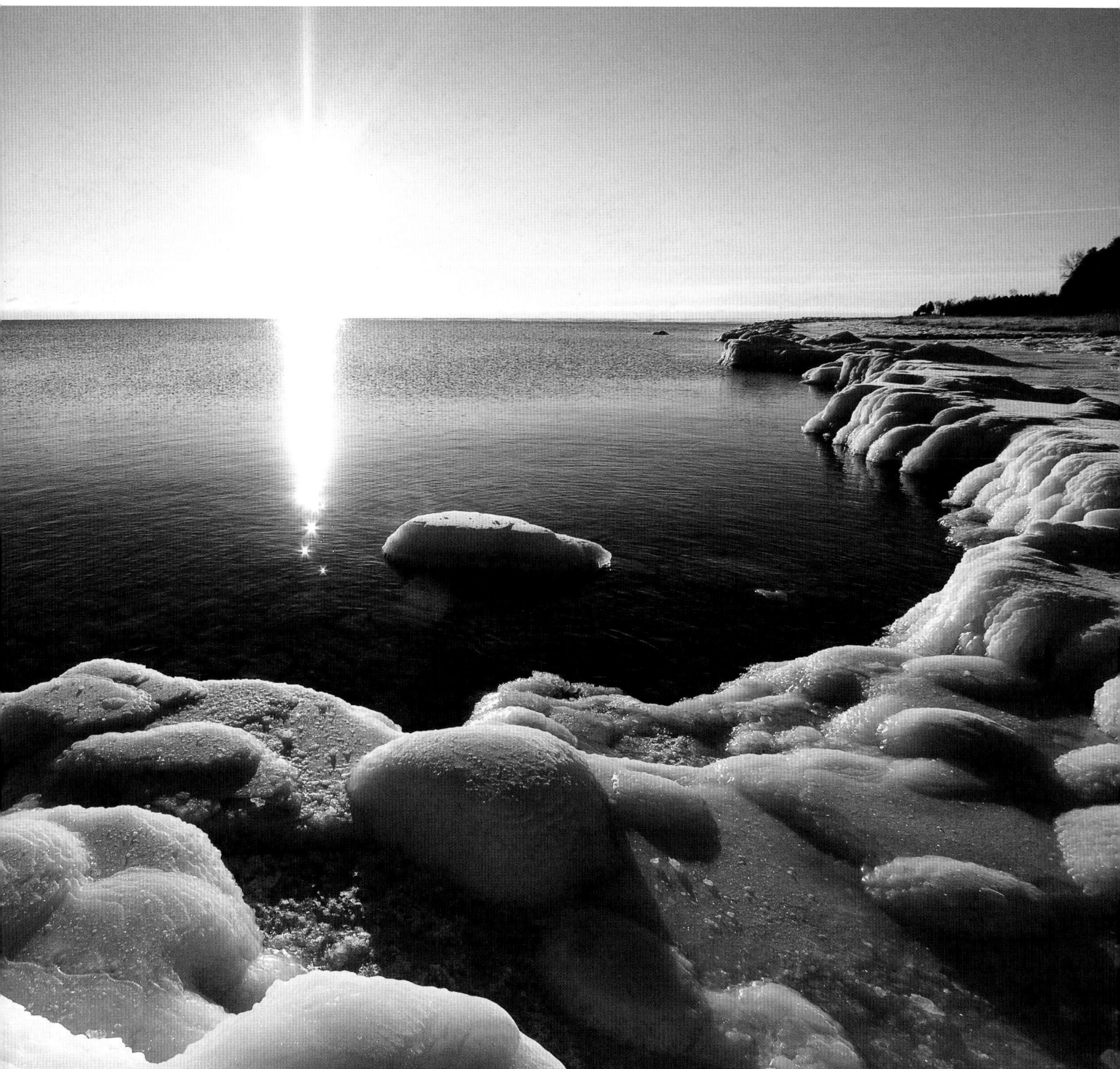

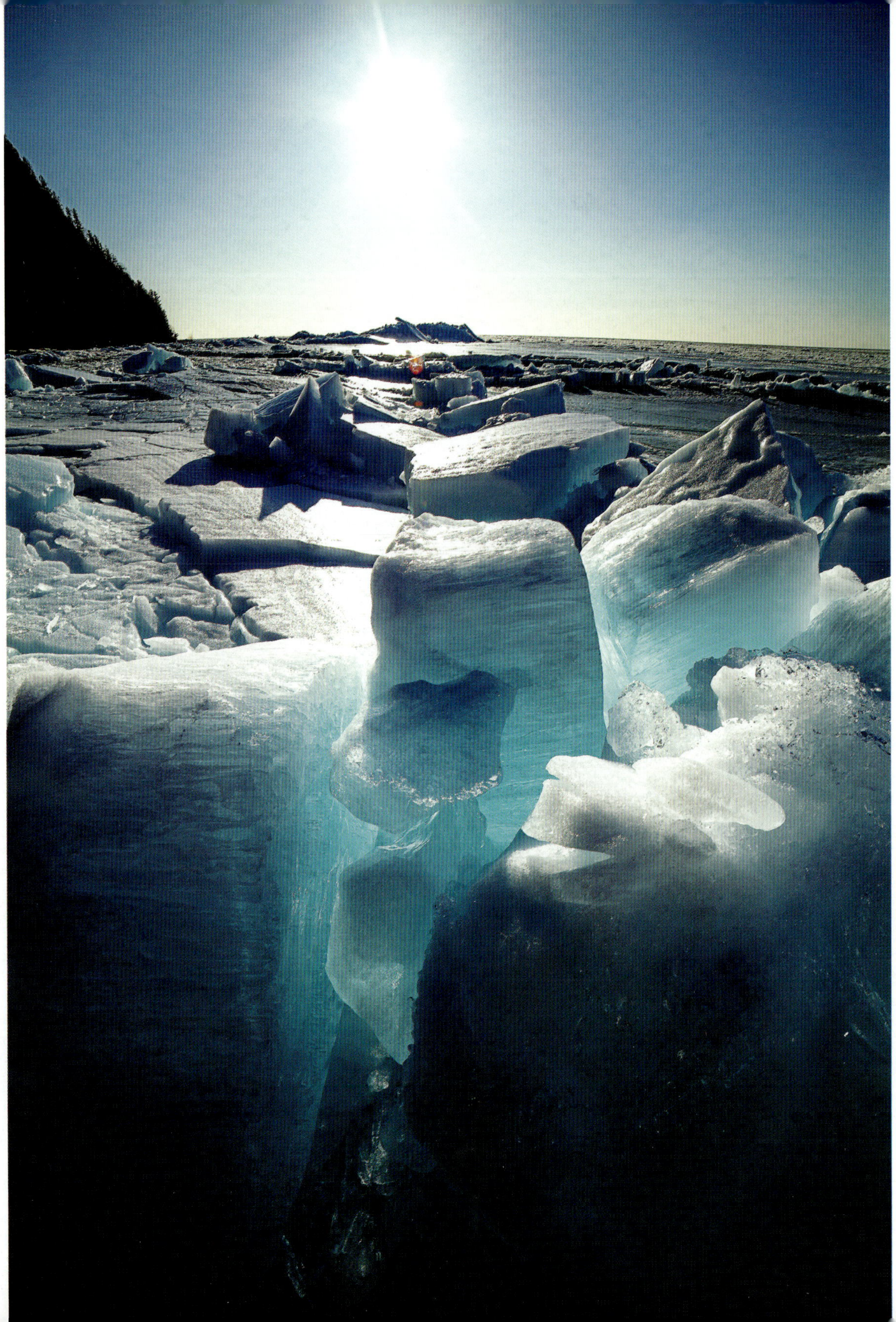

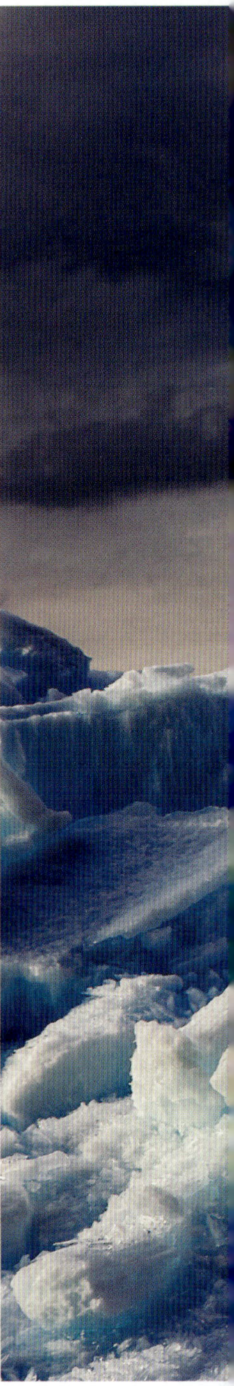

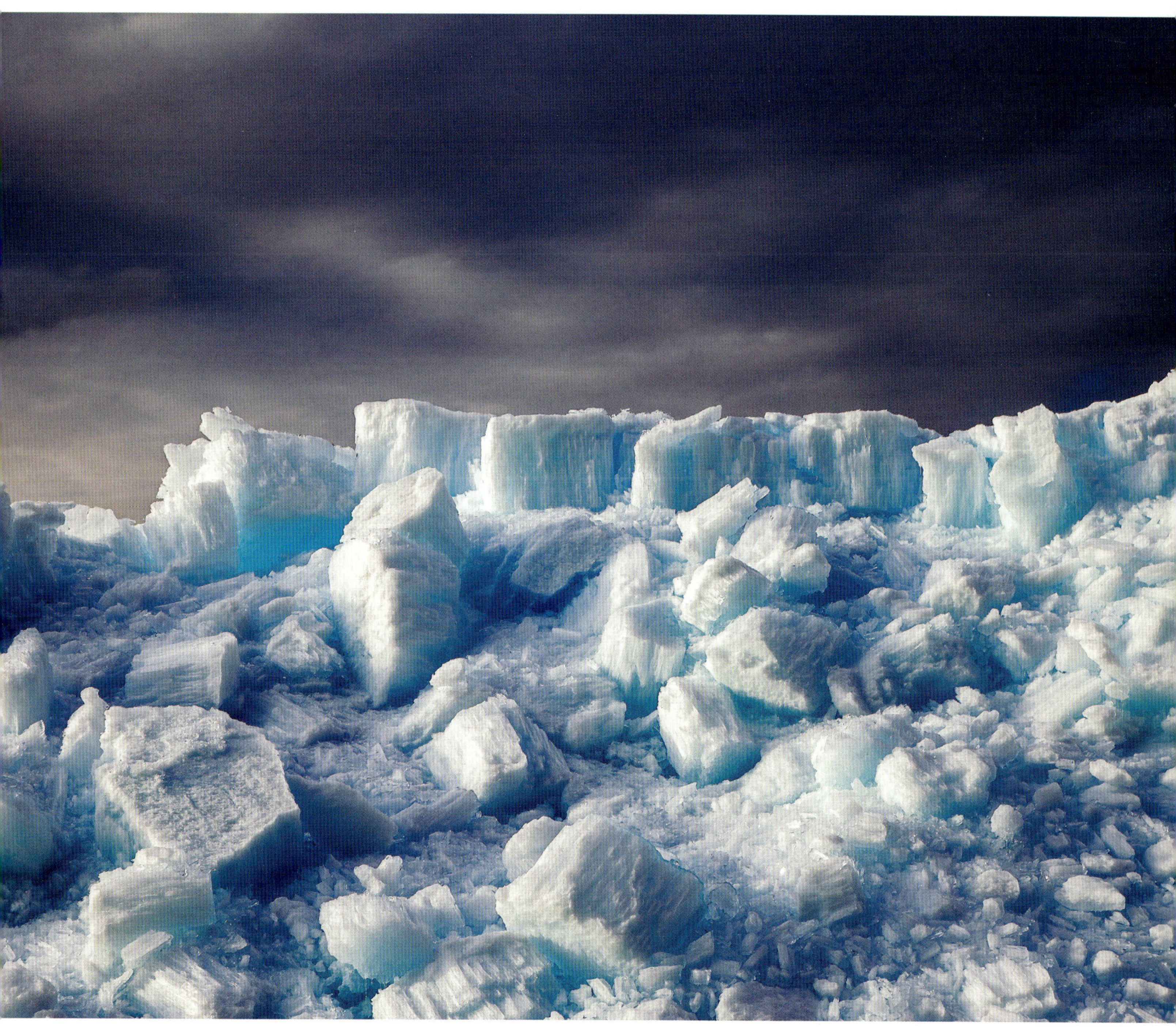

Previous page: Ice shoves, Door Bluff Headlands County Park – Lucas.

This page: Ice shoves, Door Bluff Headlands County Park – Heather.

Following pages: *Early Birds*, Washington Island – Heather; Hoar frost, Ephraim – Lucas.

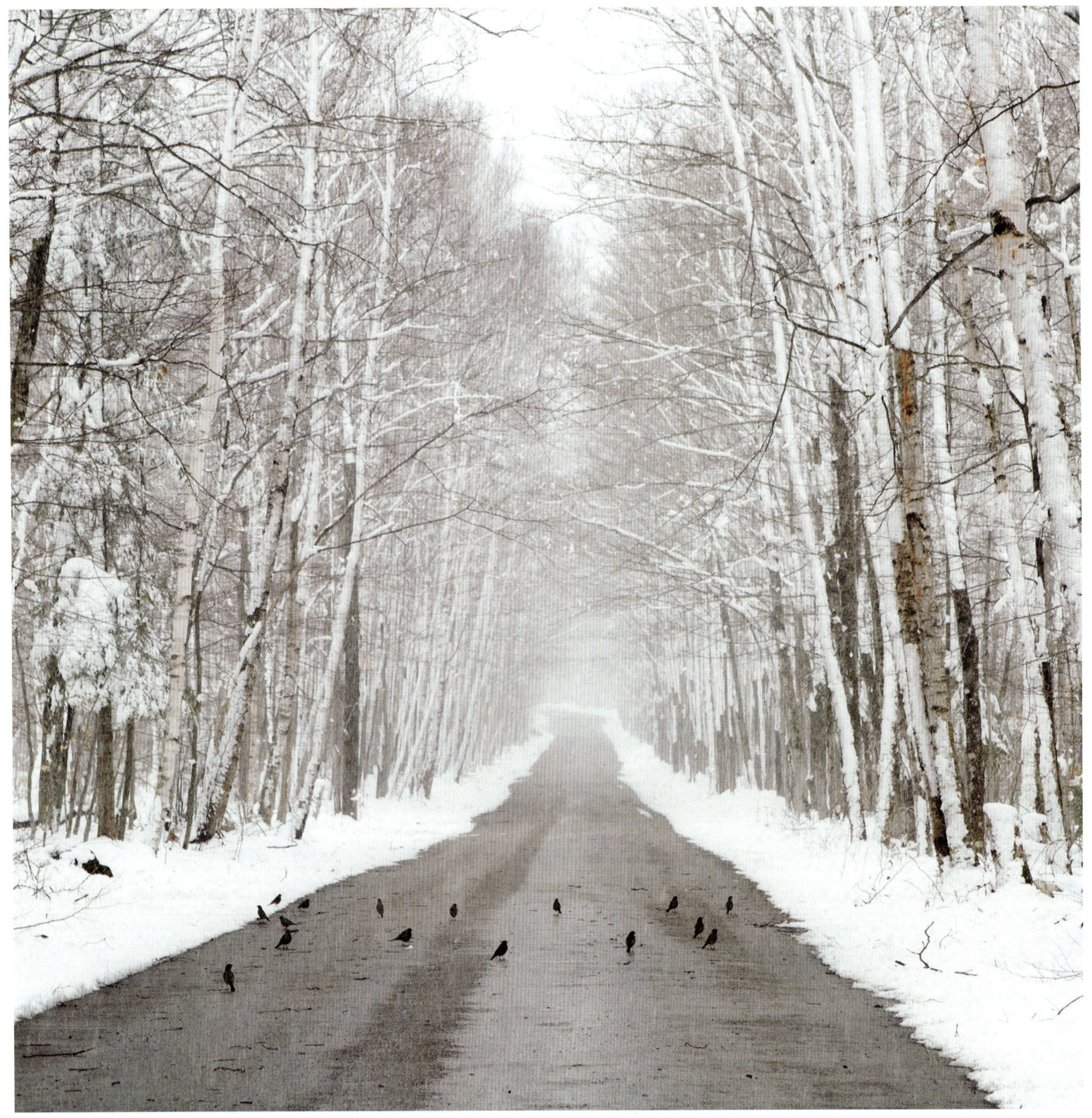

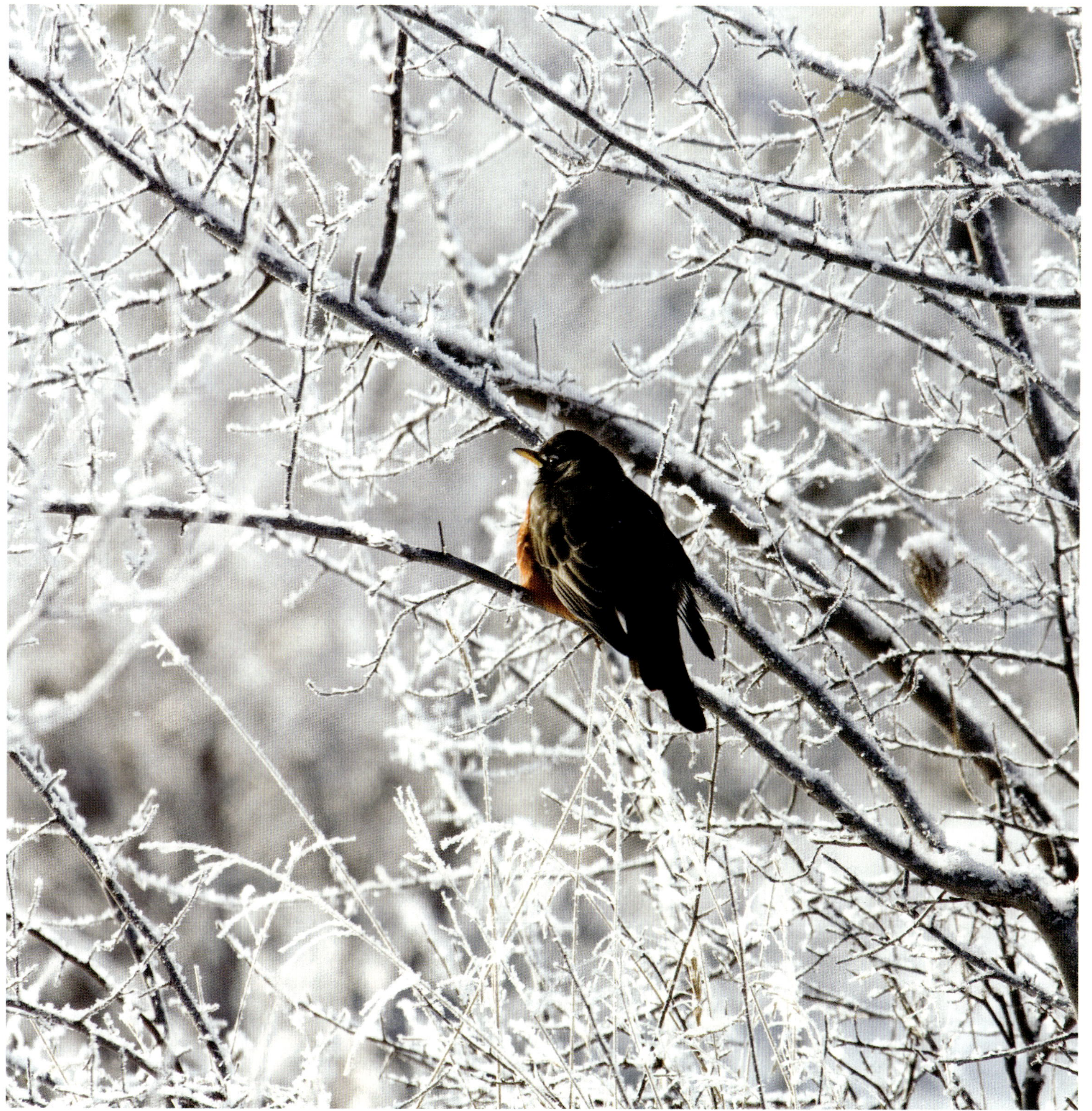

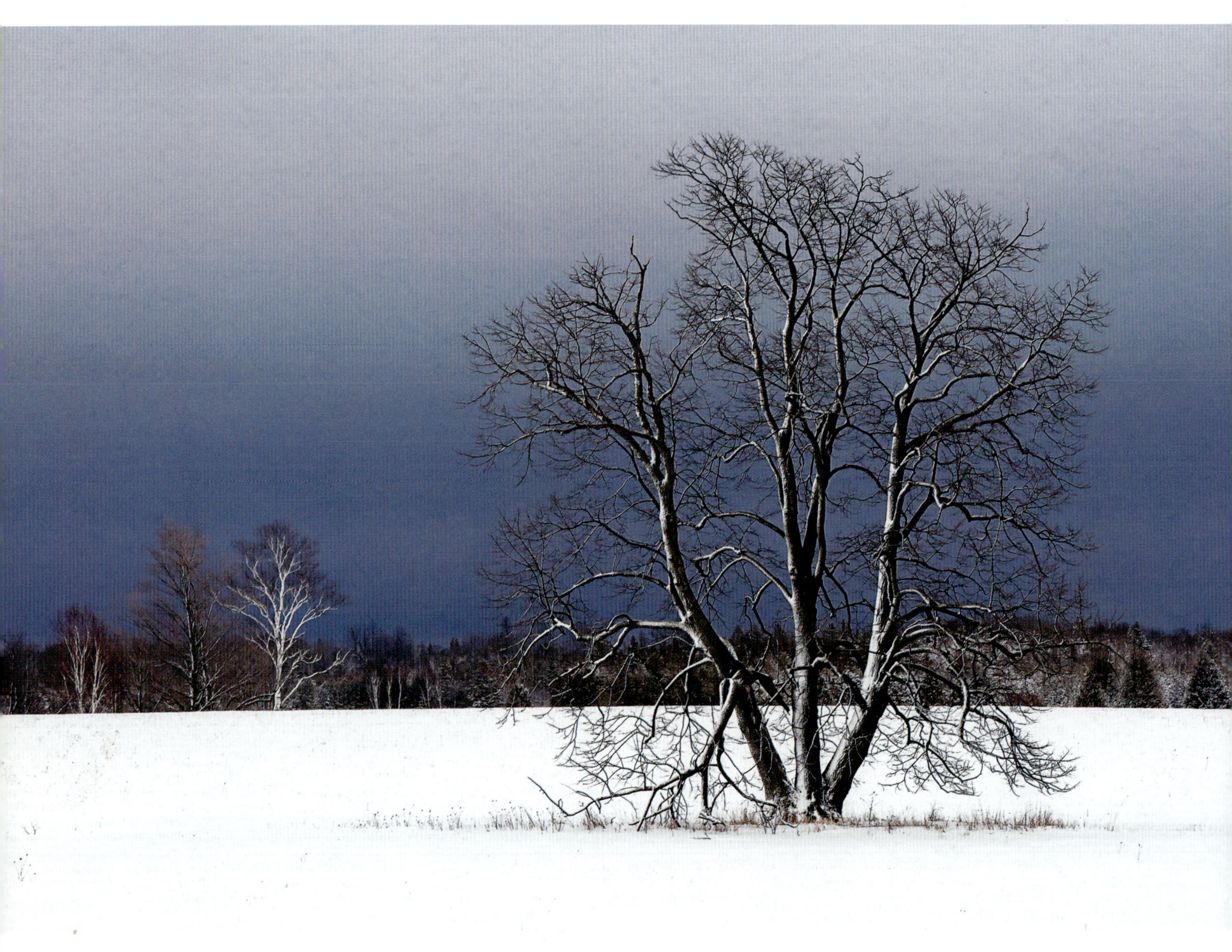

This page: Basswood, Fish Creek – Lucas.

Next page: Snow covered trees, Ellison Bay – Lucas.

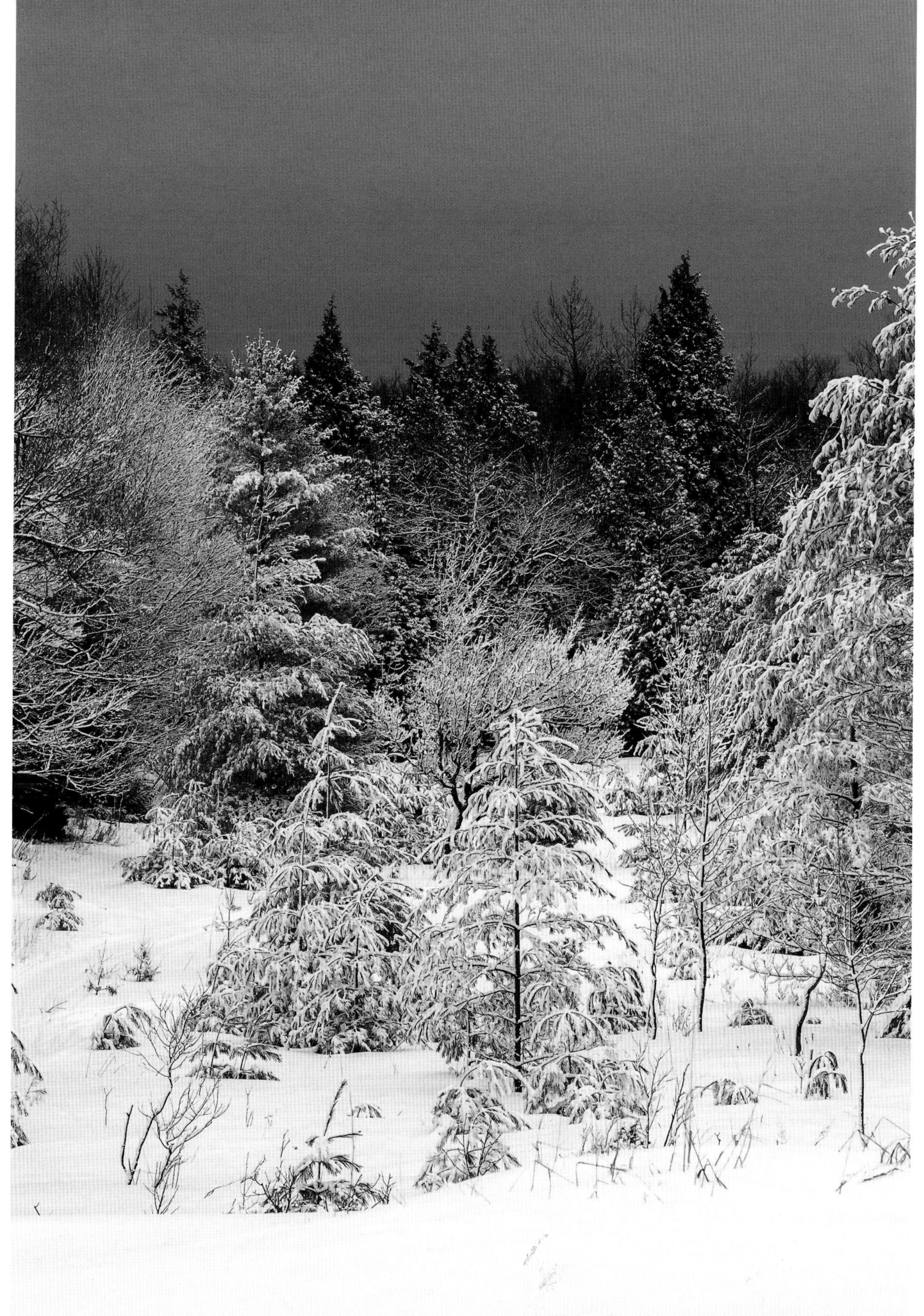

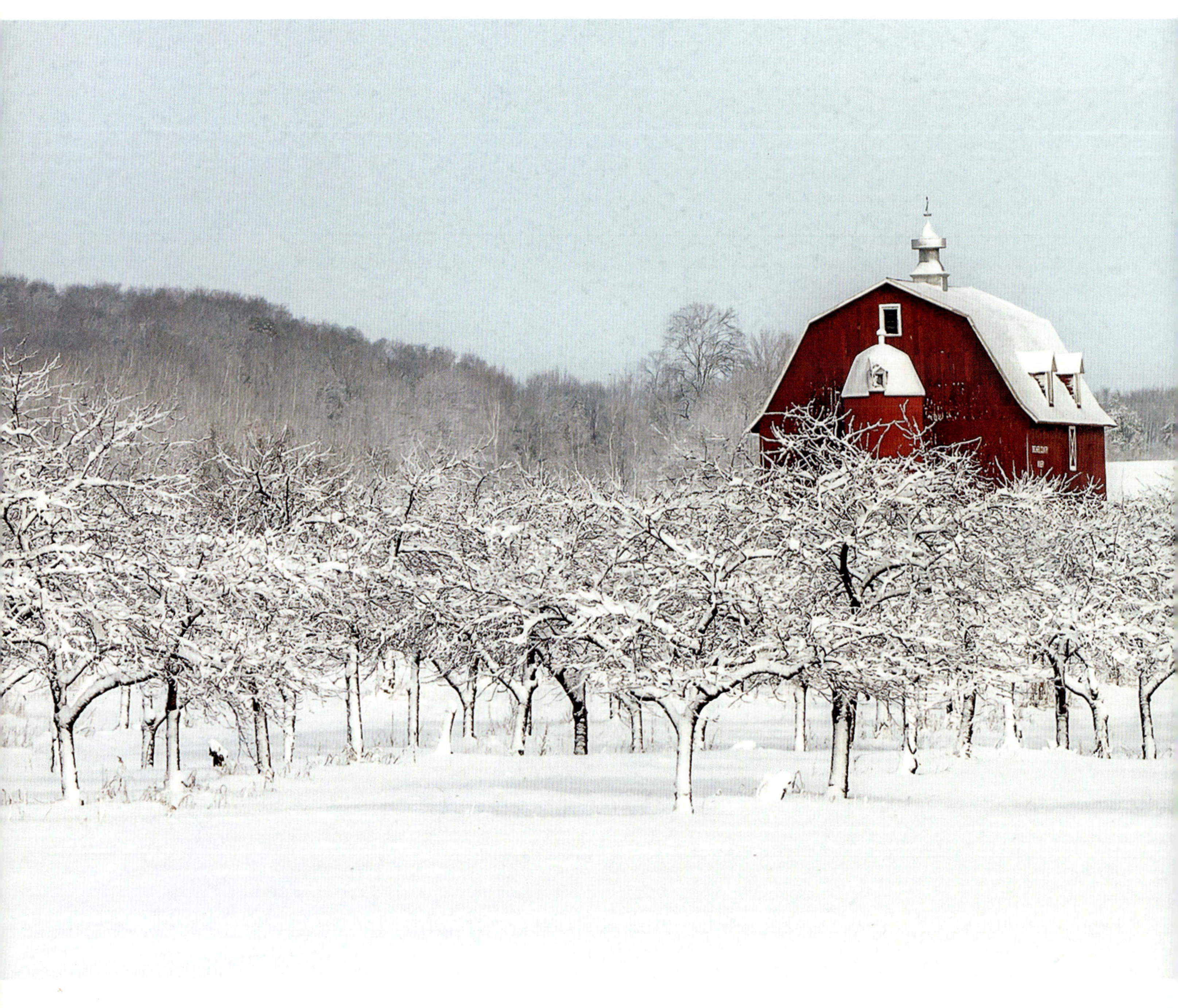

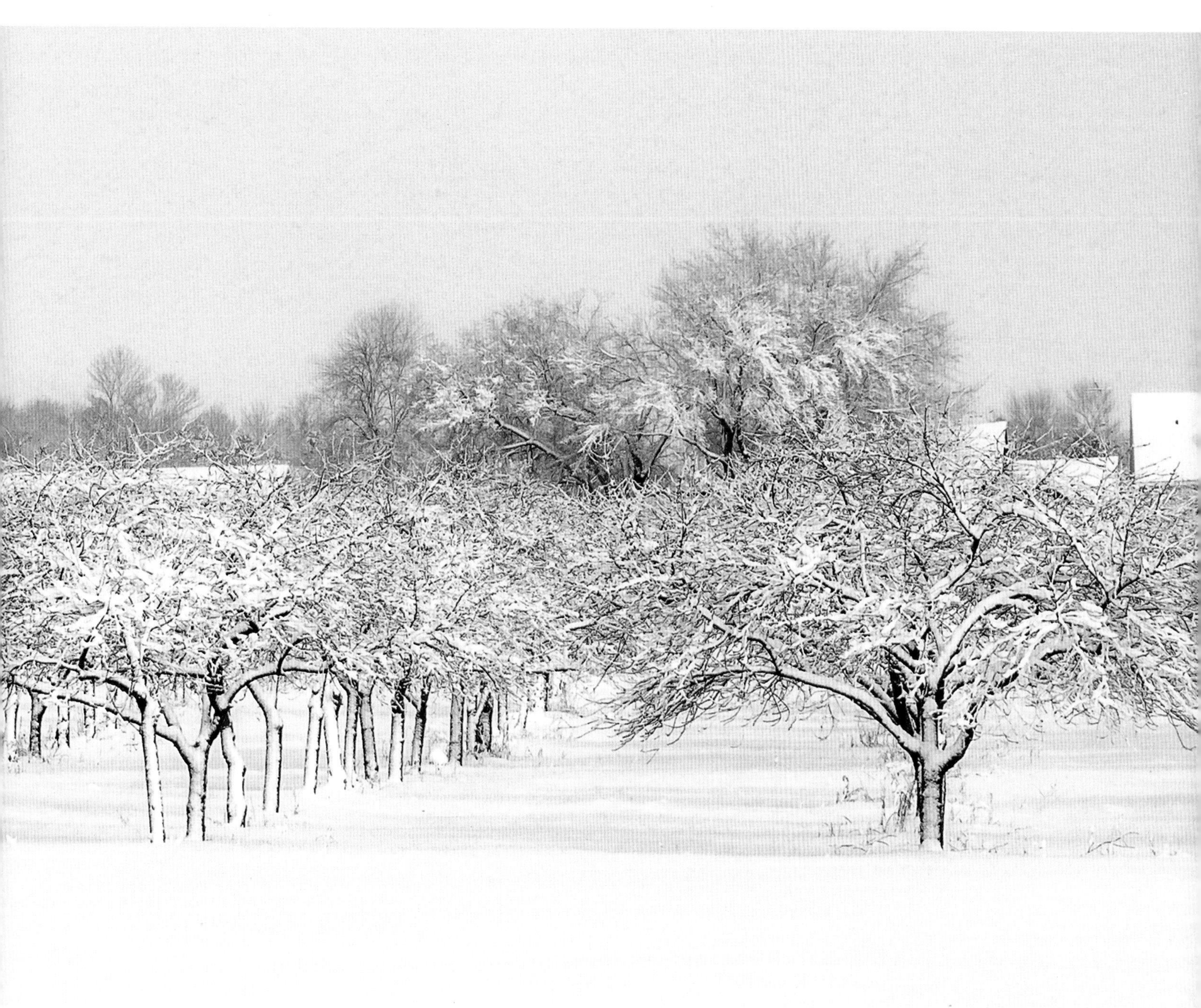

Orchard, Fish Creek – Heather.

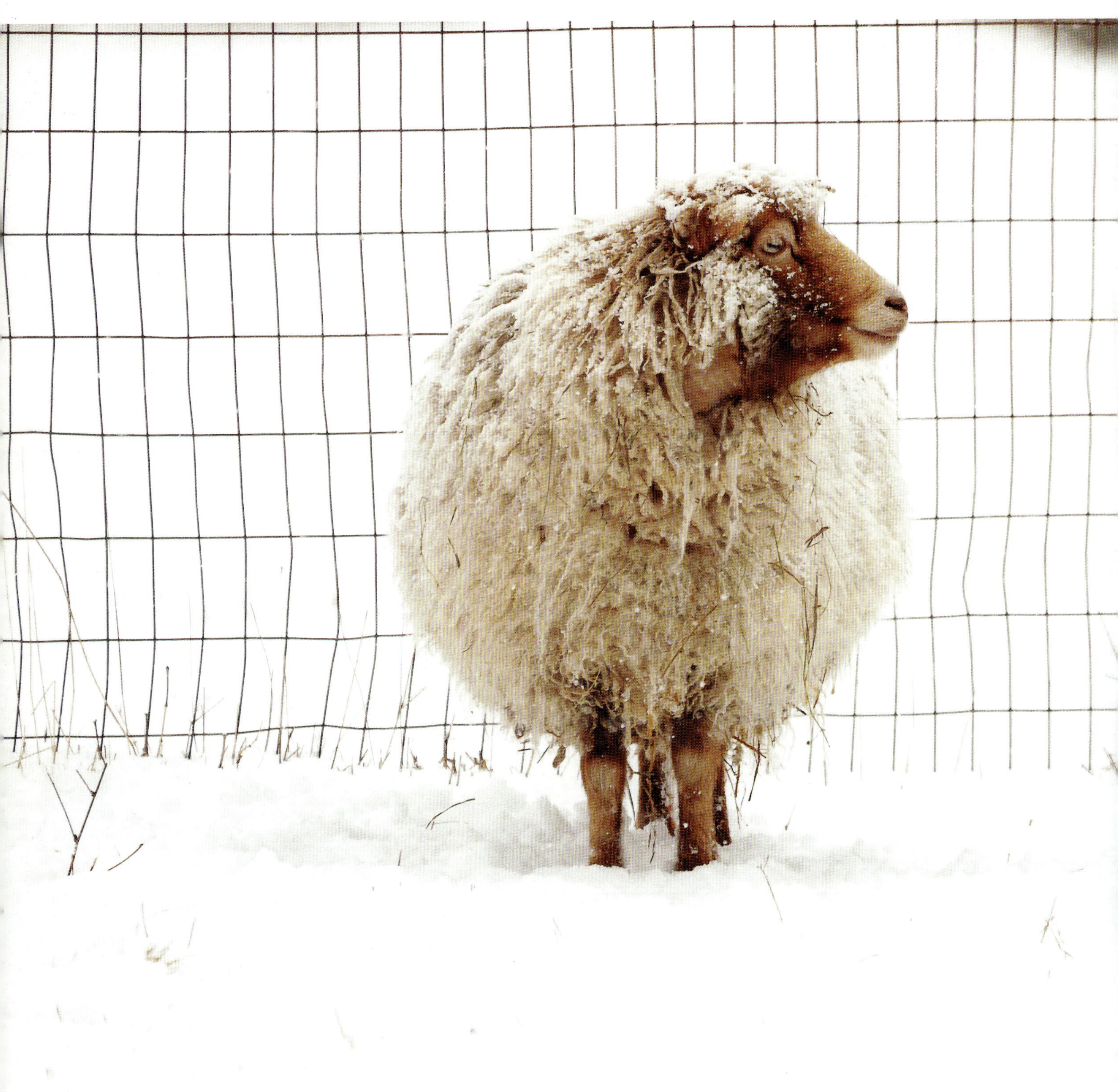

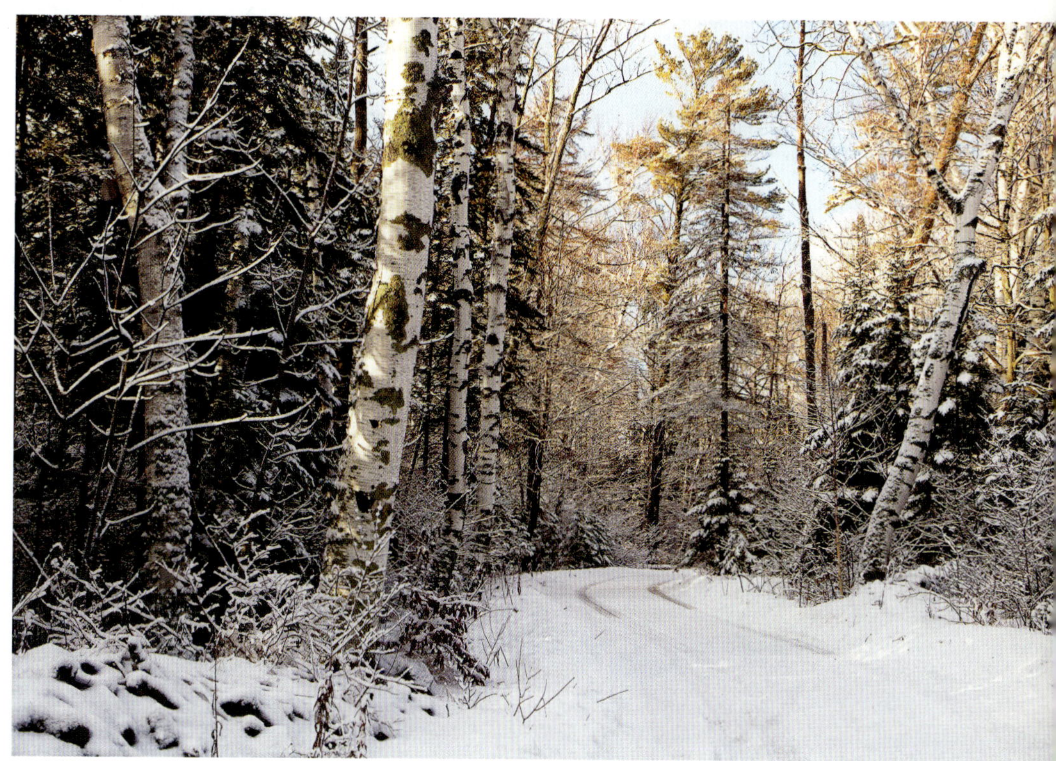

Previous page: *Frosted Shredded Sheep*, Gills Rock – Heather.

This page: The Clearing, Ellison Bay – Heather.

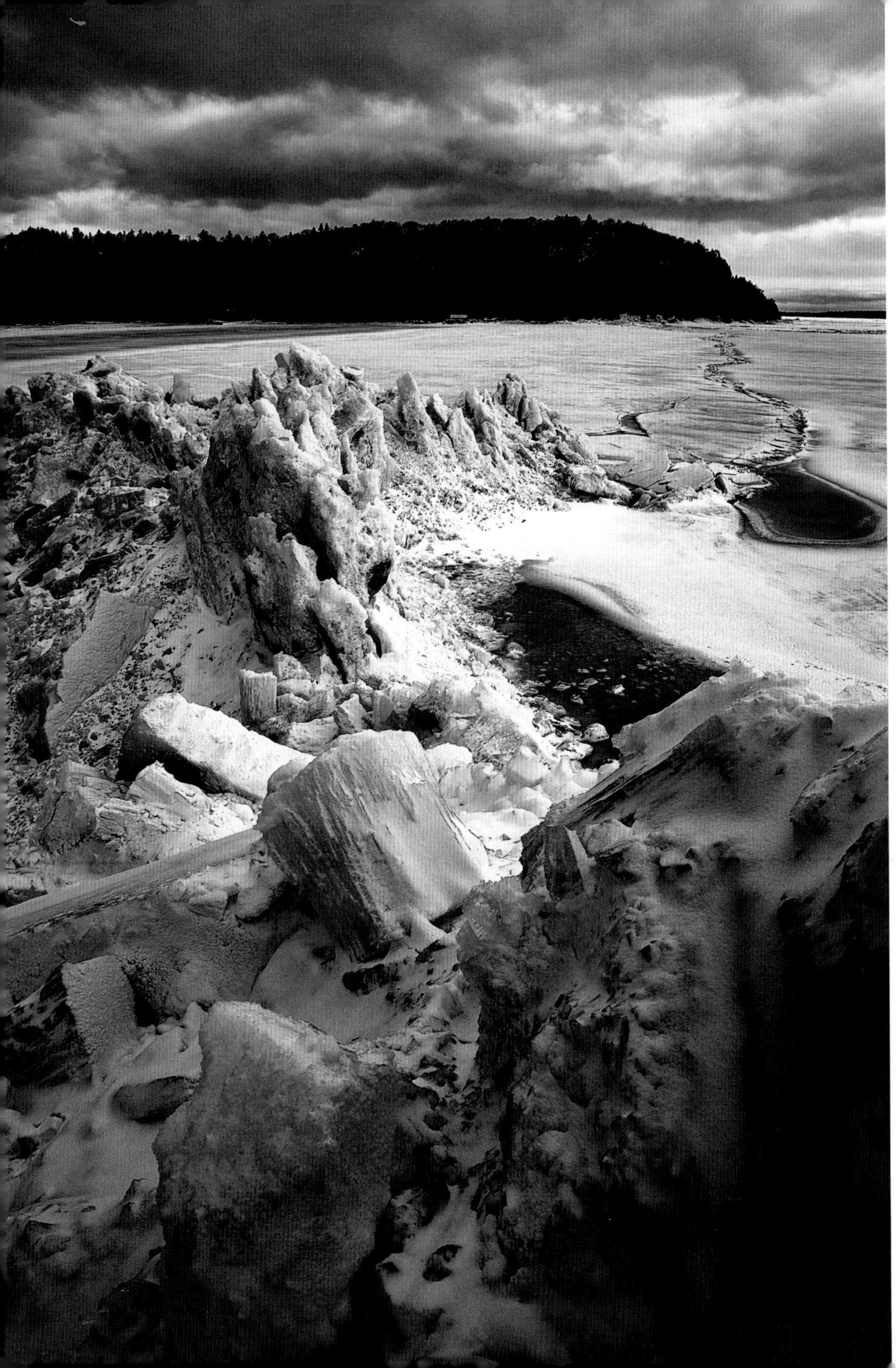

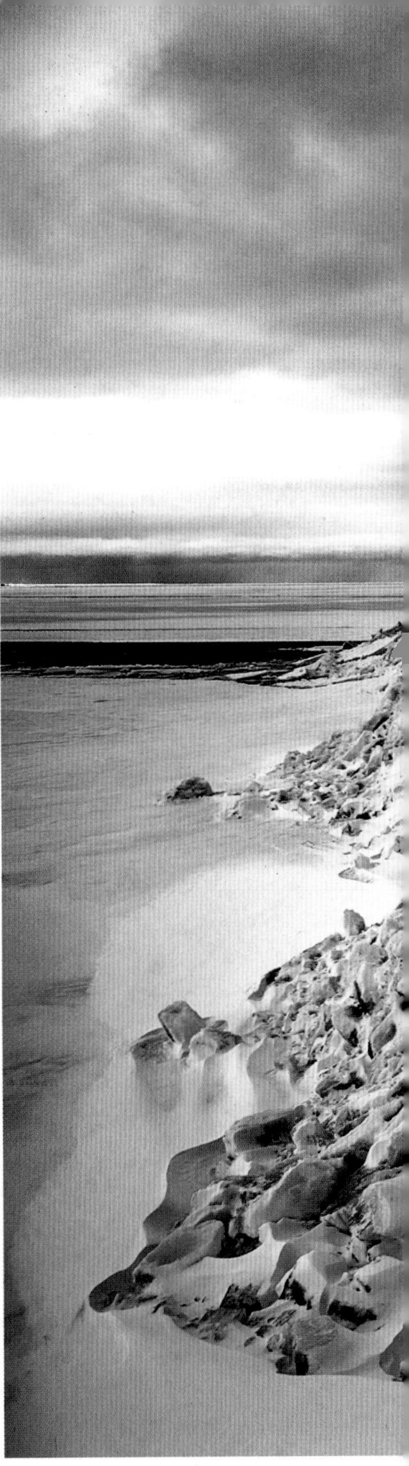

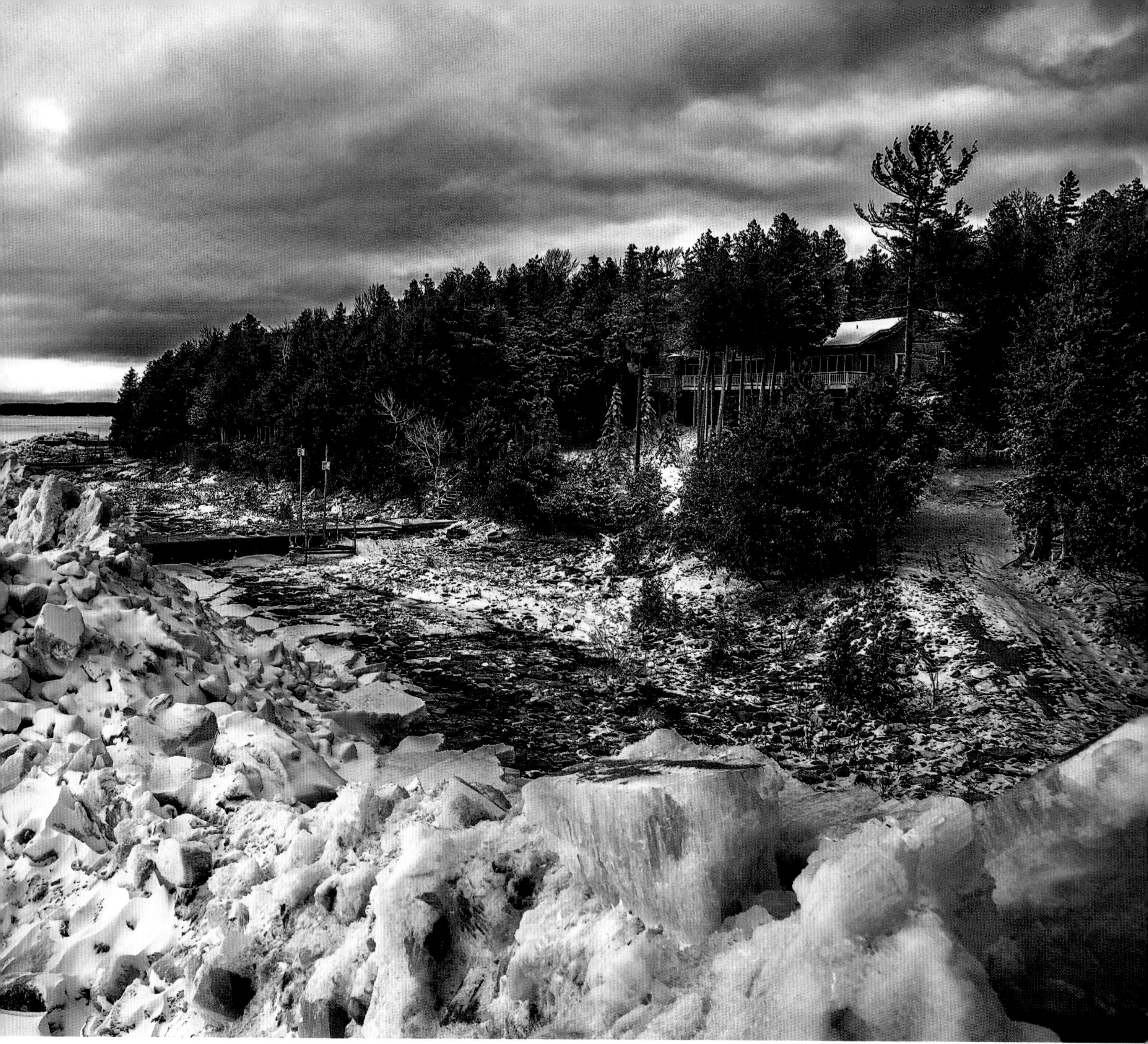

Previous page and this page: Ice shoves, Little Sister Bay – Lucas.

Following pages: Northern Lights, Cana Island Lighthouse, Baileys Harbor – Lucas.

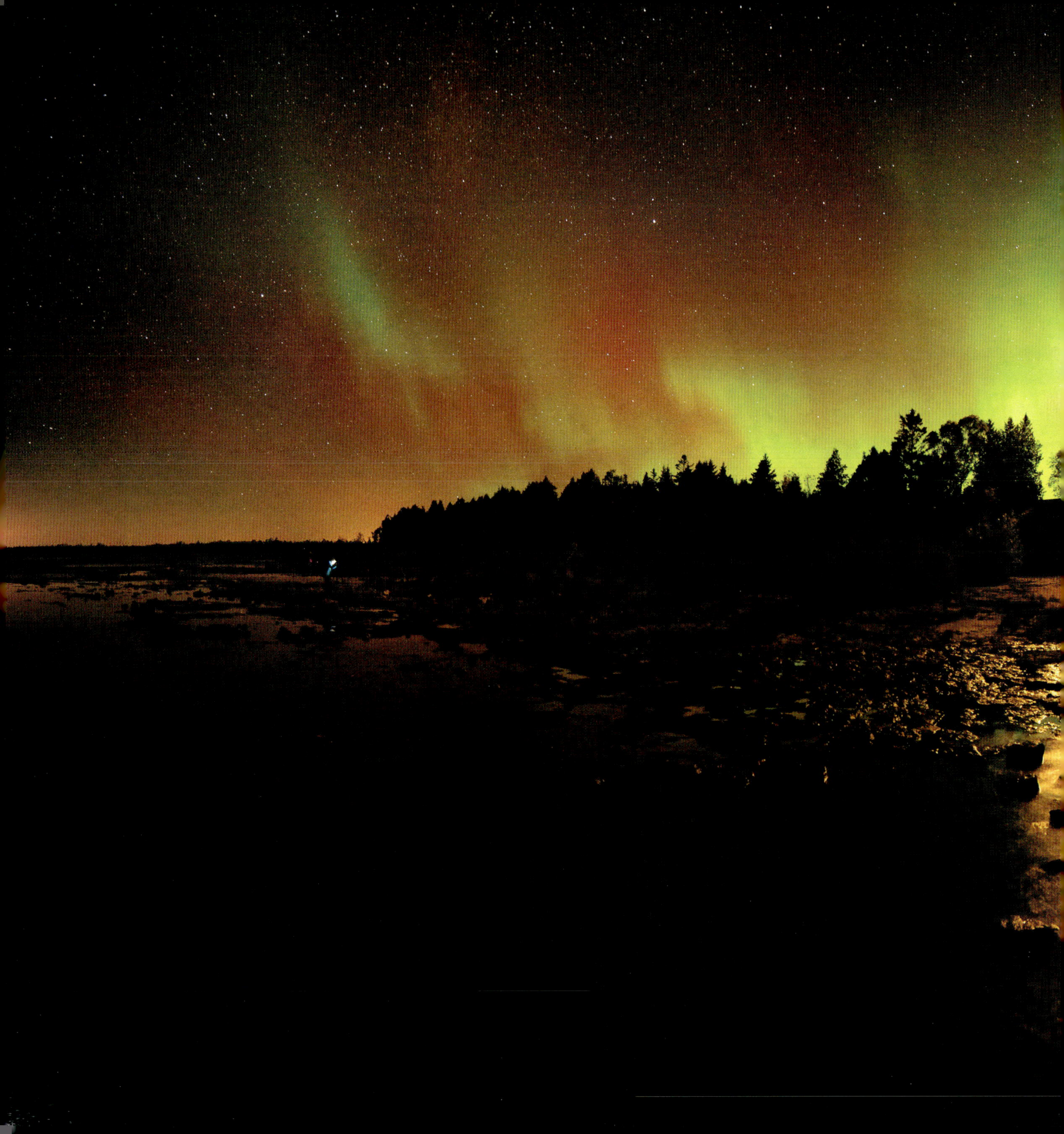

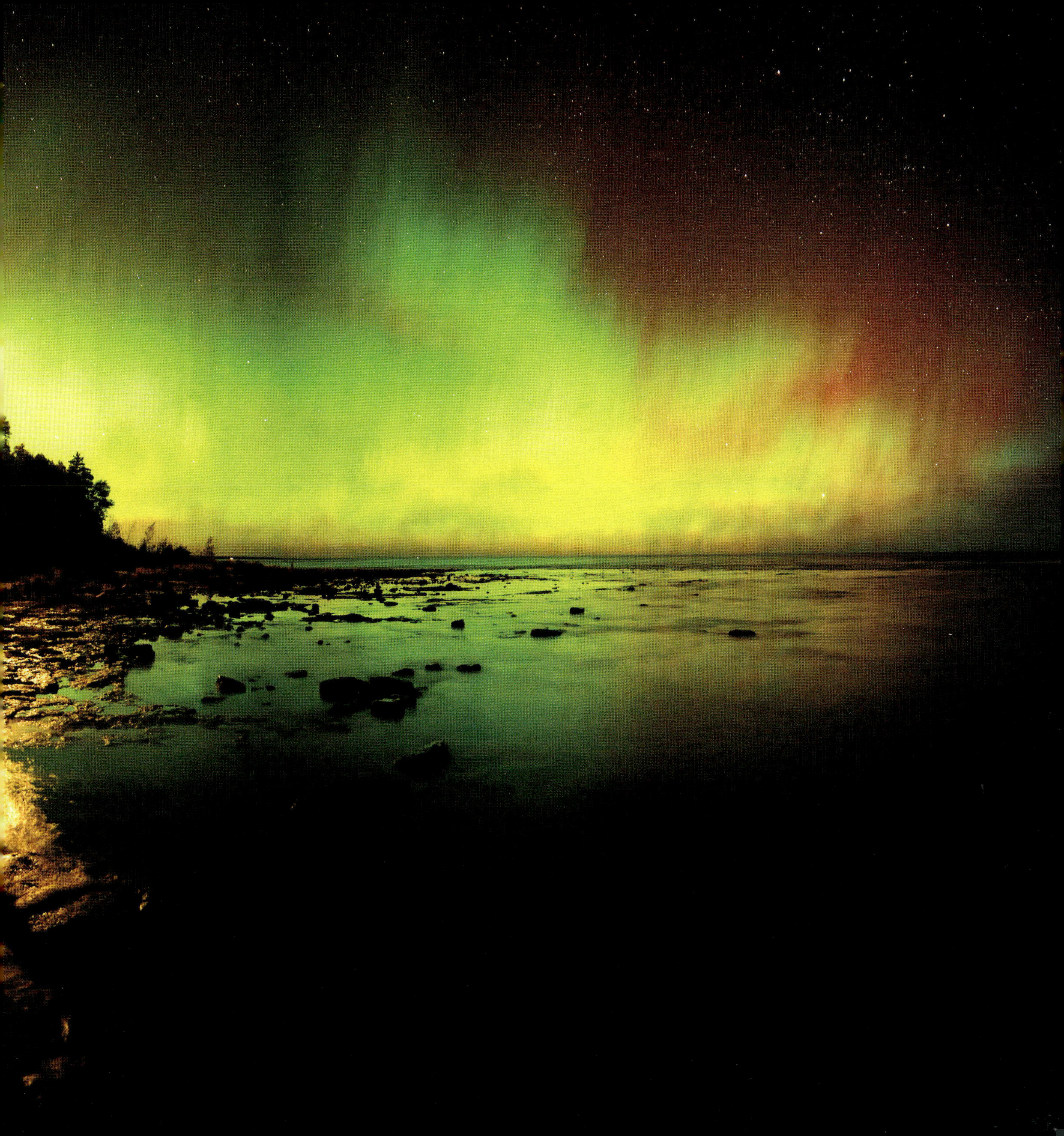

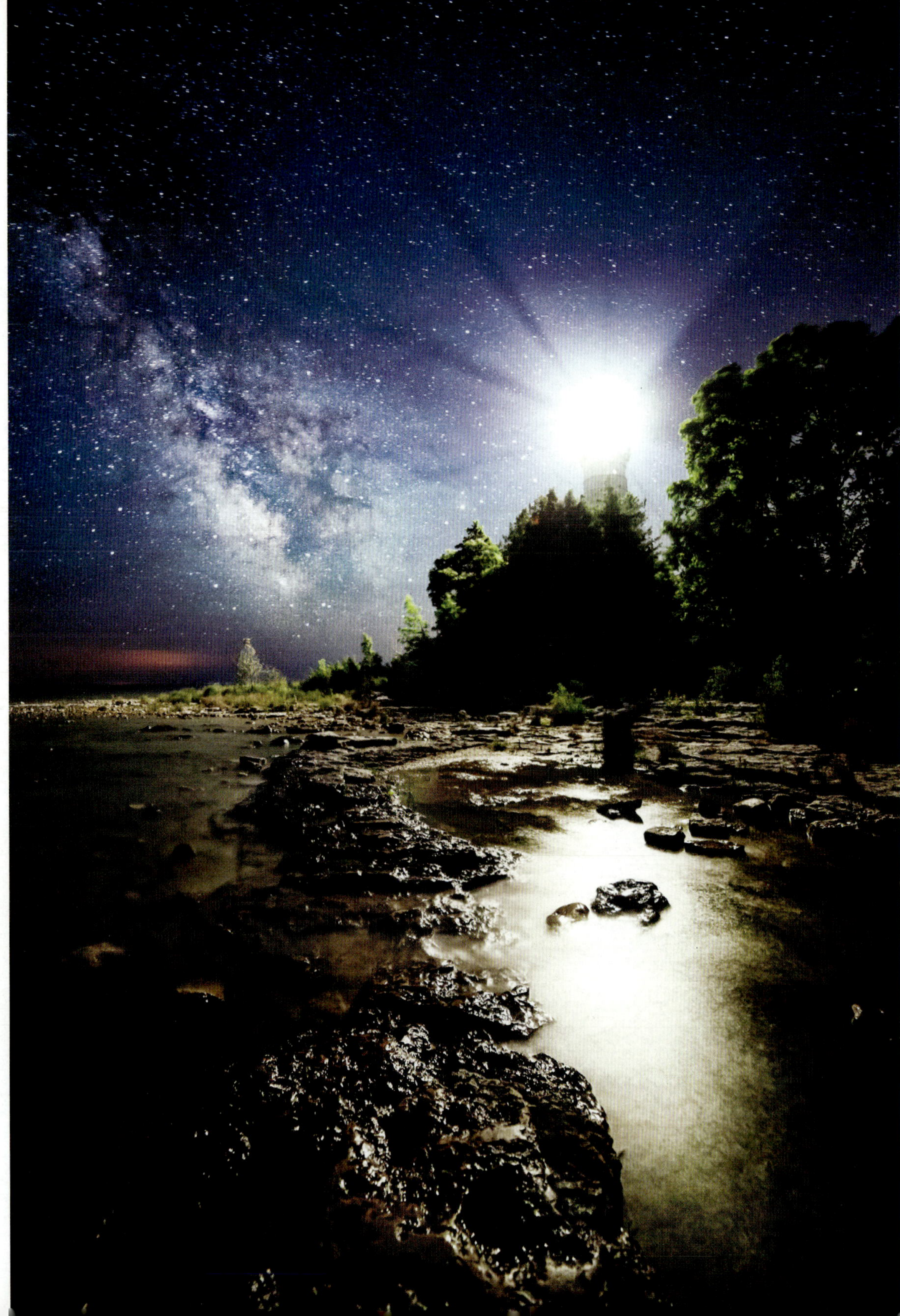

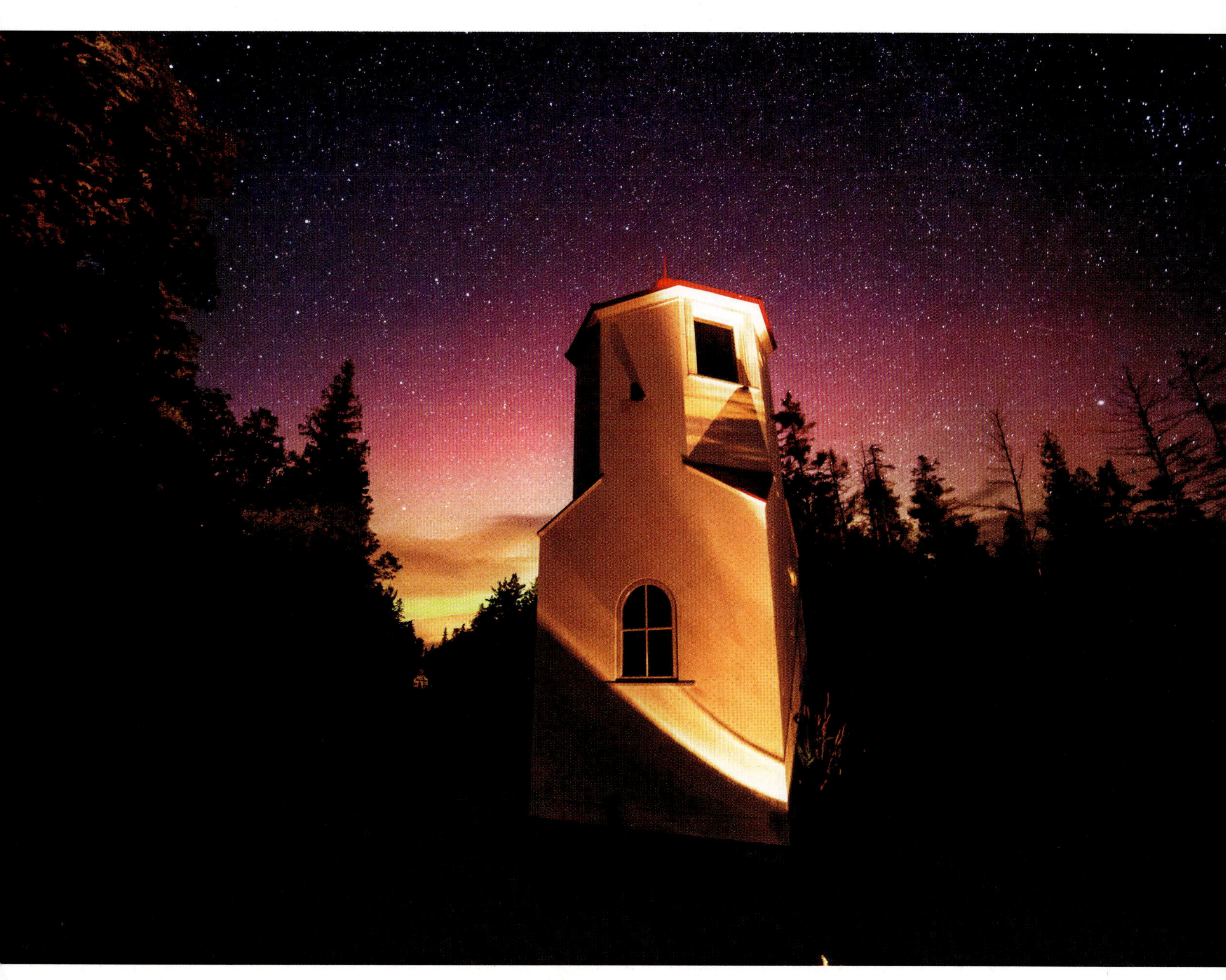

Previous page: Cana Island Lighthouse, Baileys Harbor – Lucas.

This page: Range Lights and auroras, The Ridges Sanctuary, Baileys Harbor – Lucas.

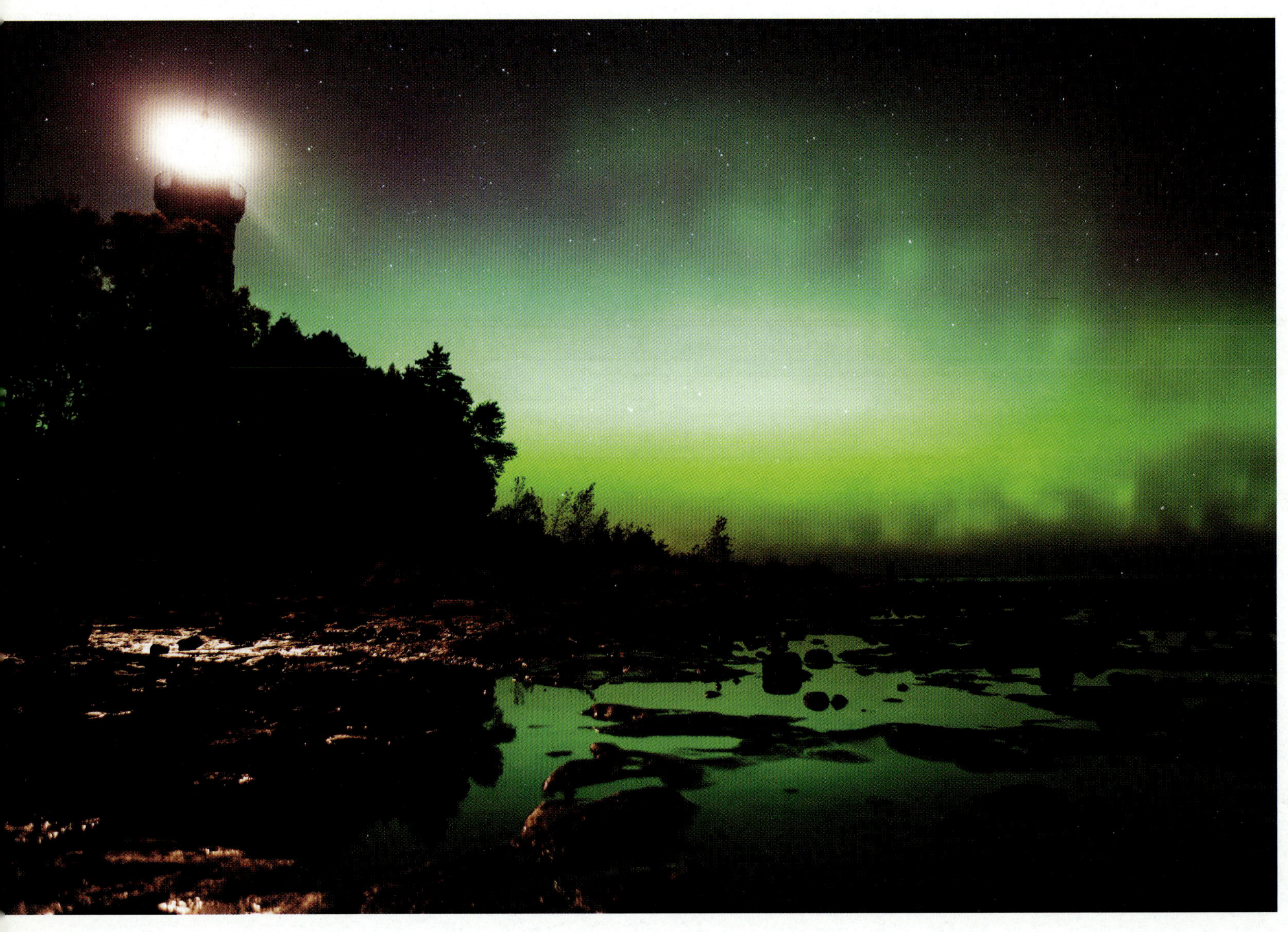

This page: Northern Lights, Cana Island Lighthouse, Baileys Harbor – Heather.

Next page: *Star Trails*, Eagle Tower, Peninsula State Park – Heather.

Following pages: Auroras, Lone Eagle Dock, Ellison Bay – Lucas; Milky Way, Kangaroo Lake, Baileys Harbor – Heather.

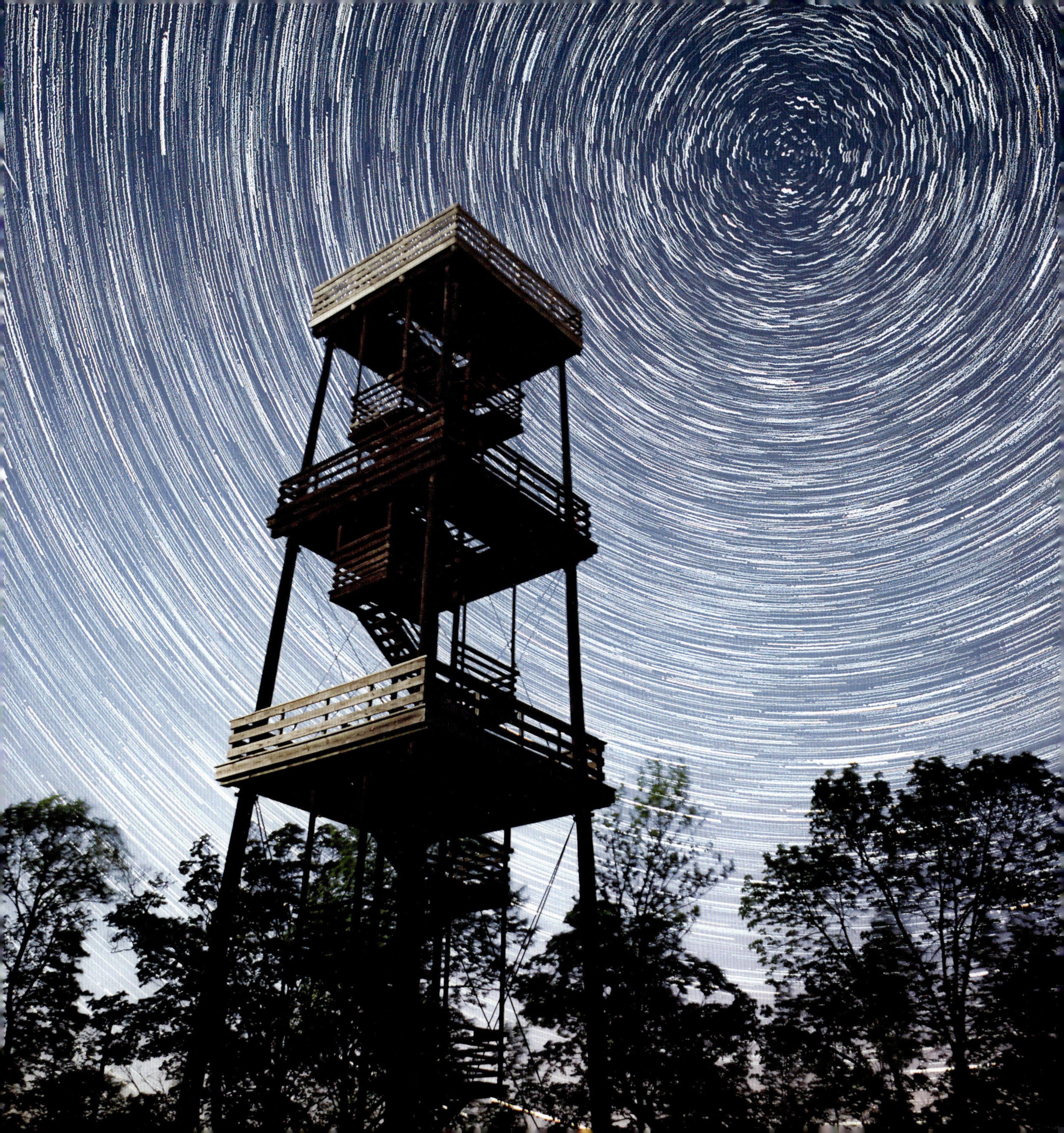

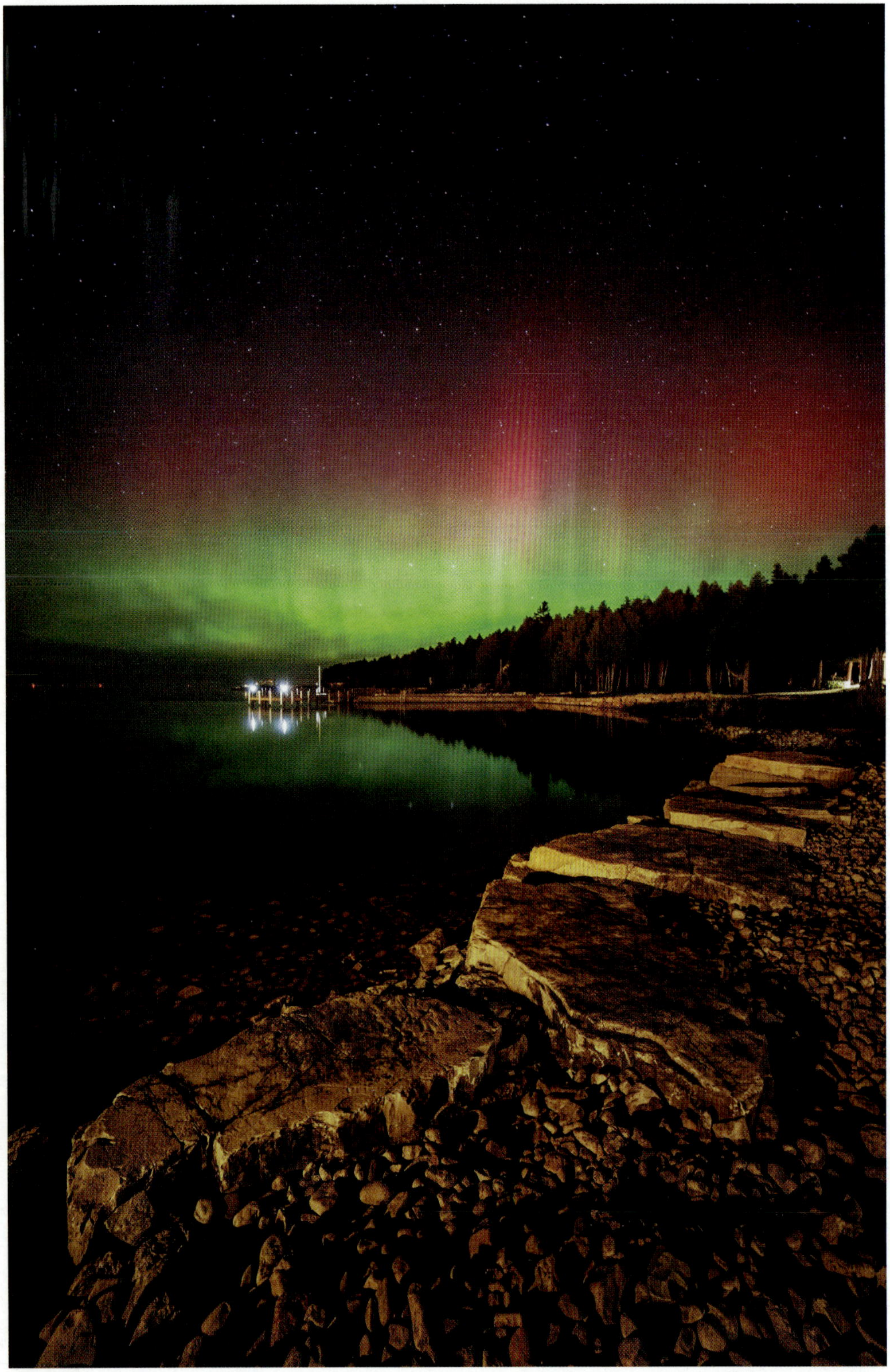

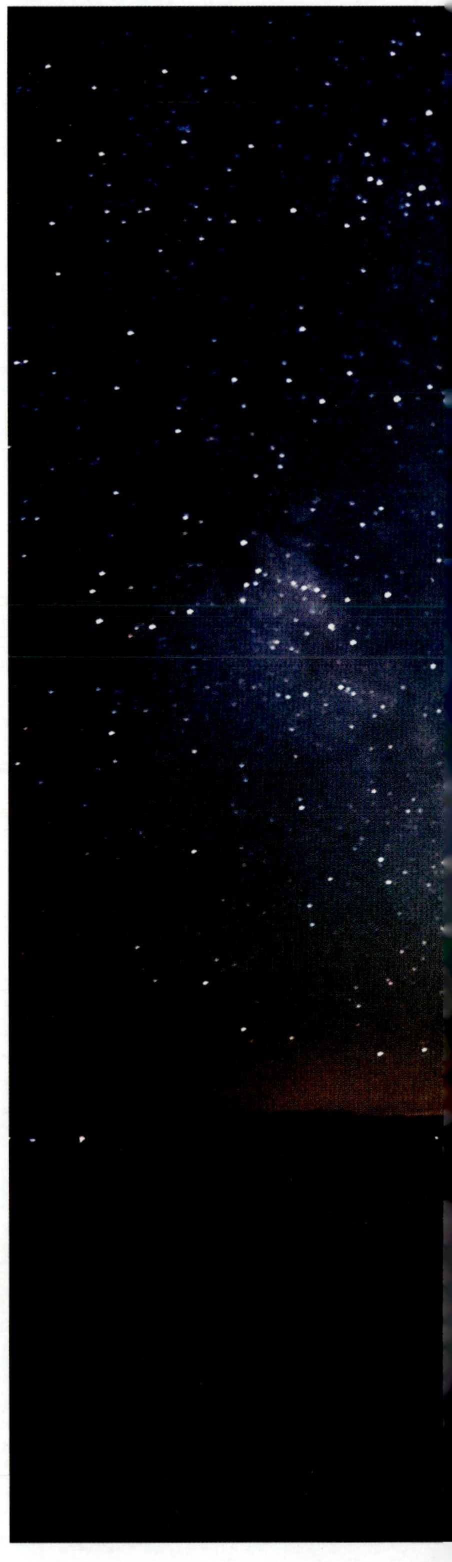

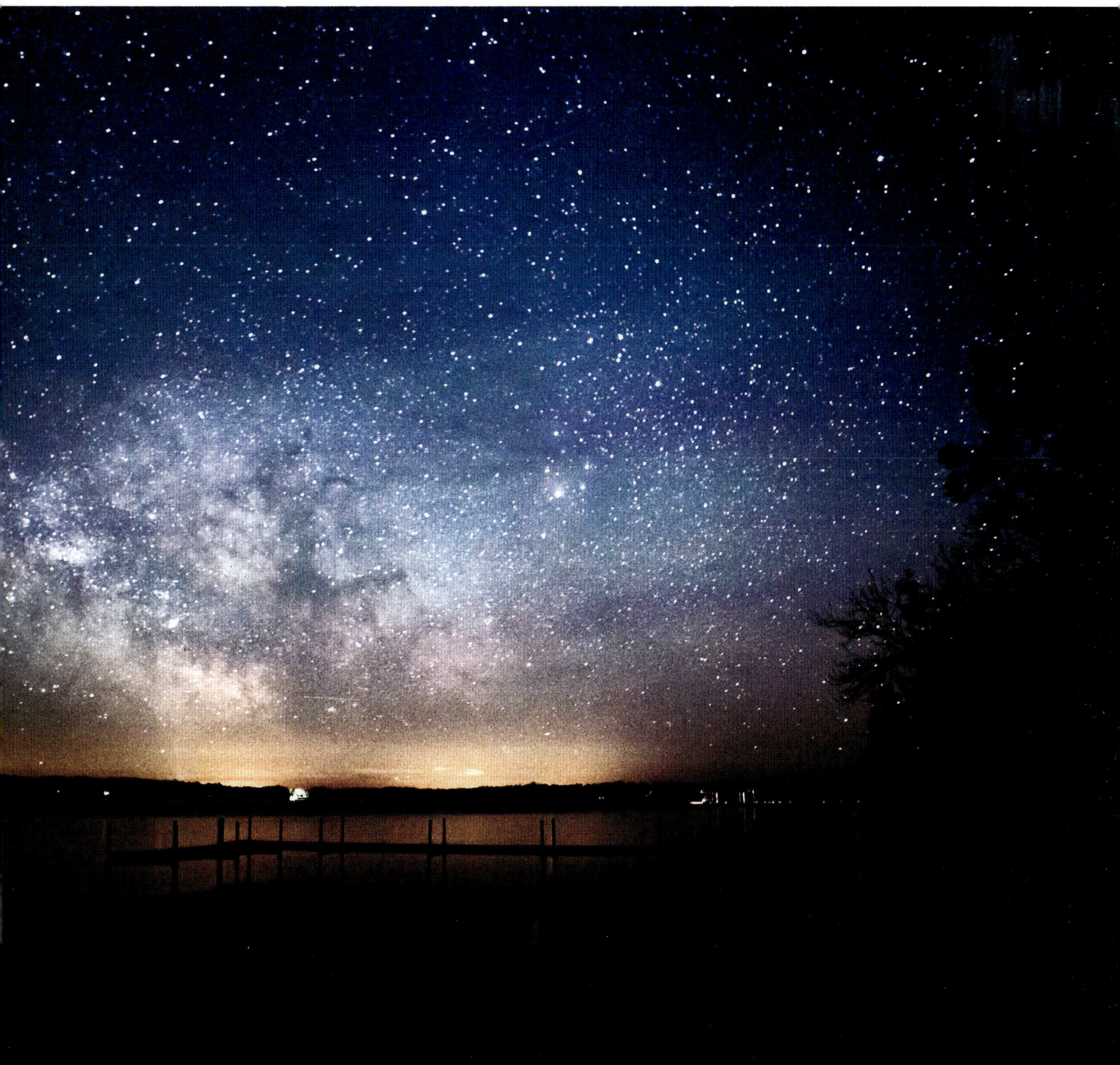

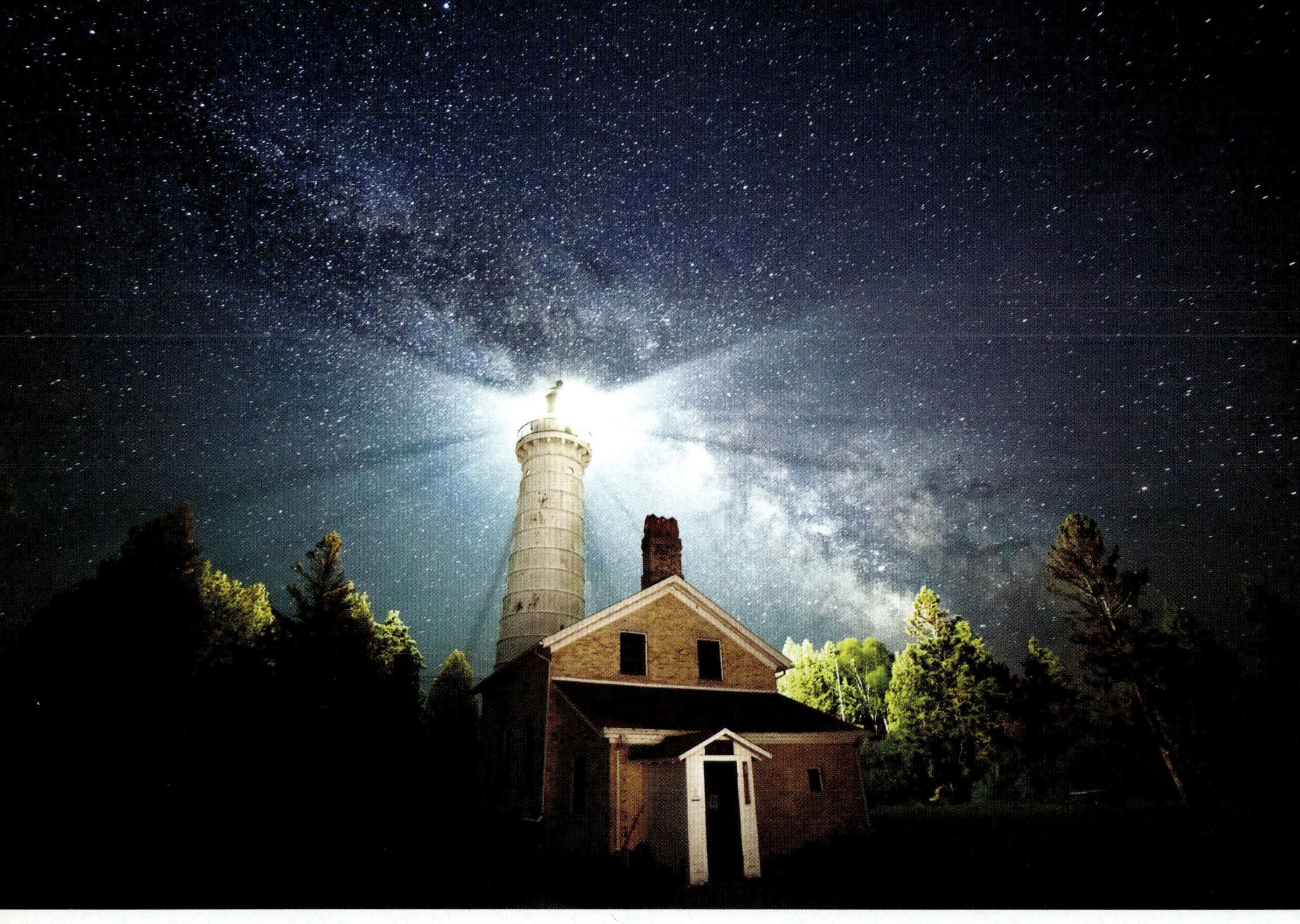

This page: Milky Way, Cana Island Lighthouse, Baileys Harbor – Lucas.

Next page: Milky Way, Cana Island Lighthouse, Baileys Harbor – Heather.

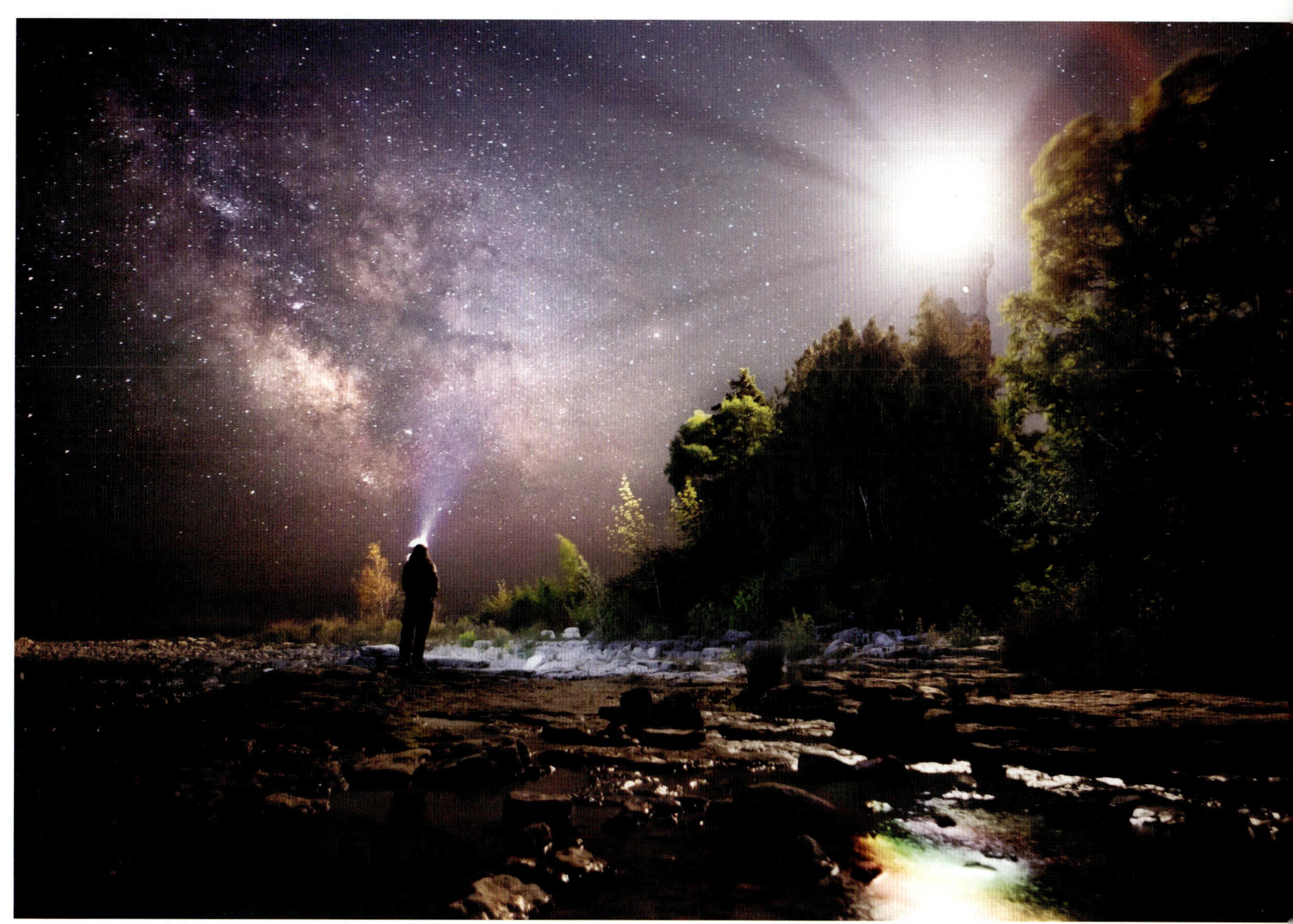

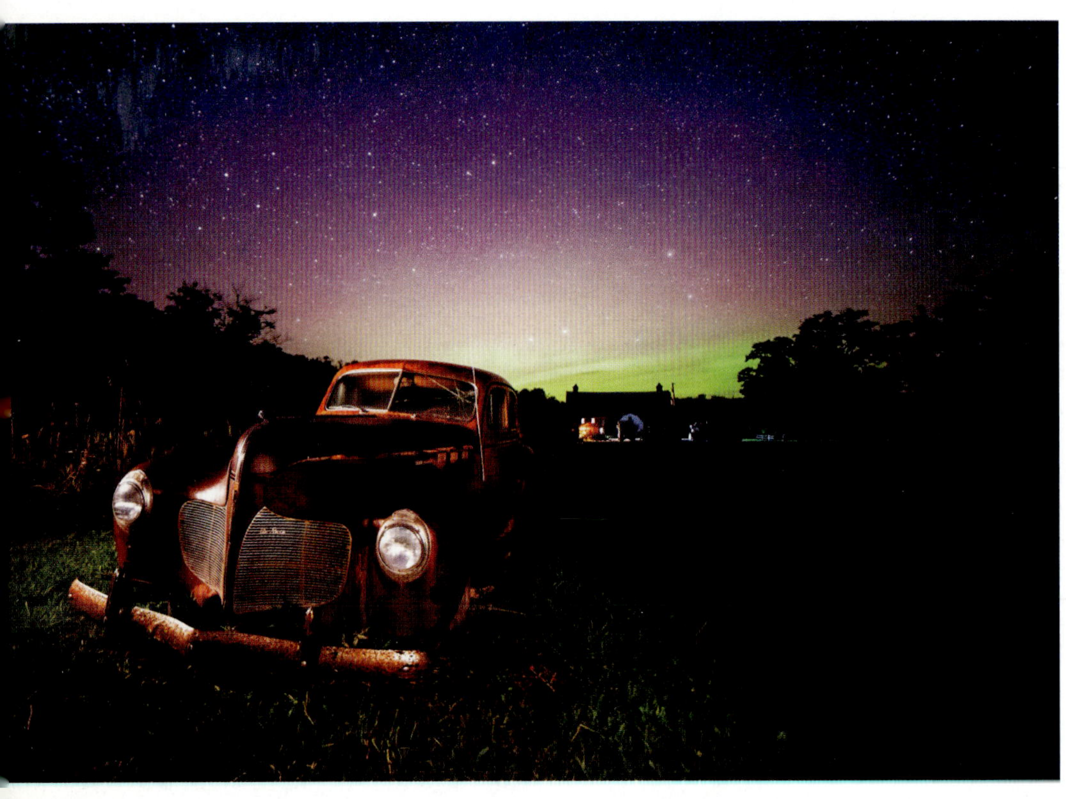

This page: 1939 DeSoto, Ellison Bay – Lucas.

Next page: Auroras, Sister Bay – Lucas.

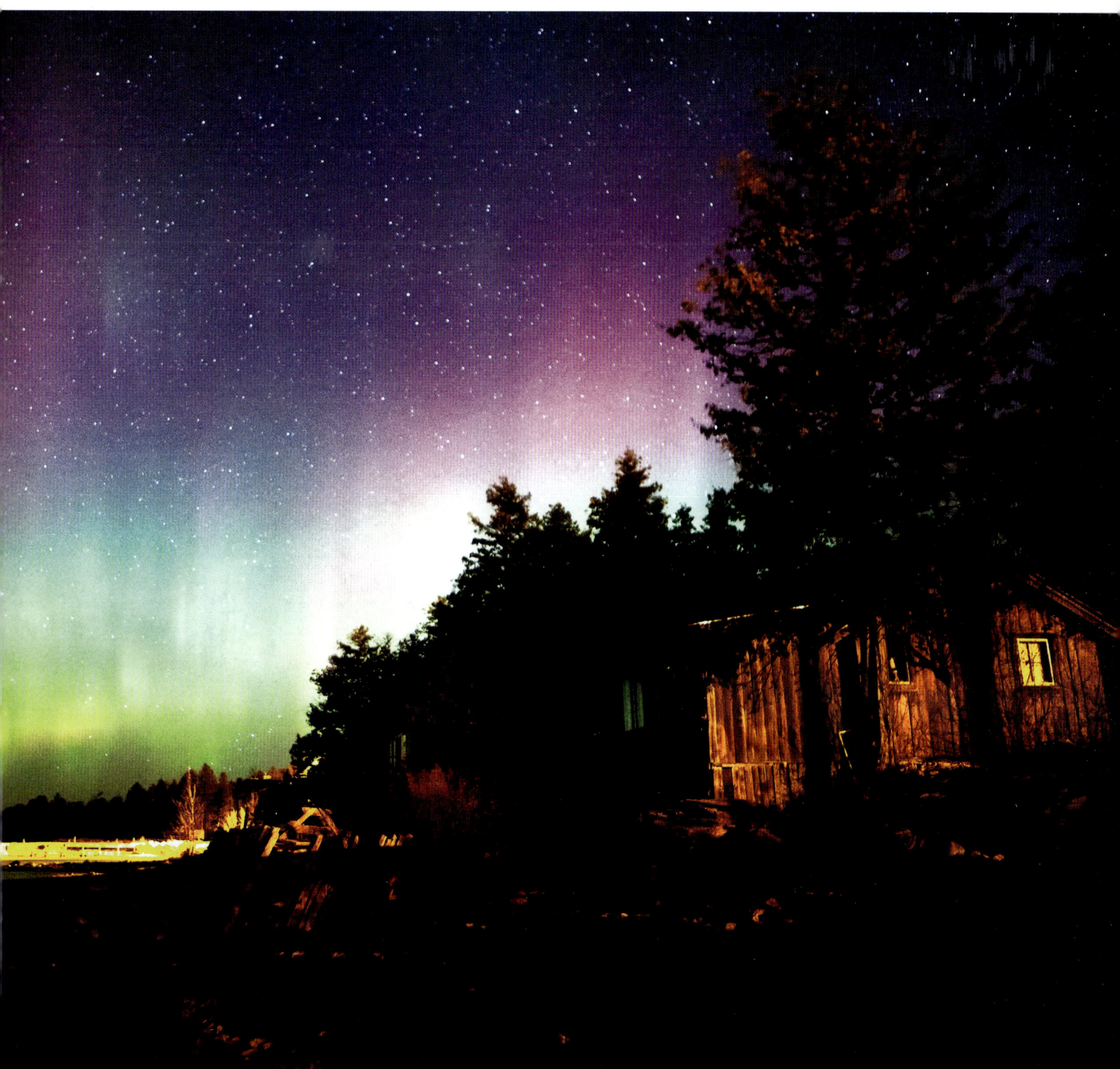

Door County Living in Pictures Volume 2

Heather and Lucas Frykman are frequent contributors to Peninsula Publishing & Distribution, Inc.'s various publications in addition to numerous other publications across the country. When not out on the peninsula with their cameras, they can be found in their gallery in Sister Bay.

What you hold in your hands is a collection of work, chosen by Heather and Lucas, which includes some photographs that appeared in the pages of Peninsula Publishing & Distribution, Inc.'s publications.

Our free newspaper, the *Peninsula Pulse,* debuted with 1,000 copies on May 24, 1996 as an eight-page arts and entertainment periodical. That first year we published 10 issues. In the intervening years the *Pulse* has grown to a circulation of over 18,000 copies in peak season and is now published weekly throughout the year.

Today's *Pulse* includes news, business, community bulletins, arts and entertainment, literature, classifieds, and sustainability coverage. In addition, each issue features a comprehensive calendar of events that is relied on by both visitors and locals.

Each issue of the *Pulse* is distributed to all mailboxes in northern Door County, to over 750 street locations from Algoma to Washington Island, and to an ever-growing subscription base.

Our sister publication is *Door County Living* magazine, a glossy, perfect bound, and collectible publication that was launched in 2003. Like the *Peninsula Pulse, Door County Living* is a free publication dedicated to telling the stories of Door County's people, culture, and lifestyle.

We publish five issues every year: four seasonally targeted issues and our annual Philanthropy Issue. Each of our seasonal issues includes articles on the peninsula's history, the arts community, outdoor activities, personality profiles, recipes, and unique habitats. These issues also include complete restaurant and lodging guides. Our Philanthropy Issue focuses on the peninsula's non-profit and charitable communities.

Our website doorcountypulse.com, offers a complete portrait of the Door Peninsula, with most of the material from our print publications available and fully linked, in addition to comprehensive guides to galleries, restaurants, lodging, and retail throughout the county. This site was completely redone and re-launched in the spring of 2015.

Door County Living in Pictures, Volume 2: The Photography of Heather Harle Frykman & Lucas Frykman is part of an ongoing series of books published by Peninsula Publishing & Distribution, Inc. The first in the series, *Door County Living in Pictures, Volume 1: The Photography of Len Villano* was published simultaneous to this volume. Both books are available for purchase through our website or at retail outlets throughout the Door Peninsula.

Subscriptions to the *Peninsula Pulse* and *Door County Living* are available by calling (920) 839-2121, by emailing subscribe@ppulse.com, or by contacting us by mail at P.O. Box 694, Baileys Harbor, WI 54202.

Likewise, if you would like to be contacted when new titles in this series are released, we can be reached in the same manner.

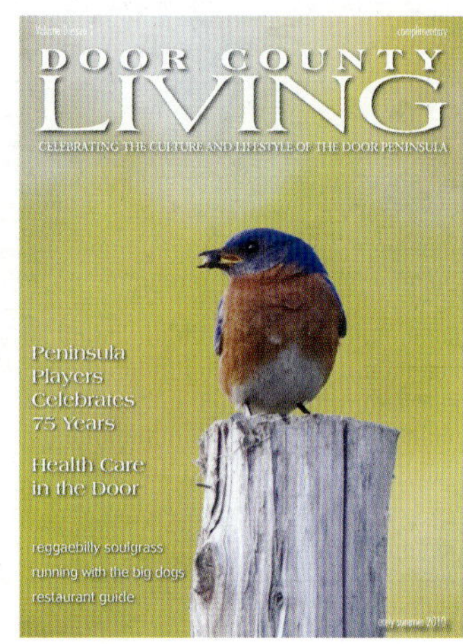

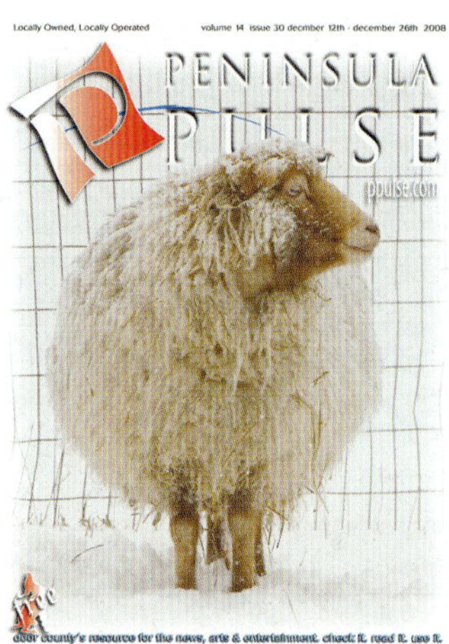

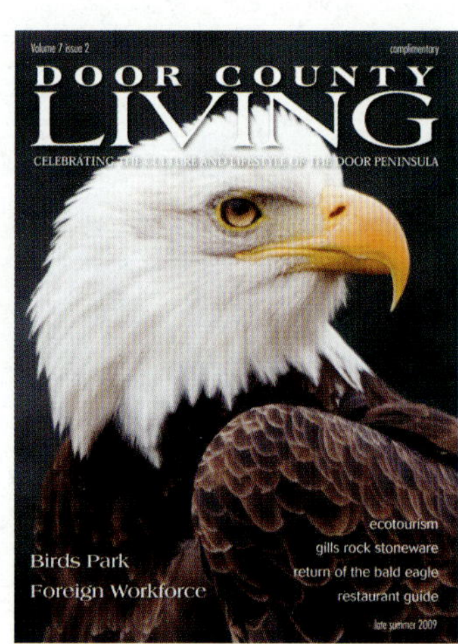